ME AND
MY MONEY

TONY MARTIN

Macmillan Canada

Toronto

This book is dedicated not only to the people whose stories appear here, but to everyone who has generously shared their investing experiences, insights and philosophies with me and the many readers of Me and My Money.

Canadian Cataloguing in Publication Data

Martin, Tony (Tony M.)
    Me and my money

Includes index.
ISBN 0-7715-7620-X

1. Investments 2. Finance, Personal. I. Title.
HG4521.M43 1998   332.67'8'0971   C98-932459-1

Cover & interior design: Kyle Gell art and design
Front cover photograph: Karen Whylie

This book is available at special discounts for bulk purchases by your group or organization for sales promotions, premiums, fundraising and seminars. For details, contact: Macmillan Canada, Special Sales Department, 29 Birch Avenue, Toronto, ON M4V 1E2. Tel: 416-963-8830.

Macmillan Canada
A Division of Canada Publishing Corporation
Toronto, Ontario, Canada

1 2 3 4 5   TRANS-B-G   02 01 00 99 98

Printed in Canada

ACKNOWLEDGEMENTS

•

This book would not have been possible without the imagination, insights and editorial expertise of many people. In particular, I'd like to thank Peggy Wente, Managing Editor of *The Globe and Mail*, David Pyette, an editor for the *Report on Business* Investing page and Ellen Roseman. Much of the credit for the thinking behind the Me and My Money column belongs to them.

The columns that you see in the paper each week, and those that appear in this book, owe a lot to the editing talents of a number of people who regularly help to craft and fine-tune the stories. They include Doug Goold, as well as the watchful eye of editors David Pyette, Karen Benzing and, more recently, Stephen Northfield.

Of course, the Me and My Money columns and this book would not have been possible were it not for the generosity with which individual Canadians have shared their stories, experiences and insights with me and with the many Me and My Money readers. My special thanks to all of you for offering up your stories so that others can learn from them.

I would also like to thank Alison Maclean, who realized the value of a book based on the columns, and Jill Lambert, for her editorial guidance and assistance.

In addition, there are many other people who have supported me in my writing over the years, including Penny Williams, Peter Volpe, David Chilton, Trish Wilson and, south of the border, Mark Butler, Kathy Welton, and Eric Tyson. Many thanks to all of you.

Finally, my ongoing and endless thanks to my wife, Jane. In addition to her now-practised role as the long-suffering spouse of someone who regularly takes on the alter-ego of a dazed and crazed writer on deadline, she helped tremendously with all her editorial assistance as well as her organizational input.

TABLE

OF CONTENTS

•

INTRODUCTION

•

This book is built around the Me and My Money columns I've written for over two years in the weekend Investing section of *The Globe and Mail's Report on Business*.

From the start, the column caught on in a big way with people right across the country. While I'd like to think it was my seamless style, wry humour and witty asides, I know better.

What Me and My Money offered for the first time was a look inside your neighbour's financial house. Previously about the only advice available on investing came from investment professionals, advisers and fund managers.

The problem with these folks is they can discuss history in a broad sense, and tell you where you should be. Everything looks pretty on their hand-outs and brochures, but it's often a very long stretch to make the connection between their optimistic charts and graphs and your personal financial and investing situation.

Various forces push and pull people financially, many of which have unhealthy results. Stores, advertisers and credit-card companies all have a sustained and powerful message pushing you to spend more. Meanwhile, the message that you can't depend on the government to support you in your retirement years is getting through to more people, with the result that many feel that if they didn't start saving madly yesterday, there is no way they'll be able to afford more than day-old bread when they leave the working world. Talk about being pulled in two directions at once!

Added to that is the code of silence that most people maintain about their financial situation. In today's label-conscious, consumer-driven world, that leaves many people with a sense of isolation, if not desperation. Often, it may seem as though everyone else has more than enough income to meet their needs, the cash on hand to fly off to the sun and sand when the first snowflake falls, and not a single worry about their long-term financial picture. And, of course, they somehow reached this idyllic, restful place in their financial lives by being on automatic pilot.

Don't believe it. For the most part, people's finances require on-going care and nourishment. And as you'll see in the following stories, even those who are truly sitting pretty have invested a lot of time and effort to gain control of their finances, and have made their share of mistakes along the way.

Thanks to the willingness of Canadians to come forward and explain their philosophies, strategies and methods, *Me and My Money* offers a rare glimpse into the real—not the abstract—world of financial planning and investing. For the most part, it's somewhat complicated, sometimes hit-and-miss and occasionally contradictory. Funny that— it almost sounds like it's human beings we're talking about!

That, of course, is precisely what we are talking about. Your money, savings and investments don't exist in a vacuum. They are influenced by—and have an influence on—your emotions, state of mind, situation, outlook and personality. You can't keep them from meddling with your financial decision-making, but you can learn to allow for them and work with them so you make decisions that are good for your money, and good for your peace of mind.

HOW TO USE THIS BOOK

This book is divided into three broad sections. The first section deals with putting your financial house in order, including ensuring that you and your family are properly protected against disaster. You'll also find some tips on how to spend less and save more—a key component of any successful long-term investor, yet one that is frequently given little play. We also discuss how to approach the world of investing and the steps to develop a workable long-term plan.

In the third section, at the end of the book, you'll find a couple of resources, including a glossary. However, this is not your typical glossary. Instead of explanations of jargon that are largely made up of even more jargon, you'll find plain-English explanations of just what all those confusing financial terms mean. You'll also find examples of how many of these terms apply to real life. There is also a short list of relevant books, newsletters and Web sites, all of which are useful weapons to stock in your financial arsenal.

The middle—and main—part of the book focuses on the columns themselves. They are grouped into six chapters, each focusing on a different type of investing.

Keep in mind a few things as you read these chapters. Many of the investors profiled don't use only one type of investment strategy. Often, a story could have been used to illustrate the principles of two or three other approaches. For example, many of the people in "The Risk-Takers" chapter also invest in conservative mutual funds. Consequently, I've tried to use the columns to draw out as many real-life lessons as possible.

In fact, most successful investors diversify by having many different types of investments, and those different investments require various strategies and techniques. For example, you may want to do your bond investing through mutual funds, hold some blue-chip stocks for longer-term steady growth, and invest a bit in small-cap stocks. You'll need a different approach for each type of investing, and you can find relevant tips and strategies in the corresponding chapters.

Just like duplicating a mutual fund's holdings by reading its reports, you won't match the returns of the investors profiled by buying the investments in their portfolio. Their portfolios are likely different today than when they were profiled. More importantly, you shouldn't try to duplicate anyone else's portfolio because what makes sense for him or her may not make sense for you.

What you can get out of the columns, however, is a great understanding of why the people profiled bought the investments they did, and what their strategy was. In short, you'll gain insights into how other people handle the real world of saving and investing, which tends to be much more confusing and challenging than the "academic" world of investing advice.

Oh, and one other thing. Don't let these people make you nuts. For the most part, they have been successful, if not very successful in their investing lives.

But in most cases, their success hasn't been a constant. All investors have to go through a learning curve, and they've made mistakes along the way. What's more, you'll never learn all there is to know, and neither will you avoid never making a bad investing choice again.

In fact, much of all investors' real wisdom turns up, funnily enough, in the "Worst Move" section. This is where they confess to a mistake or two. If there is one overriding theme here, it's the importance of having a long-term plan and sticking to it. If you only learn one lesson from our investors, it is this: your long-term success isn't so much a factor of making all the right moves as it is the end result of simply avoiding being completely wrong in your investment choices.

Finally, remember that there are many more important things in life than money. Family, friends and your own pastimes and interests offer big returns—guaranteed. Money should be just a sidebar to the rest of your life, not its main focus.

Great

PERSONAL FINANCE

MOVES

T HE MAIN FOCUS OF THIS BOOK is on investing—
the how, why and where Canadians have invested
their savings. But before you start choosing individual investments,
or even thinking about developing an overall investment plan, you
first need to take care of some financial planning basics.

Putting your financial house in order before you step out into the
wide world of investing is critical to your long-term financial success.
To build wealth, you have to start with a solid foundation. Putting the
basic building blocks of your financial house in place isn't all that
difficult or time-consuming, and once done, it will have a number
of positive results.

First, ensuring that you are making the most of your income and protecting it will actually help you put away more money. Second, it will help you understand your specific financial circumstances, which is an important step in developing your own investment approach. Finally, it will give you some peace of mind. This is an often overlooked benefit, but one that has many pleasant spin-offs. You'll feel less stress about your finances, gain an understanding of where you are and start to feel as though you are moving ahead, not just treading water. Last but not least, you'll develop a sense that you are running your finances, as opposed to your money running you. This means you'll be less likely to make costly financial decisions, and much more likely to make the right moves to make your money grow.

PROTECTING YOURSELF

A good offence starts with a strong defence. The first step in taking charge of your financial life is to make sure you aren't exposed to disasters that could prove financially dangerous. The two big areas to consider are what will happen if you can no longer earn an income, and what will happen if you die.

Protect Your Income with Disability Insurance

Illness or accidents regularly prevent people from earning a living. In fact, you're much more likely to become disabled than you are to die during your working life. You can protect yourself by ensuring that you have enough disability insurance that your payments will cover all of your regular ongoing expenses.

Many people who are employed see the words "disability insurance" in their company's benefit plan brochure and mistakenly assume that they are adequately covered. Often, however, a company's plan won't provide nearly enough income to see you and your family through a prolonged period of disability. Examine your plan, and buy additional coverage if needed. If you're self-employed, adequate disability insurance is even more critical.

Protect Your Family with Life Insurance

The second type of big-time protection is life insurance. In general, you only need life insurance if other people are financially dependent on you. In most cases, you can forget about having to take a night course in the arcane world of insurance and can simply buy term insurance. Term insurance is very straightforward. For a set amount of money—your yearly *premiums*—the insurer agrees to pay out an agreed-upon amount should you die during the *term* of your policy.

In addition to being much easier to understand than whole life, cash value or universal insurance, term insurance is also much cheaper. Buying term insurance means you'll be much more likely to buy sufficient coverage to ensure that your family is cared for.

Keep Some Cash on Hand

You'll also want to keep some cash on hand as an emergency fund in case unexpected bills or expenses pop up. In general, try to put aside about three months' worth of salary, but you can get by with less if you have investments that can easily be turned into cash, family members whom you can call upon for a loan or a line of credit.

Where There's a Will...

Your last line of defence involves establishing a will. A will outlines exactly what you want to happen to your assets when you die. Without a will, your assets will be distributed according to provincial guidelines—with often disastrous results. For example, in many provinces, the law requires that your children receive a good portion of your assets, as opposed to your spouse receiving all of your assets. In such cases, your children could end up being rich on paper while your partner must struggle to find the money to feed and clothe them. A will is also critical in determining who will care for your children, and how.

A SIMPLE STRATEGY FOR SAVING

There is a whole bunch of talk these days about investing, this book included. But the biggest complaint of many people is not that they can't squeeze an extra 3 per cent out of their returns every year, but rather it's something much simpler. "That all sounds great, but I don't *have* any money to invest!"

Unfortunately, sometimes personal finance boils down to stating the painfully obvious. But just because something is abundantly clear, it doesn't mean it will automatically be noticed by otherwise observant, intelligent and thoughtful people such as you, dear reader.

As a friend of mine likes to say, many things are concealed by the means of the ultra-obvious, and the following points definitely fall into that category. In order to have money to invest, you must have some savings. And in order to have some savings, you must either earn more money or spend less of what you currently make.

If you can easily earn more money, do so. Just tell your boss, "Hey, there are some great new ideas on investing in this new book I'm reading, so how about tossing me an extra hundred grand a year so I can check 'em out!"

If your boss is like most of the bosses I know, *you* will be the only thing that will get tossed out the door if you try this approach. You're left with the inevitable "plan B"—saving more money.

Saving more money, however, receives very, very little play in the media, on the news, or from financial institutions. Why? It's boring, it's somewhat distasteful (how many times when you're heading out with a group from work do you hear someone say, "Hey, I've got an idea, let's go someplace that's *cheaper!*"?), it doesn't give many companies a chance to make money, and furthermore, don't we all know how to do that already?

Well, no, actually.

How to Save More

The simplest and most common method that tends to work unfailingly over the long haul is the old standby of "pay yourself first."

David Chilton applied this bit of folk wisdom and sold a gazillion copies of his highly readable *The Wealthy Barber*. (So you can see just how basic the advice on saving money that most people received from their families and schools when they were growing up!)

Paying yourself first means treating your savings like any other regular expense that can't be avoided, such as your rent or mortgage payments. The best method is to take advantage of automatic deduction or debit plans and arrange to have a set amount of money whisked out of your account on a regular basis (ideally on the same day as your pay cheque is deposited in your account).

One approach is to arrange with a mutual fund company to automatically withdraw that money from your account and invest it in a mutual fund. Another approach is to have your bank or trust company take the money and invest it in a money-market mutual fund. This will keep your money safe and earning interest. Once you've built up a few thousand dollars, you can redirect that money into more long-term investments that fit with your overall investment plan and income needs.

Dances with Credit Cards

With the power of plastic behind you, you can buy tall buildings, purchase speeding locomotives...in short, you can become a kind of Superman of spending. Credit cards give you the financial strength to spend far beyond your normal human ability.

The problem is, there's the consumer's Kryptonite to deal with—debt. There's no way to defend yourself against its ability to sap your financial strength—you have to get rid of it.

If you continually spend more than you should on your credit cards, you'll have to find a way to curtail your plastic purchases. Leave your cards at home, replace them with a debit card, tie a piece of paper to them with an elastic band and write down your purchases, or simply cut them up. It doesn't matter how you do it, but find a method that works for you and stick with it.

One reason for overspending on plastic is that it is very easy to suddenly find yourself the owner of several—if not several dozen—cards!

If you find yourself in that situation, get rid of all of them except a generic VISA, MasterCard or American Express card.

In fact, thanks to debit cards, you don't really need credit cards on a day-to-day basis at all. The big advantage of debit cards is that you must have the money in your account in order to spend it. Unlike credit cards, a debit card doesn't allow you to spend what you don't have.

The Problem with Budgeting

The basic reason that budgeting doesn't work for most people is that it's very tough to distinguish between wants and needs. Sure, food and shelter are obvious needs. But what about single malt scotch, the latest Neil Finn CD, dining out every other night at Swiss Chalet, having three TVs and top-o'-the-line Nikes for the kids...are they wants or needs? (In case you're interested, I'd rank the foregoing as yes, absolutely, no, no, and Michael Jordan doesn't need any more money.)

Even if you can divide up the world of purchases into wants and needs, those will change, particularly in stressful times. "Hey," you'll tell yourself, "if I take that around-the-world cruise, I'll be even more productive when I return in three years so that's really a need, isn't it?"

And, of course, bad things happen to even the best budgets. One impulse buy or large unexpected expense can blow your budget apart in seconds, leaving you wondering why you've spent every spare minute counting the in- and out-flow of every single penny.

Where a budget can prove useful is to get a handle on just where your money is going. You may be able to find that you are spending hundreds—or even thousands—of dollars in two or three areas that are far from crucial to your continuing survival or even relative happiness, offering you quick and painless ways to drastically cut back your expenses and supercharge your savings. That done, you can put away your budget and take it out again in a few years to see if other inefficiencies have crept into your spending ways.

Pay Off High-Cost Debt

Paying off debt is certainly not very exciting, and is definitely not an approach promoted by sellers of financial products. Nobody, in fact, earns a cent when you get rid of debt except you—and you'll win big.

Say you have a $5,000 outstanding balance on your credit cards on which you're paying 28 per cent interest. Pay off your balance, and you will have earned yourself a 28 per cent return. But it gets better—that's a guaranteed return for which you took absolutely no risk. Plus you're making 28 per cent on your $5,000 after-tax. To get the equivalent after-tax return on an interest-earning investment such as a GIC, you'll have to find one paying 47 per cent if you are in a 41 per cent tax bracket. Good luck, and let me know if you do.

Of course, paying off that $5,000 also works for you in other ways. Over a one-year period, you'll save yourself $1,400 in interest charges—money that you can direct into your investments, rather than doing your bit to bolster the bottom line of The Really Big Bank. And suppose you're in a 50 per cent tax bracket and you direct that money into your RRSP. You'll also save $700 on your tax bill.

Paying off your credit cards will also give you a wonderfully free feeling, sort of like that first time in the summer when you get up on the weekend and instead of throwing on slippers, sweaters and leg warmers, you jump into shorts and a T-shirt.

Get to Know, Understand and Love Your RRSP

Contributing money to an RRSP is by far the easiest and most effective way to build wealth and reduce your tax bill along the way. Too many people, though, come at RRSPs backwards—they know the importance of saving for retirement and know RRSPs are a good way to go, but they can't seem to get started or contribute enough to their plan.

Try motivating yourself by coming at your RRSP from the other direction—as a way to actually put more money in your pocket and cut down on your expenses.

THE BENEFITS OF AN RRSP If you earn an income—either as an employee or as your own boss, you likely have earned the right to contribute to an RRSP. The actual amount is capped at $13,500 or 18 per cent (whichever is less) of what's called your *earned income*, essentially what you make from working. (The amount may be reduced if you belong to a registered pension plan.)

To understand just how RRSPs work, think of them simply as a special kind of savings account. As long as the government knows you have put money into this account (and that you won't withdraw the money without it being able to hit you up for taxes), you get two benefits. First, you can deduct the amount contributed from your income when calculating your income tax each year. For example, suppose you are in the 41 per cent tax bracket. If you put $6,000 into your RRSP, that means you no longer have to pay tax at 41 per cent on that $6,000 of income, saving you almost $2,500 in income tax.

The second benefit of RRSPs is that any money you make on the funds inside your plan—whether in the form of interest, dividends or capital gains—aren't taxed each year. Every cent that you earn can be reinvested and earn further untaxed profits for you. Over the years, this has a real snowball effect, and the amount in your RRSP will start to grow faster and faster even if you don't invest any new money (which, of course, you should be doing every year you are allowed to!).

Now I'm going to stop beating you about the head and shoulders about the benefits of putting money into your RRSP, and instead neatly tie it back into what we were discussing earlier about saving more money.

SAVE LESS TO SAVE MORE WITH RRSPS RRSPs pull off the neat trick of allowing you to actually save less and save more at the same time. For instance, you could put $5,000 into your RRSP by only cutting back your spending by around $3,000. Here's how. (Unfortunately, we'll have to deal with a few numbers, but hang in there. They aren't all that complicated and the results are more than worth the trouble.)

Say you're in the 41 per cent marginal tax bracket. If you put $5,000 into your RRSP, you'll save yourself around $2,050 in taxes. If you are in a salaried job, that will likely mean an extra $2,050 in your annual tax refund. In effect, the government is subsidizing your contribution to the tune of around $2,000.

If you cut back your spending by $3,000, you would still have to lay your hands on that extra $2,000 to actually make the contribution, and make this approach work. But that may not be all that hard. You may have a Canada Savings Bond or two stashed away, for instance. You may be able to borrow that money from a family member, or you might want to consider taking out an RRSP loan, which are widely available at very competitive interest rates.

However you do it, try to take advantage of the RRSP rules, and put in as much of your allowable contribution as you can pull together every year. You'll get a tax break on your contributions, your money will grow tax-free, plus once the money is inside your plan, you'll be much less likely to think of it as money you can spend—a necessary step for saving for the future.

LIVE FOR TODAY,

INVEST FOR

Tomorrow

N OW THAT WE'VE DISCUSSED protecting yourself, reducing debt and saving more, we can
begin looking at how to go about investing those savings.

You have to start somewhere, and that somewhere is probably just
behind where you currently are standing (or reclining, if you're reading this book in your favourite comfy chair).

Far too often, people begin investing by, well, investing! Going out
and buying funds or stocks or, yikes, limited partnerships is kind of
like going grocery shopping when you're tired, hungry, have the kids
in tow and haven't had time to make a list.

By the time you're finished, you will have spent too much, bought
many things you don't need, not enough of the staples you're going

to require to make the next meal, and you won't have bought things on sale or in the right quantity. You're also likely to have loaded up on a bunch of junk food that seemed to offer a quick fix when you were starving, but that's not only unhealthy, it is so insubstantial that you have to turn right around and go buy some "real" food that you can make decent meals with.

HOW TO SHOP FOR INVESTMENTS

The answer, of course, is to have a plan. Before you go to the grocery store, you take a look at what you've got, what you want to eat over the next week or two, who will need to be fed and what days you'll be home. Then you make a list, figure out what's on sale, decide what you can buy in quantity to save even more and then go shopping.

Similarly, you can't go shopping for stocks, bonds, funds or GICs without drawing up a list. Just what investments make sense for you—and even if you should at present be investing—can only be determined by looking at your circumstances, near-term and long-term needs, and your personality. You can deal with a lot of these factors by grouping them together in two areas—time and temperament.

A Matter of Time

There are two areas you'll need to address here. One is your own time, and the second is how much time your investments have.

SPARE TIME—WHO'S GOT ANY?!! Beyond savings, it seems that for most people, spare time is the one thing most of us lack. Who's got time to spare?

Consider the demands that are made on your time. If you don't have any spare time currently, but if you plan to actively invest and trade in stocks, for instance, you'll have to find a way to free up some time to regularly monitor and fine-tune your investments. And don't kid yourself about being able to find that time on an ongoing basis.

If you put together a stock-trading portfolio but then are too busy with other tasks and concerns to watch over it, you simply have set yourself up nicely to lose a good deal of money.

Even if you have some free time currently, you should consider how much of it you want to spend managing your portfolio. You may be better off banging out book shelves in the basement, practising your golf swing or just gazing contentedly at your navel, or the navel of someone close to you.

The more time you have and are willing to devote to investing, the more active your approach can be, right down to day-trading stocks on your own. On the other hand, if you're feeling constantly rushed, you are far better off choosing a much more passive approach. At the most extreme, that might be working with an adviser to assemble a portfolio of conservative mutual funds you can hold on to for many years.

HOW MUCH TIME DO YOUR INVESTMENTS HAVE? The other time element to consider is how long you will be investing your money. This period is usually dictated by what you plan on using the results of your investing for.

Say you're younger and are investing money in an RRSP for your retirement. You may have a couple of decades to leave your money alone. The longer you wish to leave your money invested, the more you can direct it into ownership-type investments such as stocks or real estate.

Why? Typically the way these investments increase in value is sort of like a roller-coaster in reverse. They start at a certain level, and then go up and down, sometimes with stomach-churning velocity. But over time, the level of the dips should steadily be higher, as should the peaks. (Think of one of those slippery serpents on a Snakes and Ladders board, only you get to ride it up, not down.)

You need a long time-frame, though, because you'll want to be able to choose to step off when you're near or at the top, not down in the trough. The shorter your time-frame, the less likely you'll be able to pull this off. For example, if you need your money in two years, you should not put it in the stock market. It may very well be worth more one, two or three years out, but the market could just as easily be in a real downturn at that point.

By contrast, the sooner you will need your money, the less time you have to ride out those ups and downs (and choose a higher selling point when you want to sell your investments), so the more you need to focus on conservative and guaranteed investments. For example, say you're hoping to buy a home in a few years. You should keep your money in safer investments such as money-market mutual funds so that you know that all of the money you started with—your principal—will be there for you when you need it.

Your Temperament

An objective assessment of how much risk you should take with your savings is a valuable exercise to go through. For example, if you are relatively young and saving for your retirement, much of your portfolio should be in equities. The flip side is if you're on the verge of leaving the working world and need a regular source of income to live on, you should have the great majority—if not all—of your money, in safer, lending-type investments.

But most of us live in the real world. Beyond objective assessments, you have to consider and factor in your own personality, and how well you deal—or don't deal—with risk.

ALL INVESTMENTS HAVE SOME FORM OF RISK ATTACHED Unfortunately, risk is part of any investment. Buy high-flying Internet stocks, and the risk is pretty obvious. One day the market could decide the whole business is just too much smoke and mirrors, and before you know it, it's "Hey Honey, I Shrunk Our Savings!"

But even so-called guaranteed investments such as GICs have risk. In this case the risk is that inflation will actually diminish your buying power. Especially if you are paying tax on your interest income, your savings may end up growing at a slower rate than prices are rising, meaning you'll actually have less purchasing power.

You first have to take a little time to consider how well risk sits with you. You'll also need to look at which risk poses a greater danger to you—the risk of losing your principal or the risk of missing out on better long-term growth and even losing out to inflation.

Having done this, you can look at different types of investments that have the level of risk you're comfortable with, and that are suitable for your time frame and needs. You may find, of course, that there's a gap between the level of risk you're willing to take on and the returns that those investments offer. Don't worry, it's a tug-of-war that most investors have to deal with, as you'll see as you read through the columns. You'll need to find your own balance between your desire for higher performance and lower risk.

EASY REAL-LIFE RULES
FOR SUCCESSFUL INVESTING

DEVELOP A PLAN: Use the above advice to put your plan together. Factor in how much risk you can comfortably live with, and how active or passive you want to be in managing your investments. Next, develop an idea of how you want to divvy up your savings between the three major types of investments—cash or cash-type investments, guaranteed investments and equity investments.

STICK TO YOUR PLAN: Almost to a man and woman, our investors usually only stumble and bruise their financial knees when they don't follow their own advice.

From hot tips to soaring blue chips, there will inevitably be endless opportunities that catch your eye daily. However, your long-term success will depend not on how quickly you jump on these investments, but on how resolute you are in ignoring those that don't fit into your plan. Buy only those investments that meet your big-picture needs, and add to them slowly over time to benefit from dollar-cost averaging.

DON'T FEAR RISK: To make your money grow, you'll need to invest in "ownership"-type investments. That means the value of your investments can not only go up but down as well. Over time, though, these investments, such as stocks and real estate, offer the best long-term growth potential.

BE REALISTIC: Especially when stock prices have soared over the last few years, investors often have an exaggerated idea of what their money can earn. Historically though, 10 per cent—or slightly less—is the average for ownership-type investments. And while that may seem almost negligible given recent returns (in 1996 and 1997 for example), over the longer term, 10 per cent compounded is more than enough to help your savings grow exponentially.

CONSIDER THE LONG TERM: For your money to grow, you'll need equity-type investments such as stocks. But you'll also need to leave your money invested for longer than when purchasing other types of investments. Five years is a minimum, but seven to 10 years is better.

THE SHORTER YOUR TIME FRAME, THE LESS RISKY YOUR INVESTMENTS SHOULD BE: Match the investments you select to when you'll need your money. If you're saving to buy a home in the next few years, put your money into safe investments such as a dividend or money-market fund. That way, you at least know that your principal will be safe and there when you need it.

DIVERSIFY: Spreading your money among different types of assets lowers your overall risk, allowing you to hold higher-risk–higher-rewards investments such as stocks, which are critical to earning strong returns over the long term.

TUNE OUT THE NOISE: With the Internet, 24-hour business television shows and even hourly reports on mutual-fund returns, there is no end of nitty-gritty details available on the daily trials and tribulations of the financial markets. But trying to take it all in is like listening to three different radio stations at once. You'll know there's a lot going on, but not much else. You don't need to try to follow everything that's happening in the financial world. Even if you could (and, trust me, you can't), it won't help you much in your long-term planning.

ALLOCATE YOUR ASSETS: Before you choose individual investments, you need to decide how to divide—or allocate—your savings among different types of investments. The younger you are and the more money you want to invest for the long term, the more funds you should have in investment-type investments such as stocks. The older you are, and the sooner you'll need your money, the more secure your investments should be.

KEEP YOUR PERSPECTIVE: The most important investments you can make aren't financial. The returns you'll get from devoting time and energy into your personal relationships and your health will always beat the returns from any financial product.

YOUR

Investment Options:

AN EASY-TO-UNDERSTAND

OVERVIEW...HONEST!

I F PHRASES LIKE "Buy me two lots at the ask, day order and throw up a stop-loss at yesterday's close" roll easily off your tongue, then you can probably skip over this chapter.

If, however, you feel that a different kind of English must have been taught in public school on the days you were away, then this chapter has a lot to offer you.

Getting your head around the basic types of investments can be a bit of work, but gaining a general sense of how they work and what sort of returns they generate is critical to putting your money to work effectively. Some of the jargon may seem daunting, but much of it is surprisingly simple. More importantly, once you learn the basics about your investment choices, you'll be better able to fend for yourself in the woolly investment world, plus you'll be a better judge of just which investments are best for you.

THE BENEFITS OF THINKING BIG

Even somewhat knowledgeable folk often start looking at investments through a microscope. You're much better off though, as you'll see in the next chapter on asset allocation, looking at the big picture. So pack a picnic lunch, and let's drive up into the hills and gaze out over the investment landscape.

Familiarizing yourself with the various broad types of investments has a number of benefits. First, you'll gain a clearer understanding of the specific pros and cons of different uses for your savings. This, in turn, will prove helpful when developing or fine-tuning your own investment strategy. Understanding the different types of investments is also critical if you are to buy those investments that suit your specific needs, ability to handle risk and retirement plans.

You can use this chapter as a reference to check in with from time to time. You can also read through it at one go to acquaint yourself— or reacquaint yourself—with the range of investments out there. You'll find a description about each basic type of investment, as well as its relative liquidity (how easily it can be sold) and risk, and the potential for rewards.

TWO—COUNT 'EM *TWO*— BASIC TYPES OF INVESTMENTS

Although many different investments are available, they fall into two broad categories: "lending" investments and "ownership" investments.

1. "Loaner" Investments

With these types of investments, you loan your money to a company, financial institution, government or an individual. In return, the borrower agrees to pay you interest and promises to return the original amount—the principal—at an agreed-upon date in the future. If the investment is held outside a registered—and tax-sheltered—plan such as an RRSP, the interest income is taxed at your marginal tax rate.

2. "Ownership" Investments

As the name suggests, with ownership investments, you actually buy something—or a piece of something—with the hope that its value will rise and you'll be able to sell it at a profit.

Those profits are known as capital gains. If the investment is held outside of your RRSP or other tax-deferred savings plan, any capital gains you make will be taxed, but at a lower rate than interest income. (Capital gains are taxed at your marginal tax rate, but you only have to include three-quarters of your capital gains in your taxable income.)

Equity investments such as common or preferred shares also often pay you dividends, which are simply a portion of the company's profits paid out to shareholders. Because dividends are paid out of a company's after-tax profits, dividends receive a tax credit that results in their effective tax rate being lower than that on capital gains.

YOUR INVESTMENT CHOICES

SAVING AND CHEQUING ACCOUNTS: These aren't investments as much as they are places to park your cash for easy access. If you need money, it's there and you can get your hands on it immediately. You can also be sure that what you put into your account won't shrink. But in return for this liquidity and the safety of your principal, you get very low returns, currently around 0.25 to 1.00 per cent.

GUARANTEED INVESTMENT CERTIFICATES (GICs): These once served as the backbone for many a Canadian's portfolio. With the introduction of mutual funds, the ease of investing through discount brokers and the Internet, and, not least, the low rates of return, GICs have fallen out of favour.

When you buy a GIC, you are loaning your money to the financial institution you purchase it from, typically a bank or trust company. Your principal is guaranteed—you can be sure you'll receive the full amount you've handed over when the GIC matures. In the meantime, you'll receive interest payments at a rate you will have agreed to when you purchased the GIC. GICs are usually available for periods from three months to five years. In most cases, the longer the term, the higher the rate of interest you will get.

Most standard-issue, white-bread GICs are non-redeemable, meaning you can't get your principal back until the GIC matures. However, to make them more attractive, financial institutions have developed all sorts of hybrid GICs, including ones that can be turned in early. In addition, many GICs are dubbed "mutual funds with training wheels." These allow you to earn a return based on how the stock market is doing.

TREASURY BILLS (T-BILLS): Treasury bills are another kind of investment where your principal as well as your rate of return are guaranteed. They are short-term investments, issued for a term of 91, 182 or 364 days. T-bills come in large denominations ($100,000 and up) but some financial institutions will sell "pieces" of their T-bills to consumers for amounts as low as $1,000.

Unlike GICs, though, you don't actually receive interest payments from T-bills. You buy them at a discount from their face value. The difference between what you pay and what the T-bill is worth at maturity (its face value) is your return. Over the past several decades, T-bills have paid an average annual compound return of 6 per cent.

CANADA SAVINGS BONDS (CSBs): This is another popular guaranteed investment that manages to pull at the heart-strings of patriotic Canadians.

CSBs go on sale every fall for a few weeks. They come in two basic flavours—regular CSBs that pay you interest every year, and compound CSBs that don't pay you interest but allow the interest to compound over the life of the bond.

Canada Savings Bonds have two notable features. Unlike many other fixed-income investments, you can cash in your CSBs anytime after the first month or two in which they were issued, and get all your principal back without paying any penalties or fees. You'll also get paid any interest you've earned up to the end of the last month as long as its after a defined (usually 3 month) period from the issue date. If you cash in a CSB early, try to do it early in the month rather than late in the previous month to get the most interest.

Another great feature of CSBs is that they are cashable. Consequently, the government has to keep the interest rate competitive, otherwise canny investors (just like yourself, once you've read this book!) will cash them in and reinvest their money elsewhere. CSBs are usually available in denominations of $300, $500, $1,000, $5,000 and $10,000.

BONDS: These are lending-type investments issued by governments— from the federal government down to municipalities—as well as corporations.

Bonds have a maturity date—the day on which the organization that issued the bond will repay your interest. The interest you will earn on a bond is known as the coupon rate. For example, a $1,000 10-year bond with a coupon rate of 8 per cent will pay you $80 a year for 10 years. After 10 years, you will receive your original $1,000 back.

Bonds, however, often have very different returns than the coupon rate. Here's why. Say you bought a five-year bond paying 8 per cent last year. So far, so good. But this year, rates for five-year bonds coming off the printing presses have an interest rate of 10 per cent. Bad news!

Why? If you want to sell your bond, you won't be able to get $1,000 for it. Nobody's going to hand over a cool thousand to earn 8 per cent when they could get 10 per cent elsewhere. So you have to offer the going rate of 10 per cent. You do that by selling your bond at a discount, so that the 8 per cent interest payments actually work out to 10 per cent. (Of course, if going interest rates are lower than what your bond is paying, you can sell it for more than the $1,000 face value.)

Two other things to point out about bonds: First, the longer the term of the bond, the more its market value will fluctuate with current interest rates. A bond that has a high interest rate locked in for 10 years will command a higher premium than one on which the buyer will only get a high interest rate for another six months.

Second, none of this affects you if you buy a new bond and hold it until it matures. You will receive the interest as stated on the bond, and get your principal back when the bond matures. You only need to be concerned about interest rate swings and their impact on your bond's market price if you don't plan on holding it until it matures. Otherwise, your rate of return will be fixed by when you buy your bond and what you pay for it.

There are two methods of determining the return on a bond. The current yield is the annual interest paid by a bond divided by its current market value. Take a 10 per cent (coupon rate) bond with a par or face value of $1,000. The annual interest payment would be $100. If interest rates have risen, the market price of the bond may fall to $800. Its current yield—the yield an investor who bought it today would receive—would be $100 divided by $800, or 12.5 per cent.

The second return measurement is called yield to maturity. If you buy a bond at anything but its face value, this will tell you your overall return. The yield to maturity is a rather complicated formula, but essentially it takes into account both the interest payments you'll receive and the difference between what you paid for the bond and what you will receive when the bond matures, its *face value*. The actual formula used is quite convoluted, as it also includes an assumption about the rate at which you can reinvest the ongoing interest payments.

Bonds are very liquid, meaning that they can be easily bought, or sold and turned into cash. Bonds have historically had an average rate of return of 8 to 9 per cent over the past several decades.

PREFERRED SHARES: These are stocks that behave much like bonds. Preferred shares pay dividends at a set rate. This rate seldom changes, but companies are free to alter the rate, or even suspend the dividend altogether if they run into deep trouble, known in the investment world as financial difficulties.

The share price of preferred shares fluctuates with going interest rates, just like bonds. If interest rates go down, the effective return on a preferred share rises, so their value also goes up. Preferred shares can be bought and sold easily any day the markets are up and running.

COMMON STOCK (OR SHARES): When people discuss the performance of the stock market, they are usually referring to how common shares are faring. Owners of common stock actually own a piece—or share— of a company. You have the right to vote on major decisions such as appointments to the board of directors.

For average investors, however, common stocks are bought for one basic reason—that down the road (hopefully around the next corner, not when the road reaches the coast!) the stock will be worth more than what it cost. Compared to bonds and preferred shares, common stocks have the greatest potential for rising in value. Historically, stocks have returned between 10 and 11 per cent.

Common shares are also very liquid. As long as the markets are open, you can put in a "market" order—an order to buy or sell some shares at the going price. And if you are dealing with frequently traded companies, you'll have bought or sold your shares in minutes, if not seconds.

MUTUAL FUNDS: I've stuck funds onto this list, if only to clear up a misconception. You'll get a much better grasp of how mutual funds work and how they can be best used if you think of them not so much as an investment, but as a way to invest.

Mutual funds come in all shapes and sizes. They are really just a mechanism that allows many individual investors to have their money pooled with other investors' money, and then invested by a professional money manager. Just what that money is invested in, however,

is a function of the type of fund. Canadian equity mutual funds, for example, invest in, yup, Canadian stocks. Depending on how those stocks
fare in the market, the value of those funds—and the value of the units
you have bought—can go up and down. Money-market funds, by contrast, invest only in short-term government and corporate debt in-
struments. The rate of interest you'll earn may fluctuate, but you can
always be assured that if you want to sell your units, you'll at least get
back your original investment.

Mutual funds, by definition, are neither risky nor risk-free. Rather,
their volatility—and the type and size of returns they may provide—
depends on what the fund invests in.

CONSERVATIVE
Long-Term
INVESTING

ONSERVATIVE LONG–TERM STOCK INVESTORS
buy shares in large, well-known companies
(blue-chip companies), hoping to hold their stocks for many years
as the sales, earnings—and stock prices—of those companies rise
steadily.

Some people like a quick burger from a fast-food chain. Others
live on the culinary edge, checking out the latest Thai-Cal-Mex hole-
in-the-wall with Spice Girls concert-sized line-ups.

But a lot of folk like home cooking, and it's not hard to see why.
Every Sunday, for example, my Mom used to put together the classic
English lunch—roast beef, roast potatoes, mounds of vegetables, even
Yorkshire pudding, and lots of gravy.

Those Sunday meals have a lot in common with buying blue-chip stocks—the shares of large, well-established companies—and holding them for the long term.

Unlike speculative stock-picking, you don't get your hunger for excitement and new thrills quickly satisfied. (Of course, you also largely avoid the chance of ending up with a sinking feeling in your stomach.) Roast beef is roast beef, and it doesn't taste much different from week to week. On the other hand (health warnings notwithstanding), it's tasty, consistent, and will help you grow. Similarly, blue-chip investing should provide you with steady and (somewhat) predictable returns over time.

Blue-chip stock investing, though, does require some work. My Mom could pull together a big family dinner in her sleep, but she just made it look easy. There was a lot of prep work involved, plus she had grown experienced over the years in just what needed to be done when and how to make the whole cooking process as efficient as possible.

The same holds true for investing in blue-chip stocks. You have to put some time and effort into understanding the mechanics of the stock market, assessing a company's financial situation and selecting the right stocks for your portfolio. Just listen to the famous U.S. fund manager Peter Lynch, who kindly has quipped a quotation that fits in nicely with my investments-as-food analogy: "Spend at least as much time researching a stock as you would choosing a refrigerator."

Do your research properly, and the end results should leave you feeling sort of like you do 10 minutes after clearing the Sunday family meal from the dinner table—slightly sleepy, pleasantly satisfied and a good deal richer.

JUST WHAT ARE BLUE-CHIP STOCKS?

Blue-chip stocks are the stocks of big, well-established companies with good track records.

They are also known entities, with large and established markets—nationally and often internationally—for their products and services. The blue-chip club includes companies such as Ford, IBM and Johnson & Johnson. They are often also diversified, selling a wide range of goods and services to different types of customers in many parts of the world.

All together, these characteristics mean that revenues flow in on a regular and somewhat predictable level. It also means that blue-chip companies usually have good earnings that have increased over the years, plus they often pay dividends.

THREE IMPORTANT STOCK HIGHLIGHTS

Yup, looks like we got some 'splaining to do. Earnings and dividends are two of the most critical things to investigate about a stock. You also should look at a company's price/earnings ratio.

EARNINGS: Earnings are another word for a company's profits. To put a company's earnings into perspective, you need to look at how much profit is being earned on the behalf of shareholders. This is arrived at by dividing the company's total—or net—earnings (generally its profits after taxes and dividends on preferred shares been paid) by the number of common shares outstanding (the common shares owned by investors like you).

The resulting figure tells you how much profit was earned per share. For example, a company with earnings of $30 million that has 10 million shares outstanding would have an "earnings per share" of $3.

Obviously, a company whose earnings per share, or EPS, is rising from year to year is becoming more profitable. Maybe they are selling a lot more, maybe they've cut their costs, but whatever they're doing, they're making their bottom line bigger. Investors love to see a history of bigger earnings, and also like to hear analysts say they believe that growth will continue in the future.

But what's the relationship between a company's earnings per share and its stock price? Does a company's earnings per share make its stock a good buy or a bad buy?

Hard to say, unless you compare it to what investors are willing to pay for a share of the earnings of other similar companies. To do that, you need to know a company's price/earnings ratio.

PRICE/EARNINGS RATIO: A company's price/earnings ratio, or P/E, is its current stock price divided by its earnings per share. If a company has a stock price of $30 and its earnings per share is $3, it has a price/earnings ratio of 10.

The price/earnings ratio is also known as a company's multiple. Why? If a company's earnings per share is $2.00 and the stock is trading at $18, it is trading at nine *times* its EPS.

All sorts of factors determine a company's price/earnings ratio, essentially what investors are willing to pay for a stock given a company's earnings per share. They include the company's stability, historical growth rate and expectations for future earnings per share, as well as the price/earning ratios other similar companies are trading at.

DIVIDENDS: Dividends are simply the portion of a company's earnings that are paid out to shareholders. Of course, there's a world of difference between a stock that costs $100 and pays a dividend of $1 and a stock that only costs $10 and pays the same $1 dividend.

To assess a dividend, you need to consider just how big the annual payments to shareholders are compared to what you had to pay for the stock. This is known as the *dividend yield*.

For example, say the price of a stock is $30, and the total dividends paid for the year add up to $1.50. The stock's dividend yield would be $1.50/$30, or 5 per cent.

The dividend yield tells you a couple of things. First, if the price of the stock doesn't budge, you know what your return will be—the dividend yield. Of course, if the company stops paying the dividend, then you don't even make that return. The dividend yield is also a good way to compare the return on a stock to other investments.

THE UPSIDE

Blue-chip stocks are like a giant ocean-going cruise ship. Their sheer size and sound construction means they will weather even the toughest storms. You may get rocked about a bit, but generally, you can sleep soundly, knowing when you get up the boat will still be floating and moving forward.

Because of their reputations, established sales channels and diversified offerings, blue-chip companies are unlikely to ever disappear. That means their stocks will fare better in bad economic times than small-cap and speculative stocks. However, neither are you likely to see their stocks double overnight.

Note, though, that much of the big runup in stock prices in the mid-nineties was led by blue-chip stocks. These recent returns were, quite frankly, out of line with their historical performance. Historically, the average yearly return you can expect from blue-chip stocks is around 8 to 10 per cent.

Stay Safe

Sticking with blue chips, or at least using them as the foundation for your stock-picking efforts, has a few other benefits. First, it saves you from trying to jump into speculative shares, risky promotions or hot tip stocks. It also protects you from a much less obvious but potentially just as financially dangerous risk—the risk of missing out on potential long-term profits by sticking only to guaranteed investments.

Buying blue chips steadily over time is a good, conservative way to get into the equity markets. Otherwise, you risk sitting on the sidelines, continually waiting for the big correction or price dip. Doing so keeps you out of the market, and can rob you financially over the years as you'll miss out on compounding.

Also, with some deft stock picking, blue chips can provide you with better returns than mutual funds. As Marilyn Cottrell says, management fees as well as load charges eat away at your returns, plus even so-called "quality" funds hold "a lot of garbage."

One often overlooked benefit of buy-and-hold investments like blue-chips stocks is that you don't need to fret about short-term price movements. The share value today, last week and next Tuesday really are inconsequential to what the stock will be worth five or 10 years out.

Easy to Research, Easy to Hold

Probably the biggest attraction of blue chips is that they are low maintenance. There is a ton of readily available research to help you make your initial picks, a load of historical numbers on which to base your final selections and, once you purchase a blue-chip stock, it should hopefully continue to be a good place to have your money invested for many years.

Tuck it into your portfolio, kiss it good-night, and that's about it. Close the door, and except for checking on it quietly every now and then to make sure it's sleeping peacefully; it should reward you with long-term, steady gains.

THE DOWNSIDE

There are actually quite a few drawbacks to blue-chip investing. One, of course, is that you risk falling into a stupor. As the saying goes about famed long-term buy-and-holder Warren Buffett, his isn't so much a passive approach as it is one of near-coma-like qualities.

Still, even the soundest of blue chips can get buffeted by everything from economic storms to lawsuits to changing consumer tastes.

After blue-chip prices were driven through the roof in 1996 and 1997, 1998 proved to be a disaster, with many leading companies, including the banks, shedding half their value in a matter of months and, sometimes, weeks.

DOING IT YOURSELF

Many of our blue-chip investors pick their own stocks, and it's not hard to see why. First, you already have a ready-made short-list, since you can immediately cross off speculative stocks, small caps and many other companies, including smaller resource and precious metal companies.

Blue-chip stock-picking also has a low pain-in-the-neck factor. You don't have to be constantly monitoring your babies, and you shouldn't be buying or selling them every day, week or even month. Ideally, you're hoping to find stocks that you can hold for many years.

USING A HELPING HAND

Again, you're in luck here, as blue chips are the most frequently analyzed and reported-on investments. Using a broker gives you access to their firm's research and analysis, which means you can often obtain in-depth reports on the companies you are evaluating. In addition, an advisor can often be useful in helping you break the tie between two stock buys, for example, why you might want to buy Pepsi over Coke (not to drink, but to put in your portfolio!).

If you like second and third opinions, then blue-chip investing through a broker is also a good idea. You can cross-reference your broker's analysis with reports in the media and on the Internet, as well as your own assessment.

HOW THEY PULL IT OFF

All of our blue-chip buy-and-holders have one basic goal: To buy quality stocks that offer the potential of substantial price appreciation over the long term. Ultimately, much of your success won't depend as much on your timing and specific picks as it will from simply holding some good quality stocks for the long term. It's not how you time the market, but the time in the market that counts. Or, as Woody Allen puts it, "Eighty per cent of success is showing up."

From that statement flows a long list of good rules to follow:

- *Go Slow.* In general, blue-chips don't leap up and down like dragonflies on a mosquito-laden evening. That gives you plenty of time to decide what you're going to buy, and when.
- *Look for Value.* Especially after blue-chip stocks have risen as they have in recent years, it's important to look for underpriced stocks. One method is to look for companies with a low price/earnings ratio—the stock price divided by the company's earnings per share—compared to other similar companies in the same industry.
- *Buy Gradually.* Once you've found a blue-chip stock you want to add to your portfolio, you don't have to buy it all at once. Buy a set dollar amount of the stock on a regular basis, adding gradually to your position over time. This way you'll benefit from dollar-cost averaging—buying more when a stock is on "sale."
- *Ignore the Short Term.* Long-term investors enjoy the benefit of not having to worry about short-term price fluctuations in stocks they own. In fact, the only time this strategy seems to fail them is when they ignore their own advice, and sell a stock that has fallen. This often only serves to make sure you ring up a loss. It's also a tough job trying to decide when the drop is over and the stock is back on track and climbing. In other words, you've got to guess right twice—when to sell and when to buy back in—to beat the

returns you could make merely by holding on and never selling in the first place.

- *Do Your Homework.* The more you know and understand the business and financial situation of companies you buy, the more peace of mind you'll give yourself. In addition, if you know the story and the stock founders, you have just one simple task to tackle. Check out if there have been any significant changes to the company's story. If not, then the reasons you bought the stock in the first place are still valid, and so is your investment.
- *Look at Need-Satisfiers.* Look for products or services that we all just can't do without. In good times or bad times, people still need gas for their cars, food for their table and, more and more, computers for their tables, too!

JOVIAL ENGINEER

SERIOUS ABOUT INVESTING

•

"I TRIED JOGGING ONCE, but the ice kept falling out of my glass."

Anybody who includes a quotation from David Lee Roth, the flamboyant ex-lead singer from Van Halen, in all his E-mails obviously knows how to look on the light side of things.

But Steven Lightfoot, 32, says what he does take seriously is investing. "I believe strongly that it can provide financial and personal freedom," he says. "I encourage all of my friends to invest and manage their finances, which is rather funny, because I have the image of being a flippant artist type."

An engineer, the 32-year-old works in technical support for Pratt & Whitney Canada Inc. in Montreal, crewing on a sailboat and sculpting in his spare time.

While earning a living from your job is obviously a necessity, he says, it's what you do with the money you bring home that really counts. "I was doing all that 'Wealthy Barber' stuff like having a regular amount come out of my account each month to buy mutual funds long before that book came out," he says.

In fact, Mr. Lightfoot has been using this disciplined approach to saving and investing since he began working at age 23. "It's allowed me to assemble a portfolio that's now in the six figures, and just continues to grow."

HOW HE DOES IT: Instead of chasing junior exploration companies and the like, Mr. Lightfoot puts the 10 per cent of his portfolio he's designated as his risk money into two small private businesses. "I can honestly say I'm not able to determine if they'll be profitable," he says. However, he's actively involved in the businesses, and says the experience has provided a great education in assessing companies. "I can now read a balance sheet and analyze a profit and loss statement."

For his mutual fund picks, he relies on two investment advisers. "I largely let them come up with the ideas, and I say yes or no."

Most of Mr. Lightfoot's non-RRSP funds are invested in the United States to protect him from a drop in the Canadian dollar. "I live in Quebec and see the reality of the province's political uncertainty," he says. He also feels secure about his portfolio because the individual companies he has invested in are involved in a wide number of different industries. "It's sort of by accident, but it's kind of like a mini-mutual fund."

HIS BEST MOVES: There are few high fliers in his portfolio, because Mr. Lightfoot's goal is stable long-term growth. His biggest pop came from Milton, Ont.-based satellite television company Tee-Comm Electronics Inc. (now delisted), which he bought at $4 in late 1994, and sold a few months later when the stock hit $8. "I knew satellite television was coming in the U.S., and was starting to be seen in the media as a big thing," he says. "Whether or not it was viable, I knew it would be a hot concept, the speculators would get in, and I could make a profit."

Abbott Laboratories of North Chicago, Ill., (ABT-NYSE, 52-week high $68.94 (U.S.), low $41.37, last trade $68.37), has given Mr. Lightfoot exactly what he looks for in a stock—steady, strong growth. His broker recommended it, deeming it undervalued. "That's what I look to my brokers for," he says. He has held the stock since he first bought it at $25 in 1993.

A belief that power-tool maker Black & Decker Corp. of Towson, Md., (BDK-NYSE, high $42.50, low $29, last trade $38.75), was undervalued earned him a 25 per cent return over two years. He bought the tool maker in 1993 at $20, selling two years later at $25.

"New management was coming in at the time and it looked like the company was going to get turned around."

HIS WORST MOVE: Mr. Lightfoot's largest loss came from Italian conglomerate Montedison SpA. On the recommendation of a broker, Mr. Lightfoot went in at $8 in late 1993, thinking it was a stable way to diversify internationally. His timing couldn't have been worse. Within a couple of months, the stock tanked after executives were implicated in corruption, and Mr. Lightfoot bailed out at $5.

ADVICE: "Don't chase high returns because it's a waste of time. Look for steady, long-term appreciation."

THE PORTFOLIO

Date:	Saturday, July 5, 1997
The investor:	Steven Lightfoot, 32.
Occupation:	Engineer with Pratt & Whitney.
Investment personality:	"Serious."
Portfolio makeup:	Stocks: Abbott Laboratories, Toshiba, Sea Containers, Royal Bank, Shell Canada. Funds: AGF Canadian Equity, BPI Canadian Small Companies, O'Donnell Canadian Emerging Growth, Templeton Global Smaller Companies.
Portfolio size:	"Low six figures."
Rate of return:	"Probably 10 per cent to 15 per cent."

Have fun in life, take your money seriously, and have even more fun in life. That about sums up Mr. Lightfoot's approach. But if you're already thinking you're not the type to wrinkle up your brow, say goodbye to enjoyment and engulf yourself in dry financial matters, don't worry. You don't have to.

What Mr. Lightfoot does is take his money seriously, but that doesn't mean he lets it take over his life. In fact, quite the opposite. As he remarked to me, he'd almost prefer to hire a trustee and say, "Deal with my investments and give me a certain rate of return, and take a percentage off."

All he's done is apply some very simple, basic and easy-to-implement strategies to build a large portfolio, take care of his future and take a lot of worries off his back. Consider this:

- He already has a net worth in the six figures. He's a real-life example of the benefits of regular investing and the power of compounding. For example, if you put $6,000 into an RRSP every year, and you earned an average return of 11 per cent, you'd have passed the $100,000 mark in just 10 years. Start early, contribute to an RRSP regularly, and your money truly does take care of you automatically.
- Even when the bull market was storming ahead, he wasn't particularly interested in big returns. "I don't even think about it," he said to me. As he puts it, as long as he makes a half-decent return, he'll do more than well because of his regular savings and compounding.
- Those regular savings were started when he was young, and it's become a habit he hardly even knows he has. "You don't see the money, so you just forget about it, and all of a sudden, you've got this big chunk of savings."
- He is broadly diversified. That helps him worry even less about his investments, and levels out his portfolio's performance. Not only does he have a selection of stocks from different industries, but he has also spread his money among stocks, mutual funds, GICs and two small business investments.
- He further increases his comfort level by limiting the high-risk part of his portfolio—his small business investments—to just 10 per cent.

INVESTING IS KID'S STUFF

TO B.C. BROTHERS

•

HAVING A PAPER ROUTE or collecting pop bottles is almost a rite of passage for suburban Canadian kids. After all, it's often the only way they can raise the money to buy the model-car building kit they have their heart set on or that shiny new bike.

But A.J. Shewan, 14, and his younger brother Ben, 12, of Mission, B.C., are a little outside the norm. If they ever wanted to begin spending what they've amassed to date—which they don't, by the way—they could skip the kid's stuff and buy themselves a life-sized Honda, with enough left over for a top-of-the-line Harley.

Sure, A.J. and Ben are a little more driven than most of their peers. Together, they run seven paper routes, bringing in $500 a month. Bottle collecting adds another $200 a month. But what's helped them amass a stunning total of $90,000 is that instead of spending their money on hobbies and junk-food habits, they've been investing in the stock market for more than seven years.

Their parents, John and Ilze, both teachers, wanted to ensure that the boys knew how to manage their money, and helped them make their first few investments. "They had $1,000 and didn't know what to do with it, so I asked them what company they'd like to buy," John recalls. "Right then, A.J. was watching a Laidlaw garbage truck, and the company became their first stock."

HOW THEY DO IT: The boys continue to like companies that they can see around them and in which they are interested. A.J., for instance, belongs to a model railway club, and loves to watch the freight trains that regularly ply the tracks he can see from his bedroom window, so CP Rail's parent, Canadian Pacific Ltd., became a natural part of their portfolio early on.

Once a company has caught their eye, their method is quite simple, depending largely on a gut feel. They'll watch the company's share price for several weeks, talk it over with their father, perhaps run the company by their broker, and then make a decision.

Sun-Rype Products Ltd. (SRF.B-TSE, high $2.95, low $1.75, yesterday's close $2.50), a Kelowna, B.C.-based juice maker, was a typical recent purchase. "We liked the company because you see their drinks in stores and people bring them to school," Ben says. Adds A.J., "They're a small company, and we think they could be taken over."

THEIR BEST MOVES: Five years ago, the Shewan seniors had to fly to New York City for business, and took the family along. "Plane travel is incredibly popular," A.J. says. "For example, it's the only fast way to cross the ocean."

They bought into Seattle-based aircraft-maker Boeing Co. (BA-NYSE, 52-week high $60.50 (U.S.), low $44.87, close $55.37) five years ago at $19. They still like the company, but sold their shares last month.

Another winner has been RJR Nabisco Holdings Corp., the New York-based food and tobacco company (RN-NYSE, 52-week high $38.87, low $25.50, close $34.87). They figured a company making so many seemingly addictive products couldn't fail to make a profit.

"I'm trying to help a friend quit smoking right now, and it's really hard," says A.J., who feels that many of the company's food products are almost as difficult to give up. They bought their shares five years back at $4.35, and are still holding on for future gains.

THEIR WORST MOVE: In 1990 A.J. and Ben picked up Bramalea at $1, hoping the beleaguered real estate company would be able to recover from the hammering it took when the real estate industry was razed. It didn't, though, and eventually the company went bankrupt. "I'll remember that one for the rest of my life," A.J. says.

ADVICE: "Get into investing in stocks. You can make good money, and it's better than wasting your money on drugs and cigarettes and candy bars."

THE PORTFOLIO

Date:	Saturday, September 6, 1997
The investors:	A.J. and Ben Shewan, ages 14 and 12, respectively.
Occupation:	Students/bottle collectors/newspaper delivery boys.
Investment personality:	"We buy companies we're interested in."
Portfolio makeup:	CP Rail, Sun Rype, Surrey Metro Savings, Hammond Manufacturing, Repap, TrizecHahn, Wall Financial, Imperial Metals, RJR Nabisco, Knighthawk Airlines, Prime Equity.
Rate of return:	"Above 30 per cent."
Portfolio size:	"High five figures."

This column garnered a lot of comments. Most people I heard from were very envious, and the older they were, the more envious they tended to be.

What can I say about A.J. and Ben, except they are lucky to have had parents that taught them about investing at an early age, and that they took to it like ducks to water.

The sad thing is, personal finance and investing basics should be taught in our school systems, and, by and large, it gets all but ignored. Knowing the basics of money management, good saving habits and long-term investing are not all that complicated. If they are acquired at a young age, they allow people to take full advantage of long-term savings and to maximize the benefits of long-term compounding. The end results will be fewer financial worries, a more stable financial life and a much larger pool of capital to retire on.

But don't let A.J. and Ben's young age put you off. The principles they apply can be used by people of all ages. As you'll see in other columns, no matter how old people are, learning the basics of money management and investing and putting them to work brings a sense of being in control, more optimism about the financial future and, of course, better long-term increases in one's net worth.

HE'S 62 AND STILL
LOOKING FOR GROWTH

•

MANY INVESTMENT ADVISERS have told Earl Fletcher he should protect his money. "Their philosophy is usually 'For goodness sake, don't lose it for the poor guy.'"

But the 62-year-old Burlington, Ont., resident has no time for traditional advice. The problem, he says, is that he's got a lot more time left than most people allow him.

"They tell me I have to protect my money for a few years, but hell, I'm going to live a lot longer than that, and the only way to make my money last is by investing it, not by lending it out with GICs."

But that doesn't mean just any investments. In the past, Mr. Fletcher has worked with several brokers using a timing strategy— or a mistiming strategy, judging by his limited success.

"We had a pretty good record of buying high and selling low, which is really not all that profitable," he says with a laugh.

But he later hooked up with financial adviser Richard Charlton of Fortune Financial Group Inc. in Oakville, Ont., who agreed on putting money in growth investments, but argued for a buy-and-hold strategy. Mr. Fletcher is delighted with the results. "I've basically doubled my money in just under two years," he says.

He now believes the best approach, even for someone his age, is to be a long-term investor, not a lender. He flatly says it's the only way to make your money grow.

"If you look at *Forbes'* list of the wealthiest people, you don't find any lenders," he says. "There must be a message in there even a guy like me can understand."

HOW HE DOES IT: Mr. Fletcher thinks the way to make money over the long haul is to follow the approach of such buy-and-hold advocates as famed U.S. investor Warren Buffett: Pick good companies and stay with them. While his investments may take a downturn or two, that doesn't worry him in the least. "If it's a good company or fund that has a track record, it will recover, so why not stay with it?" he says.

HIS BEST MOVES: Most of his money is in stocks and mutual funds that operate in—or invest in—the financial services sector. His best performer has been Fairfax Financial Holdings Ltd. (FFH-TSE, 52-week high $282, low $94), which he bought at $67 in February 1995. The stock closed yesterday at its high of $282.

"It's essentially a holding company that buys ongoing successful insurance companies," he says about Fairfax. "They've patterned themselves after Warren Buffett in that they buy companies they understand, and they understand the insurance business." His other stock winner has been Trimark Financial Corp. (TMF-TSE, high $45.25, low $18.50.) He bought it in early 1995 at $10.84 (adjusted for splits) and the stock closed at $42.40 yesterday.

He's also done well with the AIC family of funds. He bought AIC Advantage Fund in February 1995, at $20.21, and the units have since risen to over $45. In the same month, he also bought AIC Diversified Canada Fund at $9.88, and AIC Value Fund at $17.20. The two funds closed Thursday at $20.03 and $29.57, respectively.

The roaring bull market has certainly not hurt companies and funds tied to the financial industry, but he believes his investments will continue to do well even if the market corrects. "They're all in a business that will keep on growing for many years, as the baby boomers realize they don't have enough money socked away and start investing."

Perhaps more important is his strong belief in the companies' management. "I wouldn't just buy any financial stock or fund," he says. "They have to be well-managed companies that treat shareholders fairly."

HIS WORST MOVES: One of his biggest mistakes was hooking up with an investment adviser who didn't develop a strategy for him, but bought and sold investments regularly.

"It cost me a fortune in commissions, and more when I left, because a lot of the funds I owned had back-end loads," he says. "It was a bad dream and I don't want to know what that cost me."

His other mistake was buying shares of Royal Trustco Ltd. "six or eight years ago," following the advice of a broker. He picked them up at $10.50 each, and eventually bailed out at $1 to $1.50, when the company evolved into Gentra Inc.

ADVICE: "You've got to get off the fence of income investments and get into other stuff where your money can grow," he says. "When I talk to people, they don't know there's another way and they just think I've been lucky, but it's nothing to do with luck."

THE PORTFOLIO

Date:	Saturday, November 23, 1996
The investor:	Earl Fletcher, 62.
Occupation:	Part-time management training consultant.
Investment personality:	Conservative growth seeker. "Conservative to me doesn't mean putting your money in the bank. It means dealing with sound mutual funds and sound companies."
Portfolio makeup:	Almost all his portfolio is in his registered retirement savings plan, his wife's RRSP and a spousal RRSP. Half is in two stocks, Fairfax Financial Holdings Ltd. and Trimark Financial Corp., and the other half is spread evenly

among AIC Advantage Fund, AIC Diversified
Canada Fund, AIC Value Fund and Trimark
Select Canadian Growth Fund.

Portfolio size: Mid-six figures.

Rate of return: Around 100 per cent over the past
21 months.

One thing Mr Fletcher is right about is that 62 is not that old any-
more. A lot of advisers would still have Mr. Fletcher largely in guaranteed investments, but the notion that when investors hit their sixties
they should essentially be out of the stock market is passing. That old
maxim dates from when people tended to, well, die at a younger age.
On average, people are simply living longer today. This has two financial implications. Relative to your retirement, you simply have
fewer working years in which to build up your savings. And when
you do leave the working world, your savings will have to provide
for many more years of retirement living.

In addition to needing to boost the growth of your savings for the
above reasons, you also have to take some risk in order not to have
those savings eaten up by inflation and taxes. These two demons alone
can easily wipe out any gains from a guaranteed investment such as a
GIC. Yes, your principal will remain intact, but your actual buying
power may decrease. As Mr. Fletcher points out, he could easily have
another 25 years of living and breathing. "And you're not going to do
that on GICs," he argues.

Mr. Fletcher's definition of risk doesn't mean you're taking chances
just because you're buying stocks. "To me, conservative means you're
dealing with sound companies and sound funds. It does not mean
'For God's sake, don't make any money.'" As he points out, even GICs
come with a risk—the risk of not even keeping up with inflation
after taxes.

But Mr. Fletcher doesn't believe in just buying any old stocks willy-
nilly. Note particularly his experience with market timing. Buying high

and selling low is often the result of trying to predict just which way the market is heading and when. Especially for those who are older, it's a quick way to have to cut back on your more expensive hobbies.

One other note: Mr. Fletcher says he once had an adviser who didn't develop a plan for him, but did a lot of trading. "Churning your account is a great way for your adviser to earn commissions and bleed profits from your account, so don't let your broker get away with frequent trading," he says. As Mr. Fletcher argues, "If it's a good company and it has a good track record, why not stick with it?"

That strategy didn't hold much water for a few of his previous advisers, he says, which is why he parted company with them. "They just wanted to find funds that made 10 per cent and move you around, and every time they do it costs you money."

Advisers and brokers make money from you, and it should be part of their job to work out a comprehensive investment plan. You can't decide which stocks to buy and when unless you are able to judge if they make a good fit with your portfolio, and you can't do that unless you have an overall plan. And of course, there's the notion that you should get your money's worth from your broker or adviser. Look for proactive thinking, a long-term strategy and a coherent, cohesive game plan.

ENGINEERING STUDENT
DOES HIS HOMEWORK

•

EDUCATION AND INVESTING are intertwined for Kevin Fergin. In his last year of civil engineering at the University of Waterloo, the 23-year-old Kitchener, Ont., native, who lifts weights to relieve stress and is learning ballroom dancing with his fiancée, says that school work and the stock market are anything but mutually exclusive.

For starters, he is already working with a mid-five-figure portfolio, which he began assembling while working almost full-time hours when he was still in high school. Besides applying the basic discipline of research to his investing, his studies have helped him hone in on several stocks. He's also used the information on some companies gleaned from schoolmates' work terms to help him pick stocks.

And, like a true Canadian capitalist, he's not averse to taking advantage of whatever rules the powers that be have set.

For example, cutbacks at his university led to many of the faculty taking early retirement. In order to give itself time to fill in the soon-to-be-vacant positions, the administration asked students to do two study terms back to back, and offered loans of up to $5,000 at the prime rate to help students with the cash crunch caused by the delayed work term.

"The bells just went off," Mr. Fergin says. "Conservatively, I thought I could make 10 per cent, so I thought it was worth an hour of leg work to find out if there were any requirements that the money be spent on schooling."

There weren't, and so he got a loan, and plunked it down on BCE Inc. (BCE-TSE, 52-week high $54.80, low $30.75, yesterday's close $54.20). His shares, for which he paid $53.70 apiece in August 1996, are now worth $108.40. (They split two-for-one last May.) "Their balance sheet was good, and revenues and profits were increasing."

So were Mr. Fergin's finances. "It even paid a dividend, which, because it was fairly large, offset my interest payments."

HOW HE DOES IT: Education, once again, is the key for Mr. Fergin. "What really struck me the most is I started to read the financial papers, and I got really frustrated because there would be a gap. I'd read something about a bank or something from a company's balance sheet."

So he set out to educate himself, devouring articles that explained the basic ways of the investing world and, later, taking the Canadian Securities Course. He now finds that education invaluable, particularly given the quick lessons he's learned about the need to do his own assessments.

Take what he calls an unnerving experience with his first stock purchase, Cypress Semiconductor Corp. (CY-NYSE, high $18.87 (U.S.), low $7.37, yesterday's close $8.71), a mid-sized U.S. electronics manufacturer. "A friend of mine had a work term with them and he was bullish on them," he says.

What could be better than a fly right on the company's wall sending back reports of orders flowing in every day and new hires appearing seemingly on the hour, right? Well, problem is, those reports weren't good indicators.

Mr. Fergin, who bought his shares at $15.62 in February 1996, watched the stock tread water for many months before throwing in the towel in July 1997, selling his position for $15.50 a share. "I chalk it up to the fact I didn't research it enough individually," he says.

His approach now is to always make sure that he gets a second opinion from someone he can trust, namely himself. "I don't think basing information on one person, whether it is a friend or a broker, is the best way to go," he says. "If I take time to look into a company and do a few calculations myself, I'll make a better investor."

HIS BEST MOVES: For evidence that recommendations don't necessarily mean losses if they are followed up by his own research, Mr. Fergin can turn to Synergistic Industries Ltd., a Mississauga-based company involved with polymers. (It was delisted after being taken over by a private company in the fall of 1997.) At the time, Mr. Fergin was taking a course that touched on polymers—compound materials used for everything from wiring to race car bodies—and felt they would be in big demand.

Applying his new-found, nose-to-the-books credo, that still wasn't enough to make him buy in, but after taking a look at the company's financials, and its low price/earnings ratio, he purchased shares at $6.80 in March 1997. The stock quickly moved up, and he sold at $12.55 that August. "The company's fundamentals were still good, but I didn't feel like being greedy."

A course with a focus on entrepreneurs helped him pick out another winner. "The professor said, when looking at companies and trying to find the next success story, to look at whether they are a leading competitor or are creating new markets," he says, and that led him to Newbridge Networks Corp. (NNC-TSE, high $95, low $26.75, close $39.95).

He picked up the stock at $43 in February 1997, and sold in July at $70. While the Kanata, Ont., company subsequently hit its high, Mr. Fergin also was spared its recent collapse to the $30 range before its latest rebound. "I got out because it had a high price/earnings ratio so the threat of it having large fluctuations was there," he says.

HIS WORST MOVE: After Cypress, his non-starter starter stock, Mr. Fergin moved on to Dallas-based Paging Network Inc. (PAGE-Nasdaq, high $15 (U.S.), low $5.75, close $13.19) on the advice of a broker, picking up the stock in May 1996 at $24.72. The company got hit by falling paging prices and competition from new wireless phones, and

Mr. Fergin finally hung up on it in January 1997 at $14.91. His belief in the need to do his own research strengthened.

"The broker was very bullish, but I didn't understand all the numbers he was throwing at me," he says.

THE PORTFOLIO

Date:	Saturday, March 14, 1998
The investor:	Kevin Fergin, 23.
Occupation:	Master's engineering student.
Investment personality:	Long term.
Portfolio makeup:	Stocks: BCE, Bombardier, Midland Walwyn. Funds: Templeton Growth, C.I. Pacific, RoyFund U.S. Equity, Fidelity European Growth, Altamira Equity, Altamira Resource, Altamira Japanese Opportunity.
Portfolio size:	"Mid-five figures."
Rate of return:	"About 30 per cent over 20 months."

Mr. Fergin's biggest mistakes have occurred when he didn't understand why a "buy" recommendation on a stock made sense, but put his money into the stock anyway. His biggest profits have come from stocks that he analyzed himself and understood.

Education, not a good stock-picking instinct, is at the root of the success of most long-term investors. But that doesn't mean you have to actually be taking high-finance courses for the rest of your natural life. Your goal can be as simple as educating yourself about the different types of funds available, and how to assemble a conservative mix of funds. What's critical is that you equip yourself with the appropriate knowledge in order to be able to assess the investments that best fit your needs and investing approach.

TEACHER DOES HIS
INVESTING HOMEWORK

•

LEARNING IS A LIFE-LONG AFFAIR, says Sechelt, B.C., teacher Jack Pope, who uses his summers away from the classroom for intensive research to keep his investment portfolio on track.

A self-proclaimed information junkie, Mr. Pope treats managing his portfolio as a part-time job, and says the more research he does, the more risks he can take, and the larger his comfort zone. "If you do a good job of picking stocks, over the long term you'll do well."

The 51-year-old father of three teenaged boys, Mr. Pope says he has a lot in common with Sang Kim, another teacher profiled in *Me and My Money* this past summer. Not only do teachers have the holidays to plunge into the investing world, but also their guaranteed pensions give them a solid and safe financial base from which to enter the world of equities.

HOW HE DOES IT: *The Globe and Mail*, business television programs, his investment club and the *Investment Reporter* (a newsletter), along with his broker's updates, all serve as part of Mr. Pope's data base. He also uses the Internet a lot, especially for the Stockwatch Web site www.canada-stockwatch.com, from which he gets E-mailed corporate updates.

He continually scans all of these sources for any mention of the 25 to 30 or so stocks he watches, summarizing the latest news for his own files. "It's a great way to become very familiar with companies," he says.

If a particular company gets a few positive hits—an analyst's rec-ommendation, strong mentions in the media, and so on—it then becomes a potential buy.

He also keeps an eye on larger demographic and economic trends. For instance, he's currently looking to pick up a telecommunications company, and is keeping a watch on BCE Inc., Bruncor Inc. and Telus Corp. "I really think it's a growth industry, because we're demanding more and more telephone services, plus there's the growing demand from the developing world."

If and when he finds a potential winner, he parlays patience into better performance. "You have to wait for your entry point. If you can pick up a stock when it goes on sale, that's part of your return."

HIS BEST MOVES: Mr. Pope nicely timed the seemingly endless cycles that Newbridge Networks Corp. (NNC-TSE, 52-week high $95, low $35.75, yesterday's close $84.25) throws at investors. He bought into the Kanata, Ont.-based communications equipment maker at the end of March at just under $40. He had been watching the stock for a while, and saw it get pulled down when many U.S. technology stocks took a beating.

"I pulled up a price chart, and saw Newbridge was down 22 per cent in a matter of a few weeks," he says. "My broker had a target of $60 on it, and nothing about the company's story had changed." While his brokerage firm moved its target up to $78, he felt the ride might get a bit rough, and sold out in July at $70.

Staying in for the longer haul helped him put some air into his portfolio with Air Canada (AC-TSE, 52-week high $14.45, low $4.85, close $13.85). He bought the stock in the summer of 1995 at $6, hang-ing on as it slowly lost altitude, falling to $4.50. Not only did he get multiple positives on Air Canada through his research, but he also saw a simple sign that it was headed for success. "I could see the economy was picking up, and friends of mine who hadn't been going anywhere were starting to take holidays."

Demographics got Mr. Pope into AIC Advantage Fund early enough to enjoy the fund's recent strong performance, resulting largely from its concentration on financial stocks. "There's a massive number of people around 35, and they're going to start investing largely in their RRSPs, and 80 per cent of that money has to stay here in Canada," he says. "AIC will benefit from that, because it's a direct play on the mutual fund industry."

HIS WORST MOVE: His portfolio is conservative enough that Mr. Pope says he hasn't had any major losses. However, he was handed a setback by Mytec Technologies Inc. (MYT-TSE, 52-week high $9.25, low $2.50), the Toronto-based developer of fingerprint-scanning technology. His investment club had picked the stock as a good buy, and he picked up some shares in the summer of 1996 at $7.50.

"I do a lot of my own banking electronically, and I thought Mytec had a great story, especially given the interest in finding a means of identification for welfare recipients."

The stock moved up a little, but then fell apart, helped by a report from his brokerage firm, RBC Dominion Securities Inc., that put a best-case scenario price of $3.50 to $4 on the stock, he says. "The key problem was that Mytec's potential sales were not as large as had been anticipated, and the company was also facing huge competition." Mr. Pope unloaded his position at $3.40, and the stock closed yesterday at $2.70.

ADVICE: "You really need to do your homework."

THE PORTFOLIO

Date:	Saturday, October 18, 1997
The investor:	Jack Pope, 51.
Occupation:	Teacher.
Investment personality:	"Growth-oriented."
Portfolio makeup:	Funds: AIC Advantage, Altamira Equity, Trimark RSP, Templeton International.
	Stocks: Bombardier, Air Canada, Canadian

Pacific, Loewen, Westcoast, CAE,
Extendicare, Xillix, TVX, Ulster Petroleum.

Portfolio size: "Low six figures."

Rate of return: "18.5 per cent in 1996, 17 per cent
year-to-date."

As a teacher, Mr. Pope knows you have to learn to walk before you
run. He educated himself in the real world of investing, but did it in
a methodical way. He began with balanced mutual funds, then stepped
up to equity funds before finally making the move to picking individual stocks. Knowing what he was getting into was important for
him, even though he uses a full-service broker, another good lesson
for sound investing. "Make sure you understand what you're buying
before you buy it. Don't rely on anyone else."

He also knows what he puts into his investments and what he gets
out of them: a useful motivator. "I spend an hour a day looking after my
investments. It's like a part-time job that provides a pretty good salary."

There's an interesting corollary to his statement about doing well
long term if you pick the right stocks. In the short term, you might
not do so well, but that shouldn't deter you. Mr. Pope is dead on
when he says, "In the short term there's some volatility, but over time
good stocks rise." Mr. Pope tries to take advantage of that short-term
volatility by exercising a key quality—patience. Once he's found a
stock he wants in his portfolio, he'll still wait—perhaps for months—
hoping to buy it on a dip.

However, he told me that he doesn't believe that true market timing—buying into lows and selling on the highs—is really possible. As
he puts it, "When stocks move they move very quickly particularly
on the upside and if you're not there you've missed it."

In short, like all good buy-and-holders, he'd like to get a stock
cheaper if possible, but he knows that in the long run, it's not so much
a matter of when you get into a particular stock, but how long you've
been in that stock.

QUEST FOR VAN
PUTS VET ON TRACK

•

IN 1993, SCOTT HANSON and his wife were trying to rationalize the purchase of a new van for their growing family, which now includes two young children. "We did a whole lot of searching about whether that was the best use of our saved-up capital," he says, before snorting derisively that a new vehicle isn't exactly a terrific investment.

In the meantime, he stumbled across Gordon Pape's book, *Building Wealth in the 90s*. He devoured it, and a small library's worth of books, prospectuses and newspapers, as he discovered he was a latent natural investor. About the same time, Mr. Hanson, who lives in Burlington, Ont., and works as a veterinarian in nearby Oakville, helped found an investment club.

Today, Mr. Hanson is one informed investor who uses his own research, that of his broker, Keith Richards of Midland Walwyn, and his investment club's brain trust to make his financial moves.

HOW HE DOES IT: There are some minor differences to the approach Mr. Hanson takes with his own account and that of his investment club. For example, the investment club steers clear of resource stocks, but Mr. Hanson will hold them personally. "My broker has a really good working knowledge of oil and gas companies," he says. In general, though, whether on his own or with his fellow clubbers, his approach focuses on four basic criteria when evaluating companies.

Admitting that they drew a lot from storied U.S. investor Warren Buffett's approach, the first criterion is that the company has to be doing something they can understand before they'll look at the stock. Second, the company must have excellent business economics. That means avoiding companies whose product or service is a commodity, and targeting those with brand-name recognition and proprietary technology or other assets that give them some monopoly-like qualities. A good example, Mr. Hanson says, is Imax Corp. "They are the only company that can provide the giant screen, giant film experience."

Third, they want the management to be committed to adding value for shareholders either through dividends, stock buybacks or, most critically, a wise investment of earnings. "We want companies that are shovelling earnings back into the company." Finally, they also look for long-term profitability: "We like to see companies with a return-on-equity higher than 18 per cent, and earnings growth at the same level."

HIS BEST MOVES: In his own account, a big winner for Mr. Hanson has been Calgary-based Barrington Petroleum Ltd. (BPL-ME, 52-week high $6.60, low $3.90, yesterday's close $4.05), which he bought at $3.25 in early 1996, and sold that fall for more than $5. (Mr. Hanson always includes commissions in his cost base.) In addition to a favourable take on the company from his broker who liked its fundamentals, as well as its technical charts, Mr. Hanson also felt the company had made some wise acquisitions, and had avoided getting suckered into buying overvalued properties. "We sold because my broker felt it was heading into a cyclical downturn."

Bank of Montreal (BMO-TSE, high $67.70, low $44.85, close $67.70) also has made him some nice change since he bought it last fall at $53.47. "I wanted to add some stability to my portfolio, and I liked their acquisition of Harris Bank and the way they were moving into the U.S." Of course, yesterday's announcement of the merger between Royal Bank and Bank of Montreal makes him look like a genius.

His investment club has done well with Royal Group Technologies Ltd. (RYG-TSE, high $43.50, low $26.50, close $35.25)—formerly

Royal Plastics Groups Ltd.—which makes plastic just-about-anything. The club picked it up in the spring of 1996 for an average cost of $21.89.

"We thought the potential from developing countries for their plastic houses was phenomenal, and they make a lot of money from vinyl siding and window blinds," he says. The club sold its holding in August 1997, for a 43.6 per cent gain after they saw that president and chairman Vic De Zen had sold some of his shares. At the time, Mr. Hanson says, there were also rumours floating about—since proven untrue—that Mr. De Zen was considering leaving the company to set up another organization.

HIS WORST MOVE: Not understanding the company was where he says he erred in investing in SR Telecom Inc. (SRX-TSE, high $9.50, low $5.05, close $6.50), which he bought at $15.15 in 1995. The Montreal-based company makes wireless telecommunication systems using microwave technology, which it largely sells to developing countries. "The market was really worried about all these other telecommunication technologies," he says. "I didn't understand the industry well enough. I should have looked at the alternatives other companies like Nortel were offering." The stock was soon beaten down, partly because many analysts were disappointed by the company's inability to improve its earnings. Mr. Hanson sold in July 1996, at $8.50 for a loss of 44 per cent.

ADVICE: "Be patient and tune out the stock market because it's often noisy and very irrational."

THE PORTFOLIO

Date:	Saturday, January 24, 1998
The investor:	Scott Hanson, 32.
Occupation:	Veterinarian.
Investment personality:	Patient "Buffett-ist."
Portfolio makeup:	Personal: Philip Services, Bank of Montreal.

Investment club: Bank of Montreal, Trimark,
Intel, Imax, Bombardier.

Portfolio size: "Five figures."

Rate of return: "Average annual compound return of 14.8
per cent in the investment club, and around
15 per cent on personal account over three
years."

Like many *Me and My Money* investors, Mr. Hanson has found being in an investment club a terrific way to learn more about investing. The big attraction is that you can divvy up the research work, meaning you'll end up with more in-depth analysis, as well as enjoying the insights and observations of the other club members. One other great benefit about getting together with others to learn more about what to do with your money is they can provide a useful sounding board for your own ideas, helping you clarify your thoughts. This can be useful in helping you overcome your own resistance to risk, for example, or conversely, reining you in when you want to take a flyer on a risky investment.

SO MANY STOCKS,
SO LITTLE TIME

•

FAITH IN HIS BROKERS and hope for his equities means Don Richardson will likely never have to depend on charity.

"My approach is mostly about having trust in my advisers and trying to pick something that's got a half-decent chance of making some money," he says.

Although he's at the age when many traditional asset mixes would have him heavily into fixed-income securities, the 61-year-old Brampton, Ont., man still has more than 80 per cent of his portfolio in stocks, either directly or through equity mutual funds. "They simply pay off better than fixed-income investments, especially in this market."

Mr. Richardson doesn't like to spend a lot of time tracking his investments. Not only does his job overseeing mining projects with Kvaerner Davy Canada Ltd. keep him busy, but he says he's just plain lazy when it comes to the markets. And, he adds, "I know enough to know I don't know a lot."

So Mr. Richardson sticks to engineering, and hires his own financial consultants to help him with his money. "I've only got a little spare time so I'd rather depend on somebody who worries about my money full time."

HOW HE DOES IT: One key member of his team is Christine Butchart, now a broker with C.M. Oliver & Co. Ltd. in Erin, Ont. Mr. Richardson first hooked up with her when she was with Investors Group Inc. in the mid-eighties. In addition to directing his mutual fund investments, says Mr. Richardson, "she basically does all the financial planning for my wife and myself."

For example, she helped Mr. Richardson and his wife use income-splitting to minimize their tax bill when he stops working.

"Our savings are nicely divided so when we go into retirement it's not all in my name," he says. "That kind of thing only takes a half hour to get through, but the benefits last a lifetime."

He also has a second broker, Sharon Kubicek, who is with Nesbitt Burns Inc. in Toronto. Many of his stock picks come from Nesbitt's recommendations, and while he says he knows that means there is often an inherent promotion behind many of his investments, "I depend on their research and on my brokers' honesty."

HIS BEST MOVES: Mr. Richardson has done well with QLT Phototherapeutics Inc. (QLT-TSE, 52-week high $39, low $17.12, yesterday's close $30.50), the Vancouver-based biotechnology company whose flagship product is Photofrin, a light-activated drug used to fight cancer. "I liked it because it was health-oriented and that's something that has been growing, especially in the U.S.," he says. He bought his shares in January 1996, at between $12 and $13.

Montreal-based Bombardier Inc. (BBD.B-TSE, high $27, low $17.50, close $25.50) has been another strong performer. In addition to the company's leading offerings of planes, trains and jet skis, Mr. Richardson says what attracted him was the company's focus on the bottom line. He has seen his investment increase more than 200 per cent since he bought his shares in February 1995, when the stock was trading in the $25 range. The stock split two-for-one last July.

Mr. Richardson has also managed to enjoy some of the recent runup in bank stocks. He bought Bank of Nova Scotia (BNS-TSE, high $57.40, low $30.12, close $53.65), at around $33 last July. "I didn't think the banks would do that well, but they were undervalued, and everybody was talking about their profits."

HIS WORST MOVE: With the market steadily marching upward, Mr. Richardson says he hasn't had any real setbacks over the past few years, just a few investments that have lagged more than he would have liked.

His worst recent performers have been two funds, Dynamic Global Bond Fund and Dynamic Income Fund. He bought both funds in January 1996, and the funds have one-year returns to the end of February of 5.5 per cent and 7.7 per cent, respectively. "With interest rates so low, bond funds haven't done well," he says. While he is considering switching out of these two, "I don't jump from fund to fund, and if interest rates rise, I don't want to miss another cycle."

ADVICE: "Start off by sitting down with a financial planner to set a proper financial course, because looking after your financial health is just not taught in schools."

THE PORTFOLIO

Date:	Saturday, March 22, 1997
The investor:	Don Richardson, 61.
Occupation:	Senior project manager for an engineering contracting firm.
Investment personality:	"I'm a moderate to conservative investor, mostly because of my age."
Portfolio makeup:	Stocks include Bombardier, Seagram, Thomson, Bell Canada, BCE, Bank of Nova Scotia, Nova, CIBC. Mutual funds include BPI American Equity Value, BPI American Small Companies, Elliott & Page Equity, Fidelity Far East, Fidelity Growth America, Trimark Select Canadian Growth, AGF American Growth, Templeton Growth.
Portfolio size:	Six figures.
Rate of return:	"Around 15 per cent or more a year."

One of the common characteristics of people who are successful in life is that they often are good at knowing just what they are not good at. As Mr. Richardson points out, he knows enough to know he doesn't know a lot about picking stocks.

For an investor, that statement carries a lot of wisdom. If you don't know a lot about stocks and realize it, then it greatly clarifies your path. You either need to stay out of individual stocks and stick to mutual funds, spend some time educating yourself about equities so you can make informed investment decision, or join forces with an adviser who can serve as your stock-market guru.

Mr. Richardson also consciously made one key decision that many people skip over—deciding just how to use his free time. Like many of us, Mr. Richardson says he has little spare time, and has chosen to let somebody else worry about the full-time concerns of how his investments are doing.

Life, as the saying goes, is short. You do need to set out your financial goals, and find a way to achieve them. But you have to make sure they don't conflict with your goals for other parts of your life, which are just as important. You may find that the best investment of your time is to spend it with friends and family, and to use an adviser to help you get where you want to go financially.

INSTINCT, INSIGHT
GUIDE STOCK PRICER

•

TWO YEARS AGO, Frank Parise decided to bid farewell to his financial adviser, and take over his portfolio himself. "Everything I picked out went well, and everything he picked out went flat or down."

Throw in commissions and that was all the 56-year-old needed to make the jump from relying on his broker to depending on his "gut instinct" to pick his stocks.

But a little gentle probing reveals that his success to date—including being on the right side of a profitable takeover bid—depends more on some sharp insights than on instinct.

In addition to ringing up a healthy 25 per cent return in the 18 months he's been handling the reins of his own portfolio, the Woodbridge, Ont., Toronto Transit Commission worker has discovered he enjoys steering his own financial ship. "I get a kick out of doing my homework and being proved right," he says. "There's a lot of personal satisfaction in that."

HOW HE DOES IT: Mr. Parise favours blue-chip stocks that he knows and understands. "I shy away from high-flying mining stocks and technology companies like Hummingbird that I don't understand."

And while he says he simply buys companies he's familiar with, that familiarity must be accompanied by a strong, consistent track record and, if possible, the potential for a takeover.

He also looks for companies that have a low debt ratio because he feels they will fare better if the economy turns down, or interest rates shoot up. "It's just like a family," he says. "If mortgage rates go from 5 per cent to 15 per cent, you don't have any money to buy butter any more."

Perhaps most important, though, is that the company be a recognizable—and large—feature on the economic landscape. "I figure it doesn't matter what happens to the economy with big, well-known companies," he says. "People will always drink beer, go to the bank and need cement to build houses."

HIS BEST MOVES: His standout winner so far has been Calgary-based Suncor Energy Inc. (SU-TSE, 52-week high $49.90, low $22.18, yesterday's close $46.75). He bought it at $22 last summer. Mr. Parise thought the stock would benefit from all the positive reports he was reading about Suncor's involvement in the Alberta oil sands. He also felt—and continues to feel—there's a good chance a Shell or a Petro-Canada will buy up all of Suncor's gas stations, which will "make them a bundle and be great for the shares."

Living in Woodbridge, he became intrigued by Royal Group Technologies Inc. (RYG-TSE, high $38.75, low $19.40, close $37.20) because he saw the locally based company's name everywhere. Royal makes vinyl and plastic alternatives to metal and wood building materials. "Some people around here know the management personally and say they're good people.

"I also know people who work in the factory, and they had three shifts going full-time and were starting to sell into China and Central America," he says. "So I thought this was a company going somewhere."

He picked up his shares at $20 in February 1996, and enjoyed a nice move, selling half of his position at $37.65 recently.

Mr. Parise's "gut feeling" for potential special situations led him to buy National Trustco Inc. (NT-TSE, 52-week high $35.05, low $20.90, close $34.25) this spring. "I thought, 'Gee, CIBC is No. 2 in size, and I bet they want to be No. 1,'" he says.

To get to the top spot, he figured that Canadian Imperial Bank of Commerce would have to acquire a trust company, and the obvious target was National Trust, the country's last major family-controlled trust company. Well, he got the target right, but the potential buyer wrong, as Bank of Nova Scotia, not CIBC, made an offer for the company in June.

Not that that hurt the stock. He paid $24 for his shares. "It seemed like a low-risk investment, because even if my takeover idea didn't pan out, it was still a good company."

HIS WORST MOVE: His biggest loss to date came from betting on a drop in the U.S. market. His adviser got him into put warrants on the Standard & Poor's 500-stock index. He paid $2.50 for them in August 1995, and sold them for just 22 cents in December 1996, in order to lock in the capital loss before the end of the year. "The bet was the S&P would dive and these things would double, but of course things happened in reverse."

ADVICE: "Buy household names and keep your eyes on the news."

THE PORTFOLIO

Date:	Saturday, August 2, 1997
The investor:	Frank Parise, 56.
Occupation:	Toronto Transit Commission work assignment clerk.
Investment personality:	"I take a moderate amount of risk, but want to preserve my capital."
Portfolio makeup:	Imasco, Royal Bank, Royal Group Technologies, St. Lawrence Cement, Suncor, National Trustco, Molson.
Portfolio size:	"High five figures."
Rate of return:	"25 per cent over the past 18 months."

Mr. Parise was one of my more memorable interviews. Each time I asked him why he bought a stock that had turned out to be a winner,

I could almost hear him shrugging his shoulders as he replied, "It seemed like a good company," or some variation thereof.

It was only after a long, long time that he finally cracked. All of a sudden he started spilling out loads of information about all the critical ways he assessed companies before he invested in them. The problem was, I think, that he simply assumed that others would know what he meant when he said a company looked "good."

And in that lies the difference between smart investors and, well, *less smart* investors. Those doomed to see their investments underperform will hear somebody call a company a "good" company, and invest in it. Those who will see their net worth increase over the years, like Mr. Parise, know that to call a company "good" means that it rates well against a range of well-defined, quantifiable measures.

PATHS TO RICHES
PAVED WITH DIVIDENDS

•

PUMPING THEIR STOCK-MARKET PROFITS into luxury cars is usually a tribal rite reserved for junior stock jockeys. But retired Regina pharmacist Reg Lawrence has just bought himself a shiny new Infiniti with part of his gains from 1996, thanks to his dull and undemanding focus on investing for dividends.

"I started buying for dividends in the early 1980s, and my portfolio has done nothing but grow," he says.

Grow, indeed. Mr. Lawrence says the most he ever made running a pharmacy was $52,000 a year, and his pension is only $1,110 a month. Yet he's managed to accumulate a portfolio that's now in the mid-six figures.

In addition to some solid picking, part of that growth he attributes to his heavy use of borrowed funds. Because his investments are so conservative, he doesn't see much risk in drawing on his line of credit on his home and using the money to increase his returns.

HOW HE DOES IT: Once a year in January, Mr. Lawrence sits down with the *Report on Business* year-end investing summary and reshuffles his portfolio.

He begins by picking out every company that has a dividend of between 3 and 6.5 per cent. He then looks for companies that possess his four key indicators: rising revenue, increasing profit, a climbing share price and, most importantly, steadily rising dividends.

"I'm a great believer that if a company has regularly raised dividends in the past, then that's the approach of the board, and they'll continue to do it."

He also favours conglomerates because he says they tend to keep the dividends flowing more than other types of companies. "If something goes slack, they've got something else that makes money."

This detailed screening usually turns up just under 20 stocks. He then further trims his list by only looking at those companies with revenues of at least $400 million. "That means they're big enough to survive any problems that come along," he says.

His final list is likely to include many of the companies he is already holding. In general, he sells two underachievers each year, replacing them with two more promising candidates, keeping his portfolio to about 15 or 16 companies overall.

HIS BEST BUYS: TransCanada PipeLines Ltd. (TRP-TSE, 52-week high $26.85, low $18.87, yesterday's close $24.90) is one of Mr. Lawrence's favourites, which he picked up five years ago for $16 a share. The dividend has been increased 8 cents every year since then, and is currently at $1.16. "I'm getting 8 per cent raises, and I never got that at the hospital where I worked," Mr. Lawrence says.

Beyond the dividend increases, Mr. Lawrence approves of the company's growing international profile and its ability to keep revenue on the increase. "My guess is they're going to earn more than $10 billion this year, and I think they'll raise the dividend, and it will be around $1.24 by next January."

Another favourite is Power Financial Corp. (PWF-TSE, high $29, low $16.93, yesterday's close $25.05), the Montreal-based management and financial holding company. "They're owned by Power Corp., who want to force the dividend up so they get the money in the parent company, and I just go along for the ride."

A more recent acquisition is St. John's-based Fortis Inc. (FTS-TSE, high $34.70, low $27.60, yesterday's close $31.75), which he bought in early 1996 for $25. "They have a history of increasing dividends, and their revenues are growing," he says.

Mr. Lawrence also likes the fact that beyond its Atlantic electrical utilities, the company has diversified into Ontario, and is involved in real estate, including ownership of several hotels in the Maritimes.

HIS WORST MOVE: Mr. Lawrence's biggest mistake dates back to when he was still dabbling in junior stocks. He bought into Toronto-based Westfield Minerals Ltd., because of the promise of a property it owned in Chile. However, the company was controlled by the Toronto Bronfman group, which moved the mine over to Northgate Exploration Ltd., another company it had an interest in, through Hees International Bancorp Inc.

"That left Westfield as a cash-rich company with nothing in terms of prospects," he says. Mr. Lawrence had paid around $2.50 for his shares and finally bailed out when the stock hit $1.75. "I took a bath, and said, 'I'm never talking to the Bronfmans again.'"

ADVICE: "Buy stocks that pay dividends, because when the market is down, you'll still have the income."

THE PORTFOLIO

Date:	Saturday, April 12, 1997
The investor:	Reg Lawrence, 58.
Occupation:	Retired pharmacist.
Investment personality:	"I'm conservative. Any investment house would classify me as ultra-conservative."
Portfolio makeup:	Bank of Montreal, BC Telecom Inc., Canada Resource Trust Units, Pengrowth Energy Trust Units, Fortis Inc., IPL Energy Inc., Power Financial Corp., TransCanada PipeLines Ltd., Westcoast Energy Inc., Crestbrook

Forest Industries Ltd., TVI Pacific Inc.,
Novopharm Ltd.
Portfolio size: "Mid-six figures."
Rate of return: "Around 12 per cent over the past 22 years."

Investing for dividends typically gets little coverage, but it is an excellent way to earn tax-favoured income, thanks to the dividend tax credit.

Here's how dividends end up being taxed at a lower rate than capital gains and interest on your investments. At tax time, you actually increase the amount of dividends you've received by 25 per cent. For example, if you receive $1,000 in dividends, you "gross up" to $1,250, and calculate your federal tax on that amount. However, you then get a dividend tax credit of 13.33 per cent of the grossed-up amount. This amount then gets subtracted from your federal tax and usually earns you a reduction in your provincial taxes as well.

The result of all this smoke and mirrors is that dividends have the lowest investment tax rate compared to stocks (capital gains) and interest earned on bonds, CSBs and the like. For example, if you're in a 41 per cent tax bracket, your dividends will be taxed at around 25 per cent. That is much lower than interest income, which is taxed at your marginal tax rate, and even capital gains, which for someone in the 41 tax bracket would be effectively taxed at around 31 per cent.

A portfolio like Mr. Lawrence's that focuses on companies that pay strong dividends offers the best of both worlds—a combination of strong income, as well as the potential for steady, if not spectacular, growth. Stocks that pay dividends tend to be those of conservative companies, so they likely won't fall as drastically as more growth-oriented stocks when the market drops, plus you'll still have your income.

Mr. Lawrence's first criterion is a good one to focus on—is the company committed not only to regularly paying out dividends, but also increasing them? Actions speak louder than words, so you need to follow Mr. Lawrence's example and see if the company has raised its dividends in the past.

Another quality to look for is growth on many fronts, including revenues, market share and profits. Often, the increases go hand in hand. For example, if a company boosts its dividend payment, that may be a sign the company expects its earnings and share price to increase as well.

When assessing dividend-paying stocks, you should also keep an eye on a company's dividend payout ratio. This is the total amount it pays out in cash dividends on common shares divided by net income. If the ratio is too low—say below 30 per cent—you're not getting enough of the company's profits passed on to you. If the ratio is too high—getting up to 100 per cent or even above—the company may not be keeping enough cash on hand to help pay for future growth.

EX-FIREMAN CAREFUL
NOT TO GET BURNED

•

YOU PROBABLY DON'T NEED to visit too many fires before you realize that when things go up in flames, they really go up in flames. And
unless you were brought up in a cliché-free zone, it's hard to forget
that business about what happens when you play with matches.

So it only seems appropriate, somehow, that retired fireman Richard
Cresswell has spent his investing life avoiding situations where he
could get financially burned and putting his money into the most
flame-proof investments available.

"I guess my approach is dull and conservative but over the long haul
prices go up and dividends rise, so it works," says the 72-year-old, who
spent 31 years with the Toronto Fire Department before retiring in
1978. He moved to Calgary where he worked as a chauffeur for a Royal
Bank executive for several years. He and Florence, his wife of 48 years,
then settled in Vernon, B.C., where he busies himself with church activities, including cooking up hearty dinners for the homeless.

HOW HE DOES IT: Mr. Cresswell bought his first stock in the fifties, purchasing a few hundred shares of Stafford Foods, which promptly went
from $5 to $7. "In the mid-fifties when salaries were low, several hundred dollars was a lot of money to make," he says. "I immediately bought
a White Owl cigar, and everybody thought I was swaggering."

But he quickly set himself up with a very conservative broker, and
has steadily built his portfolio with big-name, dividend-paying blue-
chips. "I used to look for things I could see around me like CP and

utilities that people need every day," he says. "No matter what happens, the trains still run, and when it gets cold, people still turn on the gas."

The Saturday crossword looms large in Mr. Cresswell's plans, but after that he uses the weekend to devour the business press and review his stocks and his strategy "to reinforce where I'm going."

Most of the stocks he currently holds he's had for many years, the one big exception being Calgary-based TransAlta Corp. (TA-TSE, high $20.25, low $15.10, yesterday's close $20.10), which he picked up when he moved to Alberta.

Lately, he's been keeping his eye on another western company, Vancouver-based Versacold (ICE-TSE, high $12.30, low $6.65, close $11.25), the largest public refrigerated warehousing and distribution company in the country.

If there's a common theme running through the stocks in his portfolio, he says, it's that they are all Canadian companies, but own large operations that have a lot of potential and are working internationally. "For example, TransAlta owns a utility company in New Zealand, while Edper has vast holdings in Brazil," he says. "My strategy is a long-term process, and certainly not a get–rich–quick method."

Of the markets' recent volatility, Mr. Cresswell says that people who hold good stocks should just stay calm. "No matter what happens over the next six months, ride out the storm," he advises. "Then if you're still uncomfortable, look around for different investments."

HIS BEST MOVES: The latest runup in bank stocks is just one chapter in Mr. Cresswell's profitable position in Royal Bank of Canada (RY-TSE, high $77.65, low $44.00, yesterday's close $74.85), which he picked up in 1984 at $12.50 a share, adjusted for splits.

"There's nothing wrong with (Bank of Montreal president) Matt Barrett, but I knew people who worked for the Royal, they were the No. 1 bank, and they have their fingers in many different pies," he says.

Another long-term winner has been Canadian Pacific Ltd. (CP-TSE, high $43.85, low $31.80, close $41.50), which he bought in the 1970s in the single digits, adjusted for splits.

Given his extremely long-term buy-and-hold approach, the money he's made since picking up TransAlta at $14 in 1992 and 1993 could almost be qualified as his trading profits, although he still holds the company.

HIS WORST MOVE: Mr. Cresswell still remembers the hit he took on Peace River Mining and Smelter back in the sixties. What began as a small western Canadian mining company was turned into a manufacturer of iron parts for the auto industry. The move misfired, and by 1970 the company had been placed in receivership.

The unfortunate shareholders, including Mr. Cresswell, got 3 cents on the dollar. The lesson, he says, is that the company was the same company that he had originally bought in name only, and that wasn't enough. "When I see companies change hands and change strategies, that's the end of the road for me."

ADVICE: "Don't be afraid to ask your broker questions, and be leery of what you hear."

THE PORTFOLIO

Date:	Saturday, November 15, 1997
The investor:	Richard Cresswell, 72.
Occupation:	Retired fireman.
Investment personality:	"Dull and conservative."
Portfolio makeup:	Canadian Pacific Ltd., Canadian Bank Note Co., EdperBrascan Ltd., Royal Bank, Stelco Ltd., TransAlta Corp., TransCanada PipeLines Ltd., Versacold Corp., strip bonds, CP Hotel Trust Units.
Portfolio size:	"Six figures."
Rate of return:	"12 per cent to 16 per cent a year."

Mr. Cresswell is a great example of some of the rich irony found in the stock market. He says he doesn't invest in order to get rich quick, but aside from the lucky few who get in—and out—of things like Bre-X at the right time, the stock market doesn't often reward even the most seasoned traders with ongoing profits of the eye-popping kind. Yet his long-term blue-chip approach is just the thing to build substantial wealth if you start early enough and stick to your guns.

BIG-PICTURE PLANNING
KEY TO RETIREMENT

•

FOR ALMOST SEVEN YEARS, Steve Bareham has been applying himself
to learning how to invest and plan for his retirement. While he is still
learning, he admits, the 47-year-old married Nelson, B.C., college
instructor, who also runs a communications company, says that "what
is smart and what's not is becoming more clear."

As he sees it, people have a basic choice of turning over their financial decisions to others or becoming knowledgeable in retirement
planning themselves. A self-described "Type A," Mr. Bareham chose
the latter route, and pursued it with such vigour he has laid out his
strategy in a recently published book called *The Last Resort—A
Retirement Vision for Canadians and How to Achieve It.*

HOW HE DOES IT: Living in prime retirement country, Mr. Bareham is
probably dead-on when he says his home is also one of his primary
assets—and one in which he expects to see strong returns. On the
premise that nobody is making any more waterfront, he and his wife
bought 1-⅓ acres on Kootenay Lake that included a house and a rental
cabin. "We have the option of living on the lake forever, or selling it
in 20 years to some urbanite fleeing the big city."

On the market side, he says it's a challenge for the small investor to
keep up with important information, such as sudden changes of management, insider selling or buying, or poor earnings reports. "Between
leaving for work in the morning and getting home at night, a stock

can get decimated by the mutual fund company and pension fund managers who are closer to the action."

As a result, he says, successful smaller investors need a system that builds in discipline and restricts them to companies that meet certain criteria. For Mr. Bareham, those criteria include:

- A minimum five-year track record of good revenue and earnings growth.
- A leading position in a given sector, quality goods and management.
- Debt reduction and share buybacks.
- Solid evidence backed by research—not rumour—that growth will continue at double-digit rates.

To dig up that information, he often turns to *The Globe and Mail's Canada Company Handbook* and *Report on Business.* "You'll have to fill in the blanks to get a handle on developments and watch a company to try to understand it."

He's also said goodbye to his stock-flipping days. He used to automatically bail out once a stock moved up 30 per cent, but he found he missed out on a lot of big moves that way. He also realized that his wife was making the same sort of returns as he was, without doing anywhere near as much trading or worrying. "I often think women are better investors than men," he says. "They are more patient and not so inclined to think they have great insight."

HIS BEST MOVES: It's probably a bit of hindsight talking when Mr. Bareham bemoans getting in too late and out too early with Ballard Power Systems Inc. (BLD-TSE, 52-week high $141.25, low $32.50). "If I had used my head, I'd be much closer to retirement."

He had been intrigued by the potential of the Burnaby, B.C.-based developer of environmentally friendly fuel cells four years ago when it was an $8 stock. He went on holiday, and in a matter of weeks, the stock had popped up to $20. He finally bought it in late 1996 at $26, and sold his position in October 1997, for $78.25 a share. It closed yesterday at $136.90.

He's seen some powerful money-making from his investment in Power Financial Corp. (PWF-TSE, high $54, low $24.10), which he bought in November 1995 for $31.87, before the stock split two-for-one. The company's subsidiaries include Investors Group and Great-West Lifeco Inc. He still holds his shares, which closed yesterday at $53.05. "I like their international insurance company exposure," he says. "They are so well diversified, and they are in a cash-cow business."

He's still holding on to Brampton, Ont.-based Northern Telecom Ltd. (NTL-TSE, high $77.75, low $43.50, close $77.20), which he first bought in March 1997 for $96.65 (before it split two-for-one earlier this year), despite calling it "a bit pricy."

"It just keeps coming up with new contracts and is such a well-managed company that global modernization bodes well for it," he says. He used to move in and out of the stock as he feels it trades somewhat like an emotionally charged technology stock, but is now looking at it more as a long-term hold.

HIS WORST MOVE: Lose your discipline and you get dinged, more often than not. A tip that the stock was going to $18 got Mr. Bareham into Abacan Resource Corp. (ABC-TSE, high $13.70, low $1.38, close $2.60), a Calgary-based oil and gas company, last spring at an average price of $10 a share. But instead of heading up, the stock plunged, driven down by a number of negative reports from analysts and the collapsing juniors market. Mr. Bareham readily admits that the investment runs counter to his philosophy, and the nicest thing he can say about the stock is he hopes it makes a bounce so he can make his exit.

ADVICE: "Retirement plans don't tolerate procrastination. Retiring wealthy is really pretty easy if you pay attention and use savings discipline for about 20 years."

THE PORTFOLIO

Date:	Saturday, March 7, 1998
The investor:	Steve Bareham, 47.
Occupation:	College instructor, communications consultant.
Investment personality:	Long term.
Portfolio makeup:	Stocks include Bombardier, Bank of Nova Scotia, Midland Walwyn, Newbridge, Northern Telecom, Nova, Philip Services, Power Financial. Mutual funds include AIC Advantage, Bissett Small Cap, Ivy Canadian, Templeton Growth, Templeton International Stock.
Portfolio size:	"Mid-six figures."
Rate of return:	"About 20 per cent a year since 1991."

Unless you can stay on top of your stocks every second, warns Mr. Bareham, you'll be far better off avoiding speculative shares that can be turned into dust between the time you leave for work and when you check in on your portfolio at lunch time. If you're trying and failing at stock–flipping, don't despair, because, as Mr. Bareham makes clear, there is an easier way. Just follow his clear and level-headed criteria for buying good companies. Oh, and also learn like he did from his wife, and when you buy those good companies, hold on to them and don't worry so much.

BLUE PORTFOLIO

MAKES OTHERS SEE RED

•

HIS PORTFOLIO may be bluer than blue, but returns like the 38 per cent Todd Hoyem earned in 1996 could cause those playing small-capitalization juniors to see red.

"I think you can play high-growth conservative stocks and do as well as those playing speculative stocks without the downside risk," he says.

A chemical sales representative in Lethbridge, Alta., Mr. Hoyem has been following this approach for five years. In addition to impressive returns, he enjoys following the markets enough that he hopes to work in the investment industry some day.

HOW HE DOES IT: While he reads widely, perhaps the most critical helping hand for Mr. Hoyem is *The Investment Reporter*, a Toronto-based newsletter. "They give you enough information to make a good decision," he says. "And they teach you long-term investment strategies."

The newsletter's philosophy is that if you focus on the best companies in any industry, you will be rewarded with above-average, long-term returns, which meshes beautifully with Mr. Hoyem's approach.

Mr. Hoyem typically watches 20 to 30 stocks closely, and holds around a dozen. To make his short list, a company must boast a strong brand name and all the standard good corporate finance credentials such as little debt, rapidly rising cash flow and an above-average growth rate.

Another critical figure is a strong five-year stock price growth rate. Of course, the big danger in investing in a company whose stock has been on a prolonged tear is that the day you buy is the day the run will come to an end. To guard against that, he looks for positive news, lots of money in the bank and rapidly rising cash flow and income.

A little patience also helps. Once he decides he wants in on a company's good fortunes, he will often wait on the sidelines for the usual dip in the stock price. "You have to be disciplined because a lot of people like to run with the crowd."

HIS BEST MOVES: Mr. Hoyem had software maker Geac Computer Corp. Ltd. of Markham, Ont. (GAC-TSE, 52-week high $70, low $16) on his watch list last fall when the stock took a heavy hit, so he quickly bought in at close to $16. "It was reported that the president had stepped down, but they didn't say that he was going to be working full time on acquisitions."

The president's new focus soon became more widely known. That was followed by news the company was acquiring the software division of New York-based Dun & Bradstreet Corp. for $191 million (U.S.).

That got the stock rolling along, but it really took off in July when the first-quarter results following the purchase came in much higher than expected. The stock closed yesterday at $60.60 (Canadian).

Back in 1994, he invested in Burlington, Ont.-based Laidlaw Inc. (LDM-TSE, high $22.90, low $12.30), while the company was still struggling with its waste-hauling business. "Profits were off, but I felt it was a good solid company and had a recognizable name," he says. "But what made me jump in was that the company was in the process of getting out of the waste business and starting to focus on its core transportation business where margins were better." Mr. Hoyem paid $7 for his shares, and the stock closed yesterday at $20.65.

Another winner has been SunAmerica Inc. (SAI-NYSE, high $60.04 (U.S.), low $32.12), which sells life insurance as well as annuities targeted at retirees. The stock was a big favourite of David Driscoll, editor of *The Investment Reporter*, who last August noted it had risen 132 per cent in less than 18 months.

More importantly, Mr. Driscoll saw no reason that that performance shouldn't continue, citing the company's above-average returns on investing policyholders' money, a strong distribution system and the fact that the stock was still trading at a multiple below its five-year, 18 per cent growth rate. Mr. Hoyem agreed, waited for a pullback and bought in about a year ago at $28. The stock closed yesterday at $53.69.

HIS WORST MOVE: No, it's not another tip-gone-wrong story. In fact, Mr. Hoyem's mistake came from trying to develop an asset-allocation model. "I felt I should have part of my portfolio in speculative stocks, and I got burned."

The stock that scorched him belonged to Arimetco International Inc., which was involved in copper mining in Nevada. The company had garnered a few strong reports in the media, so Mr. Hoyem bought in at $2.25 (Canadian) last year. Arimetco soon ran into production problems, the stock tanked and Mr. Hoyem bailed out after six months, getting 90 cents apiece for his shares. The company, which traded on the Toronto Stock Exchange, is now delisted. "Smaller companies just don't have the backing to ride out storms," he says.

ADVICE: "Take advantage of the worldwide shift to equities and invest in high-grade companies with large asset bases."

THE PORTFOLIO

Date:	Saturday, August 23, 1997
Investor:	Todd Hoyem, 32.
Occupation:	Chemical sales representative.
Investment personality:	"Long term and aggressive."
Portfolio makeup:	Petro-Canada, Canadian Occidental Petroleum, Geac, Cinram, Donohue, Laidlaw, Magna, Precision Drilling,

SunAmerica, SNC Lavalin, CanWest
Global, U.S. Filter.

Portfolio size: "Five figures."

Rate of return: "38 per cent in 1996, 33.5 per cent to date
this year."

There's a real bit of wisdom in Mr. Hoyem's statement that he likes *The Investment Reporter*—a newsletter—not only because of the specific stock information it provides but also because of its overall advice and encouragement to stick with a long-term investment strategy.

Here are the main ways he tries to ensure his long-term investing success:

- *Buy Strong Companies.* That means investing in companies that have an established brand name, low debt, rising cash flow and a strong growth rate.
- *Don't Buy on Rumour-Driven Spikes.* Defend against buying a stock that has just finished a strong run and drops the moment you get your buy order filled. Look for recent positive news and recommendations by analysts, as well as signs that more good announcements are coming.
- *Exercise Patience.* Because he's buying for the long term and buying more conservative names that don't jump up or dive down overnight, Mr. Hoyem never has to feel rushed to buy a stock. Take your time, evaluate the company and make sure it fits your larger investment plan before buying.

QUALITY PAYS OFF
IN THE LONG RUN

•

MANY INVESTORS follow the patient school of investing, but Willard Jamieson takes it one step further.

"I have to prove to myself an investment is good before I buy it," says the Saskatoon optometrist of his approach, which includes a long period of studying an investment—an extra "hold-on" period, if you will—before following through with the old buy-and-hold.

Given his cautious approach, it's not too surprising to find Mr. Jamieson counting himself as a GIC refugee. He's somebody who loved his security, but who had to look for better returns elsewhere when his 18 per cent GICs were maturing and the best rates were less than half that level.

He then moved on to mutual funds, but after watching the market, figured he could take on the stock picking himself: "I thought that I could get almost as good a return and not have to pay management fees."

Mr. Jamieson does his trading through TD Green Line, relying on his own reading and research to make his choices. "I'd find it hard to find an adviser who I have enough confidence in, because everybody has their own biases."

Lately, he says, his returns haven't been that terrific, because he's got a lot of money just sitting on the sidelines. "I've been waiting for the crash to come."

HOW HE DOES IT: Mr. Jamieson takes the long, patient view. He'll begin by watching a company's earnings and stock performance, sometimes for a couple of years, before making a purchase. Even then, he'll often only hold a stock in his trading account, and, if it is still performing well after one or two years, buy it for his RRSP.

What he looks for is earnings growth, as well as a strong outlook for a company's products. For example, he recently has become interested in Cameco Corp. "The stock price is depressed because the price of uranium is down, but there will probably be a shortage, and that should push the price back up."

While he holds a few speculative shares in his portfolio, his main focus is on blue-chip stocks. "They often have better returns over the long run than a lot of those flash-in-the-pan juniors," he says.

HIS BEST MOVES: Mr. Jamieson's leading mutual fund is AIC Advantage, which he bought into 2.5 years ago for less than $20 a unit. The units were valued this week at more than $52, and the fund has a two-year average compound return of 53.5 per cent. The fund has a heavy concentration of financial sector companies, such as banks and insurers, which have been on a tear recently. "When you think of all the baby boomers becoming more conscious about taking care of their money, I think this fund will continue to do well."

His best stock performer has been SNC-Lavalin Group Inc. (SNC-TSE, 52-week high $19.00, low $10), the Montreal-based engineering and construction firm. He bought in the fall of 1994 at $19 a share. The stock subsequently split three-for-one, and closed yesterday at $14.10. "They're recognized as being a leader in a lot of engineering fields, and over half of their revenues are coming from outside Canada," Mr. Jamieson says. "They've got to be pretty good to get the rest of the world to hire them to do their engineering."

Another winner has been Agrium Inc. (AGU-TSE, 52-week high $21.30, low $16.00, yesterday's close $18.25), a Calgary-based fertilizer company. He has owned it for several years, and picked up more shares in February for around $19 each. He expects the company's growth to continue and shares to appreciate further as a result of the company's share buy-back program.

HIS WORST MOVE: Years back, one of the people Mr. Jamieson bought his eyeglass frames from left the business, only to turn up as an officer in a junior gold exploration company called Consolidated Ramrod Gold Corp. (Now Quest International Resources Corp.) As a result, Mr. Jamieson kept a curious eye on the company, watching it for two years as its share price bounced between $5 and $7.50. Based on its trading patterns and some positive media reports, Mr. Jamieson thought he was making a pretty safe bet when in June 1995 he picked up some shares at $4.85. Shortly after, a financing deal fell through, and the company's stock headed south. Shares in Quest closed yesterday at $1.20.

ADVICE: "Buy quality stocks. My portfolio is holding its own because the good ones are looking after the bad ones."

THE PORTFOLIO

Date:	Saturday, May 10, 1997
The investor:	Willard Jamieson, 56.
Occupation:	Optician.
Investment personality:	"I'm pretty conservative."
Portfolio makeup:	Mutual funds include AIC Advantage, Mackenzie Industrial Growth, Trimark Canadian, Trimark Fund, Green Line Canadian Bond, Fidelity Far East, Fidelity Capital Builder and Altamira Equity, Bond, Income, and Resource. Stocks include Kensington Resources, Princeton Mining, Ibex Technologies, Circuit World, Mango Resources, Nova, SNC-Lavalin.
Portfolio size:	"Mid-six figures."
Rate of return:	"Just under 20 per cent."

Mr. Jamieson is more patient than even patient investors. Once he's zeroed in on a stock, he'll wait for months, not just hoping to pick the stock up cheap on a dip, but to ensure that his initial evaluation holds up, and that the buy still makes sense.

Note Mr. Jamieson's advice to buy good quality stocks because his good stocks are taking care of the damage done by his bad stocks. Blue-chip stocks are kind of like an outrigger on your investment canoe. You can play the speculative markets, have some perky small-cap stocks, but as long as you've got a good portion of your portfolio in quality, long-term stocks, you should easily stay afloat as well as catch a few nice waves.

LOOKING OUT FOR NO. 1

KEY TO INVESTING

•

MANY PEOPLE SAY they look for good management when making their investment decisions. But Larry Agranove is better placed than most to put that principle into action.

Not only did he teach management at Wilfrid Laurier University in Waterloo, Ont., for many years, but he currently works as a management consultant in London, Ont.

"I like investing because I'm interested in management," he says. "I like to find out how and what managers are doing, and if I like what I find, I buy into their companies."

In addition to enjoying managing his own money, it's really the only route for Mr. Agranove. He tried going the broker route for many years, he says, but found it wanting. One of the last straws came when one of his brokers called him when he was wrestling his sailboat through a huge storm on Georgian Bay. The broker tried to convince him to buy into Campeau. "I said to him: 'This is a guy who bought a department store with borrowed money with no experience in retailing.'"

Experiences like that, he says, gave rise to what he dubs his first rule of investing: Nobody cares as much about your investments as you do.

"If I could find a broker who would say things like 'Let's get out of FPI (Fishery Products International Ltd.) because the fish are all gone,' or 'I made a mistake,' I'd hug and kiss him on both cheeks," he says.

Mr. Agranove also stays away from brokers these days, he says, because their focus is largely on Canadian stocks. One of his investing laws is to direct most of his money into international investments as he doesn't have a lot of faith in Canada.

HOW HE DOES IT: "I do my own trading through InvestorLine (Bank of Montreal's discount brokerage), and I read voraciously," he says. In addition to the financial press, he also regularly follows a handful of newsletters. They include *Noram Portfolio Notes*, put out by Noram Capital Management Inc. in Toronto, and *The Successful Investor*, edited by Patrick McKeough.

For his offshore investments outside the United States, though, he relies on the expertise of others. He is a big fan of both the Sceptre and Saxon fund management companies. "They're no-load, they've got good managers, they don't flip their portfolios a lot, and their MERs (management expense ratios) are low."

As well as many of their fund offerings, he has invested a significant amount through Sceptre's Personal Investment Fund program. In addition to a very low management fee—a maximum of 1 per cent—he says he likes the personal attention he receives. "You get to talk to people and develop some trust."

HIS BEST MOVES: One of his largest holdings is General Electric Co. (GE-NYSE, 52-week high $108.37 (U.S.), low $73.75, yesterday's close $105), which he picked up in January 1996 for $70 a share. "I used to use them as an example of a well-managed company when I was teaching," he says. Beyond the company's management, he also likes the synergy he sees between its many businesses, including its involvement in manufacturing computer chips.

Another U.S. leader he is heavily invested in is Motorola Inc. (MOT-NYSE, high $69.75, low $44.12, close $56.62), which he bought at $50, also at the start of 1996. "I felt that a lot of developing economies will skip the copper wire stage and go straight to cellular phones."

Mr. Agranove thought he was making a somewhat dangerous move in April 1990, when he bought into Berkshire Hathaway Inc. (BRK.A-NYSE, high $37,900, low $30,000, yesterday's close $37,900), the Omaha-based investment company run by the legendary Warren Buffett. "I thought lightning was going to strike me," he says, because of the company's sky-high stock price at the time, a hefty $6,900. "If you set out to design a mutual fund, you couldn't do any better."

HIS WORST MOVES: Whenever his consulting work takes him around the country, Mr. Agranove's airline of choice is Canadian Airlines International Ltd. (CA-TSE, high $3.50 (Canadian), low $1.05, close $2.02), which is somewhat ironic given that it's also his worst investment pick. He bought $5,000 worth of Canadian Airlines debentures back before the company bought out Wardair. Later converted to common shares and warrants, his investment is currently worth just $400. "I maintain it for sentimental reasons."

ADVICE: "My second rule of investing is don't expect your investments to make you rich. Your business or profession should have done that already."

THE PORTFOLIO

Date:	Saturday, April 19, 1997
The investor:	Larry Agranove.
Occupation:	Marketing consultant.
Investment personality:	"I like investing because studying management is part of my business."
Portfolio makeup:	Stocks include General Electric Co., Berkshire Hathaway Inc., Motorola Inc., Nu-Gro Corp. Mutual funds include Sceptre Asian Growth, Sceptre Equity, Sceptre International, Sceptre Balanced,

Saxon World Growth, Freidberg Currency,
Phillips Hager & North Dividend Income.
Portfolio size: "Low seven figures."
Rate of return: "15.75 per cent last year, after tax."

Call 'em Larry's Two Rules. The first—that nobody cares as much about your money as you do—should be self-evident, but it's often forgotten so it bears repeating to yourself from time to time. Nobody's going to care about it more because not only did they not earn it in the first place, but the only lifestyle that will be affected by how you manage it is yours and your family's. Whether you're managing your own money or using an adviser, the more you know about investing and personal finance, the more informed and more profitable your decisions will be.

The second rule—don't expect your investments to make you rich—also carries a lot of wisdom, especially when up until 1998, it sometimes seemed all you had to do was sink some bucks into the big banks, and you'd make magnificent returns with no effort. Your investments can make you rich, but you'll need to do two things. One, regularly put money away—preferably maximizing out on your RRSP contributions—and second, manage your investments carefully.

REJIGGING PORTFOLIO

PAID FOR MONTREALER

•

IN EARLY 1996, Luc Nocente decided that enough was enough. Actually, make that enough wasn't enough.

"I looked at the rate of return I was making on my funds and it was below the Dow," says the 39-year-old Montrealer, who is general manager of a high-tech software imaging company. He promptly sold most of his holdings, including some Altamira Management Ltd. funds and some bank funds, reassembled his portfolio, and has quickly seen much stronger returns.

"I'm surprised I'm doing so well," he says. "What it tells me is it's not luck, it's doing your homework."

HOW HE DOES IT: Mr. Nocente currently has 90 per cent of his portfolio in stocks and equity funds and 10 per cent in fixed-income investments. "I've still got 25 years of investing left," he says, noting that he was unhappy the markets hadn't fallen further this past week. "If they had, I would have sold my bonds and bought more stocks."

Mr. Nocente holds individual bonds to avoid paying management fees on balanced and bond funds. "Say the management fee is 2 per cent and bonds are currently paying 4 to 5 per cent—you've lost half of your return."

He picked up this particular strategy from one of his favourite Web sites, www.fundlibrary.com, which he also uses, along with guide books, to pick his funds. He also checks out stock forums such as those on the Silicon Investor Web site www.techstocks.com to see what others think of a particular stock.

In addition to the Internet, he's a voracious reader of the business press, including *Report on Business, Barron's, Business Week* and *Fortune*. "I travel a lot for work, and whenever I have any spare time I read," he says.

He also credits his Palmpilot, a popular hand-held computing device that allows him to enter notes in his own handwriting, for helping him stay on top of the stream of information he digests. "I was looking at buying some 3Com, so I looked up the notes I keep on my Pilot, saw that I'd written that an analyst was shorting it big time, so I stayed away."

One of his favourite stock strategies is buying solid companies when they are beaten up, as he did with Discreet Logic Inc. and, more recently, with Placer Dome Inc. and Renaissance Energy Ltd. "Often, the only way to make money in today's market is to buy blue chips that everyone is spitting on."

HIS BEST MOVES: Discreet Logic (DSLGF–Nasdaq, 52-week high $28.87 (U.S.), low $5.62, yesterday's close $19.56), a Montreal-based maker of animation software and post-production systems, had a tough time in early 1996.

Rising losses and a massive restructuring plan drove the stock down from a high of about $30 to around $3. But Mr. Nocente felt the company would turn around, and when the stock started to move up, he moved in, picking up his shares at an average price of $8 in the fall of 1996. The stock hit its high of $28.87 recently before falling back to the $19 range, but Mr. Nocente just sees that as another buying opportunity.

A big short-term winner has been the Templeton Russia Fund (TRF–NYSE, high $64.37, low $20.25), which Mr. Nocente bought this past spring at around $25 a unit. The closed-end fund underscored its volatility for him by quickly plummeting to $21. Over the next three months, though, it went as high as $52, and the units were valued yesterday at $40.50.

"I read some good comments by Mark Mobius (Templeton's Asia-based emerging markets manager) about Russia, saying in 15 years it will be a big market," he says. "They have a lot of educated people, and they have a lot of natural resources, but they're still lacking on the marketing front."

HIS WORST MOVE: Mr. Nocente kept an eye on ATC Communications Group Inc. of Dallas (ATCT-Nasdaq, high $23.87, low $2.56), a company offering telemarketing services, after it was added to the Fool's Portfolio in the fall of 1996 (found at The Motley Fool investing forum on the America Online service) at almost $23. The stock then fell to $5, so Mr. Nocente figured it was a bargain-basement price. He received more positive feedback when he checked out the stock's discussion forum at the Silicon Investor Web site, and when the stock poked its head back up over the $6 mark last August, he bought in. However, it wasn't a bounce that lasted.

He sold his shares at $4.87 recently, and the stock closed yesterday at $3.37. "I shouldn't have bought it because I didn't know enough," he said.

ADVICE: "Don't trust your brokerage firm because by the time you've gotten the information it's often too late. Do your own homework and make sure what they're telling you makes sense."

THE PORTFOLIO

Date:	Saturday, November 1, 1997
The investor:	Luc Nocente, 39.
Occupation:	General manager of high-tech imaging software company.
Investment personality:	"Aggressive."
Portfolio makeup:	Stocks: BCE, BPI Systems, Placer Dome, Royal LePage, Renaissance Energy, Discreet Logic, ABL Canada, Image Processing,

> Thunder Energy. Funds: AIC - Value,
> Advantage II; Elliott & Page Equity, Fidelity
> Canadian Growth, Sceptre Equity Growth,
> Templeton Growth, Trimark Latin America,
> Templeton Russia Fund.
>
> *Portfolio size:*   unavailable
> *Rate of return:*   "27.8 per cent in an RRSP from January 1 to
> end of October."

Mr. Nocente left the fund world to pick his own stocks and is making better returns. "Hey," you may be thinking, "I should too!"

Not so fast. Mr. Nocente says his profits aren't just fated to happen; they are the result of the work he puts into his investments. He reads voraciously, keeps detailed notes of companies he's following on a hand-held computer, and turns a lot of his spare time into stock-watching time.

Stock-picking can offer better returns than funds, no doubt. After all, each year many funds fail to even beat the market averages. But you won't have success if you simply buy stocks that some analyst in the paper says is moving up. Why? Because more than likely, you'll be able to open up the following day's paper and find another expert quoted, this time saying the stock is way overpriced and bound to drop. Plus if you did buy every "buy," you'd hold most of the stocks in the known universe, since analysts tend to be a pretty optimistic bunch.

Unfortunately, the recent bull market probably had a lot of people convinced that stock-picking can be done just by reading from cursory headlines. Don't believe it. When the markets dropped, stock-picking once again became a much more difficult thing to pull off successfully. If you aren't sure what you are doing, either educate yourself, or ensure some of your money is being handled by the pros.

TEACHER CHANGES

COURSE, LETS BETS RIDE

•

ROY HU IS UNLIKELY to ever get the VIP treatment in Vegas.

The gambling industry just loves those willing to let their bets ride, because it knows the odds are in its favour and it will eventually come out ahead.

Mr. Hu's investing strategy, though—at least until recently, has been to always take his money off the table when he gets slightly ahead. "Anytime I got a 20 or 25 per cent return, I'd cash in," says Mr. Hu, a Toronto-area high-school business teacher. "I had a primarily short-term profit orientation."

While that level of returns might seem very appealing, Mr. Hu is busy switching tactics, as he says there is more money to be made by letting his money ride when he's on a winning streak. But lest any casino kings out there are quickly dispatching their private jet to Mr. Hu's house, be warned that he is also moving toward more conservative stocks. "I want to find a few good stocks and ride them out."

HOW HE DOES IT: Mr. Hu has a balanced portfolio, including GICs and a handful of mutual funds, which he likes because they are "no-brainers."

He has always applied his brains to assessing the fundamentals of any shares he buys, but he now sees certain stocks as belonging in his recently established "core" portfolio, in which he will hold shares for the long haul.

Why the switch? While Mr. Hu has made some good money in the past, he realized he could have amassed much, much more by holding for the longer term. This is particularly true given the stocks Mr. Hu likes and has invested in in the past.

Take Microsoft Corp. Mr. Hu bought Microsoft shares at $93 (U.S.) in 1995 and when it hit $125, he quickly sold. "My philosophy at the time was you can't lose by taking profits." Subsequently the stock went to $140, split, went to $140 again, and split again.

How does he feel about those paper losses? Not too bad, actually, he says, because he would usually roll his money into other investments. "Plus, I try not to look back."

To pick his stocks, he uses the same method he teaches his students. He begins by looking for sectors that he feels have strong growth potential. "Demographic changes, international trade agreements, low interest rates, these are all major changes the world is going through, and you have to look for industries that will benefit from these changes." He sees great potential in the technology, biomedical and financial sectors. By contrast, he is avoiding the heavy manufacturing and service industries.

He then starts looking for the leading companies in those winning sectors, particularly those with the ability to remain far ahead of their competition. "I look for companies that have the size, competitiveness, marketing skills, technology, consumer acceptance and innovation to win," he says. "Those are what I call key success factors."

Mr. Hu favours industry leaders because he says they are less speculative and better able to weather economic ups and downs. "Especially with the market being a little crazy right now, you want to be in quality," he says. "Industry leaders probably have more underlying value."

To find those leaders, he relies on *Barrons*, *The Globe and Mail* and CNBC, NBC's cable TV channel. Investing is becoming a hobby almost by default, he says. "Nobody wants to spend that much time just to make a few bucks."

HIS BEST MOVES: Even before the announcement of its proposed merger with Bank of Montreal, Royal Bank of Canada (RY-TSE, 52-week high $87.50, low $50.40) was already a big winner for Mr. Hu. He bought Royal shares at $40 in June 1996, and the shares closed Thursday at $87. Beyond the attraction of buying the largest Canadian bank, Mr. Hu felt Royal Bank was well run and very aggressive on the marketing front. "And when I bought them, interest rates were around 3 per cent, and it was yielding 3 per cent," he says. "It was like a textbook buy it was so perfect." He's still holding the stock, but admits it's hard not to relapse into his old profit-taking mode. "I've been very tempted to sell."

U.S. drug maker Merck & Co. Inc. (MRK-NYSE, high $133 (U.S.), low $80.62, close $126.25) gave him a nice return, despite being one of his "take the money off the table" plays. He bought the stock at $64.62 in July 1996, and sold it a year later at $103.50. "I felt there was a lot of innovation in the medical field, and it couples nicely with my belief in the technology sector." He picked up Merck because it had a lower price/earnings ratio than other leaders such as Johnson & Johnson and Pfizer Inc.

HIS WORST MOVE: "I feel really silly, but I bought Micron at $38." Mr. Hu bought his shares in Idaho-based Micron Technology Inc. (MU-NYSE, high $60.06, low $22, close $27.75) in the spring of 1996, expecting the memory-chip maker to benefit from the growth in the PC market.

Just around that time, though, a huge oversupply in RAM developed, the stock crashed and Mr. Hu sold in the summer at around $19. "I saw the balance sheet was strong, but I followed the trend," he says. "When everybody is dumping the stock, it's natural to sell, yourself, and not have the confidence to hold it."

ADVICE: "Decide which industries have growth potential and which companies are the market leaders in those industries."

THE PORTFOLIO

Date:	Saturday, April 11, 1998
The investor:	Roy Hu, 36.

Occupation:	High-school business studies teacher.
Investment personality:	In transition.
Portfolio makeup:	Royal Bank, Newbridge, Intel, Lucent. Funds: 20/20 Aggressive Growth, 20/20 Canadian Resource, AGF Growth Equity, BPI Small Companies, C.I. American RSP, Trimark Select Canadian, Trimark Select Balanced, Working Ventures.
Portfolio size:	"Six figures."
Rate of return:	"31 per cent in 1996 and 1997."

Interesting, isn't it? Here's Mr. Hu saying that he has been able to get in and out of a lot of stocks quickly and make a fast buck, but he's changing his strategy. Now he wants to buy stocks and hold them for the long term.

Why? Because he sold a lot of stocks only to see them go much, much higher. His experience—and his new long-term buy-and-hold approach—underscores one bit of wisdom that could stand repeating, oh, well, at least one more time. No one can regularly buy low and sell high. Buying solid, conservative stocks and holding them for the long haul spares you the danger of doing the opposite—namely buying high and selling low—and makes things easier for your nerves as well.

In order to succeed though, you'll need to follow Mr. Hu's advice, notably to look for "companies that have the size, competitiveness, marketing skill, technology, consumer acceptance and innovation to win."

STUDENT TURNS GROCERY
RECEIPTS INTO CASH

•

JOHN CAGGIANIELLO, a third-year accounting and finance student at Ryerson Polytechnic University in Toronto, had a highly rewarding part-time job in high school.

Not that grocery stores pay their help all that much, but sometimes the fringe benefits, even the informal ones, can add up. "The manager was into the stock market, and I got interested in investing when I saw how much money you can make."

His boss, and market mentor, was a disciplined charter of stocks, who made a lot of money on his investments, including Newcourt Credit Group Inc. and Newbridge Networks Corp. The latter was Mr. Caggianiello's first investment choice when it dropped to around $30 in early 1995. The stock subsequently soared, but he wasn't aboard for the flight. "I was scared," he candidly admits. "I was just 19, and I didn't want to throw my life savings into stocks."

But a year later he took the plunge, and found the markets so much to his liking that he is hoping to work in the investment field some day.

HOW HE DOES IT: Even though he has just started out, Mr. Caggianiello already knows that buying low and selling high is a lot harder to do than it is to say. "I'm not a very experienced investor, but if you try to do that you never time it perfectly." That said, he is still inclined to avoid the buy-and-hold approach and to try to only be in stocks making a strong move. "If you watch stocks, you can sort of see when they are moving and jump in to maximize your profits."

His favourite place to be, in fact, is on the sidelines, money in hand, waiting to take advantage of buying opportunities. At present, he only holds two stocks, Sears Canada Inc. and Nova Corp., both recent buys. He picked up Sears hoping to profit from the attention that retail stores—and stocks—get around Christmas. "I'll probably hold it for a couple of months until there's more speculation about their earnings," he says.

He bought Nova at $13.20 because he felt the market would react positively to the Calgary-based conglomerate's announcement it planned to split itself into a chemical business and a pipeline operation. "I know estimates from CEOs are biased, but Nova's CEO valued the company at $14.50, and the stock had already gone up by the time I got in."

HIS BEST MOVES: Mr. Caggianiello played his very first investment, Bank of Montreal (BMO-TSE, 52-week high $67.40, low $39.05, yesterday's close $61.90), like a pro, doing his homework, understanding his investment and getting out with a tidy profit untarnished by greed.

He targeted the banks because he realized low interest rates were helping the sector. He picked Bank of Montreal in particular because it was one of the lowest priced stocks, and was paying a 4 per cent dividend, more than some guaranteed investment certificates, he says. He bought the stock at $44 in November 1996, and sold in March 1997 at $56. "It seemed safe because even if the stock went down and I had to hold it for a long time, my money wouldn't just be sitting there."

Following in the footsteps of his grocery-store mentor, he went back to Newbridge (NNC-TSE, high $95, low $37.60, close $51) a year ago, buying the Kanata, Ont., telecommunications company's stock at $39 and selling it in May 1997 for $48. "It had been going up and down, so I tried to get it on a dip," he says.

Up until the middle of this past week, Mr. Caggianiello also thought he had made a lucky call by betting loads of play money on Pure Gold Resources Inc., one of the companies involved in exploring for diamonds in Alberta. Mr. Caggianiello and some classmates were participating in the fall Green Line Investment Challenge, in which students have nine weeks to invest a pretend $500,000. Pure Gold was the play that put them in fifth place, at least unofficially.

His team aimed for a good, not great performance, and decided to simply ride the market up through investments in companies such as Northern Telecom Ltd. and Newcourt. Unfortunately, his group, like most investors, didn't see the October correction coming, and watched their portfolio get knocked down to 15 per cent less than what they started with. That left them with no choice but to switch to plan B—speculation. They decided to play Pure Gold. They picked it up at 31 cents a share and watched it shoot up to over $1.20.

Or so they thought, until *Me and My Money* tracked down the reason for the stock's magnificent rise—a one-for-five stock consolidation that some data-base dweebs neglected to factor in. The numbers also highlight just what a speculative pick can, or can't, do for a portfolio.

After the numbers were recrunched correctly, Mr. Caggianiello's placing fell from fifth to 782nd out of 900 contestants. "We knew the stock had gone way up, but we couldn't find out why," he says. "Next time, I'd probably phone the company, because you obviously need to stay informed."

HIS WORST MOVE: Just before last Christmas, Mr. Caggianiello paid $18.70 for some shares in Agnico-Eagle Mines Ltd. (AGE-TSE, high $20.25, low $6.20), a mid-sized gold producer working largely in Canada. "At the time, it was recommended by my brokerage firm's analyst, and it was supposed to hit $25 partly because they expected gold to go up," he says. The price of gold refused to co-operate, and while the company's earnings remained healthy, the stock took sick. Mr. Caggianiello sold in early March at $13.50. The stock closed yesterday at $7.75.

The lesson Mr. Caggianiello says he learned was to seek out second, if not third opinions, and to understand and track the factors that could affect his investments. "At the time, I didn't even follow the price of gold."

ADVICE: "Don't buy something that you don't know anything about just because somebody recommends it."

THE PORTFOLIO

Date:	Saturday, December 20, 1997
The investor:	John Caggianiello, 21.
Occupation:	University student.
Investment Personality:	Momentum investor.
Portfolio makeup:	Stocks: Sears Canada Inc., Nova Corp.
	Funds: Canada Trust Special Equity, Canada
	Trust Amerigrowth, Canada Trust Bond.
Portfolio size:	"Five figures."
Rate of return:	unavailable

Yet another investor who knows that in the long run, besides the fact that we'll all be dead, you just can't consistently buy low and sell high if you are trying to frequently trade stocks. Buy large, proven and successful blue-chip companies, and—particularly if you get them at a bargain price (when their price/earnings ratio isn't off the top of the charts)—they should provide you with steady, long-term growth in your portfolio.

HIS BEST MOVE
WAS TO CALIFORNIA

•

ANDRE PETTIGREW AND HIS WIFE of 42 years live what he calls a "civ-ilized" lifestyle in an adult retirement community in Sonoma, Calif., about 125 kilometres north of San Francisco. "We came out here to house-sit in 1988, went home to London (Ont.), packed up and moved," the 74-year-old says.

It's also a very healthy lifestyle. In addition to playing tennis almost daily, Mr. Pettigrew is right in the heart of California's wine country. "I'll drink almost any kind of wine, depending on the occasion," he says with a chuckle.

The first time Mr. Pettigrew moved to California was in 1958, when he joined a U.S. health management company as a financial officer, after working for CIL Inc. in Montreal. He later returned to Canada where he served as chief financial officer of Commonwealth Holiday Inns of Canada Ltd. for many years. He then worked in the brokerage industry before retiring in 1988.

HOW HE DOES IT: Mr. Pettigrew says that one great benefit of being retired is he has the time to carry out in-depth research. He has always read the major U.S. business publications such as *Barron's*, and keeps his eyes open for what he calls a "situation"—the op-portunity to buy into a solid company with long-term growth at a reasonable price.

For every 12 situations he examines, he'll perhaps buy into two. As part of his screening process, he relies heavily on the sounding-board capabilities of friends, including a retired pension fund manager. "When you're sure of something, you should run it by somebody who can play devil's advocate."

A typical buy for Mr. Pettigrew started back in 1990, when he saw a story in *The Wall Street Journal* about St. Louis-based General Dynamics Corp. He obtained Value Line Inc.'s assessment, and found the company's book value was $47 (U.S.), but the stock was still trading at around $20. He liked that it's traded on the New York Stock Exchange, was largely controlled by the employees and a family, and that there were only 44 million shares outstanding.

When the Persian Gulf War erupted in 1991, the stock zoomed up to $31 and, while it soon fell back, Mr. Pettigrew saw opportunity. "They had perfected the technology on the F-16 (plane) and all these other toys, the research had been paid for, and I felt some friendly country would still buy their products."

He bought in at $28 two weeks after the war ended, and a few months later sold his shares at between $40 and $50. However, he says, Warren Buffett soon picked up the stock at $75, and within a year it hit $119. "The lesson was that I should have had the patience to ride it a little longer."

HIS BEST MOVES: In 1982, the U.S. auto industry was just coming out of a few years of heavy losses, when Mr. Pettigrew caught Chrysler Corp. president Lee Iacocca pitching the company on television. "I called in my wife to watch," he says. "This guy was better at selling than the professionals."

At the time, he says, interest rates were dropping, the economy was picking up, and he felt if people felt secure in their jobs they would buy cars. So he bought Chrysler warrants at $5 that December and, less than three weeks later, sold them at over $10.

Toronto-based conglomerate Trilon Financial Corp. caught his attention five years ago when he noticed a steady stream of "buy" recommendations on the company coming out. Meanwhile, the stock (TFC.A-TSE, 52-week high $11.90 Canadian, low $6.40), which had been at $10, began a long, hard slide. "When it hit $5, I bought because I thought, 'For goodness sake, this has got to be a good deal,'" he says. "Unfortunately, at that time they were still sweeping their dirt like the problems at Royal Trust under the carpet, and the stock fell to under $2."

Then the "sell" reports came out, but he decided to swim against the stream, largely because he felt London Insurance Group Inc., which Trilon had a majority share in, would keep the company afloat. His bet paid off, and the shares did come back to life, moving up strongly this past year to close at $11.35 yesterday. "I was so proud to have acquired the virtue of patience that I didn't have before."

HIS WORST MOVE: Mr. Pettigrew picked up some Hees International Bancorp Inc. and Trilon Financial warrants in 1989 and 1990, but the Toronto companies were hit harder in the recession than he had thought, and the warrants went downhill. He intended to sell at some point, but in 1991 he was preoccupied with moving to California, and the warrants expired worthless. "My broker should have been watching that for me."

ADVICE: "Apply a most important virtue called patience."

THE PORTFOLIO

Date:	Saturday, December 6, 1997
The investor:	Andre Pettigrew, 74.
Occupation:	Retired financial executive.
Investment personality:	"Generally patient."
Portfolio makeup:	Trilon Financial Corp., ARC International Corp. trust units, Potash Corp. of Saskatchewan Inc., Pengrowth Energy Trust, Barrick Gold Corp., Laidlaw Inc.
Portfolio size:	Six figures.

Rate of return: "42 per cent in 1996, 34 per cent in 1997
to late November."

Recently, Mr. Pettigrew sent me some more of his thoughts, the results, he says, of "long-term experience."

• "Some advisers say, 'Go Global.' I say, don't take the risk of investing directly in a foreign country and exposing yourself to an additional risk of currency devaluation. Instead, do it through solid
American giants who operate overseas like Ford, GE, IBM and
Coca-Cola. Being listed on the NYSE, these companies give you
another safety net, as the exchange is the most demanding in terms
of fact disclosures, plus you are still dealing with growth situations."
• "Be very careful of relatives or friends being a source of information
or tips regarding an investing situation, unless your uncle is Peter
Lynch [the famed U.S. mutual funds manager]. An investment is a
cold-blooded decision. Use well-experienced sounding boards before you move forward.
• "We have had fabulous markets in recent years. Your worst enemy,
now, is *greed*. I have known it and I have paid for that sin in the
past.

B.C. MAN HAS EARLY
START AT THE GOOD LIFE

•

WARNING: IF YOU HAVE CHILDREN, you may want to wait until just after they've done something unbearably cute before reading this story.

Malcolm Watson has just sent a book on the history of Boy Scouts in British Columbia off to his publisher, gets up to a lot of tricks with a local magician's society, and, since his house is perched right on Prospect Lake, just outside of Victoria, he naturally spends a good deal of time fishing.

Throw in a couple of trips a year to far-off lands, and it's fair to say Mr. Watson is leading the good life. The kicker is he's just 52, and has been living this way since he quit the working world more than five years ago.

Before retiring, he made a good living working as a construction safety engineer on ferry terminals, power dams and paper mills. But more importantly, he says, being a single man with no dependants, "has given me a great deal more latitude than most people."

Certainly, being able to stash away the substantial cash flow that running a larger household takes has given Mr. Watson the freedom to make a lot of financial and lifestyle moves, which are simply not an option for many family types.

In 1986, for example, Mr. Watson was downsized out of his job. Instead of seeing a headhunter, he headed to the beaches of Thailand for two years. And it wasn't to escape worries about his financial future.

Over the years he had plowed his savings into a number of investment properties in Vancouver and Victoria. At the time of his layoff, he had two homes that he rented out. Figuring real estate wouldn't run up forever, he decided to take his first step into the world of equities. He put his severance pay and what he received from his profit-sharing plan into stocks.

But even on the beaches of Phuket, he felt the aftershocks of the stock market's October 1987 crash.

"It scared me because it took away the idea my money would last forever," he says. "So I shot home to make some more." He worked for another four years, overseeing the removal of asbestos at the University of British Columbia, before calling it quits in the working world for good.

HOW HE DOES IT: Mr. Watson says that with nobody else to support and his home paid off, he's been free to put everything into the stock market, including bumping up his portfolio by buying on margin.

"With such a large buffer and a good economic outlook for at least a few more years, I felt pretty confident," he says. And to date, his strategy has paid off, giving him annual returns of 20 per cent and more.

But while aggressive, Mr. Watson is not a big risk-taker. He favours blue chips that have a clear leadership, steadily rising earnings, and that get regular, positive press coverage. "You should enjoy your investments, not fear them," he says.

Over the next few years, Mr. Watson expects to see fund management companies do well, noting that by some estimates, today's baby boomers stand to inherit in the neighbourhood of a trillion dollars from their parents. "And I think that a lot of that money will find its way into the market through mutual funds."

HIS BEST MOVES: You can't ask for much more from the market than what Trimark Financial Corp. (TMF-TSE, 52-week high $84.45, low $36, yesterday's close $71) has done for investors, especially those like

Mr. Watson who got a piece of the April 1992 initial public offering, priced at a split-adjusted $3. "What attracted me was that the company was making money from the fees whether the funds were going up or going down."

That success had Mr. Watson looking to invest in another fund management company, but instead, his broker directed him toward the AIC Advantage Fund, which has a sizzling average annual compound return of 49.4 per cent for the three years since Mr. Watson made his investment.

Another of his fund favourites, Altamira Equity, has been notably running out of steam recently. However, Mr. Watson is standing by the fund, run by stock-picker Frank Mersch.

"I've gone through their portfolio and like a lot of companies they've got in there," he says. "Sure it bothers me they're not making as much money as they used to, but it just shows you can't be in the top 10 every year." The fund has a five-year average annual compound return of 18 per cent.

HIS WORST MOVE: When Internet service provider Istar Internet Inc. (WWW-TSE, high $5, low $1.05) went public in November 1995, many thought that getting in on the then-first national Internet service provider in the country seemed like a sure trip to the moon. The shares, priced at $12, opened at $22, their high for the day, and Mr. Watson bought in at $18, just above the first-day close of $17.75.

Unfortunately, that very same day Rogers Communications Inc. announced it would be offering high-speed cable Internet access, and the next day, news came out that Bell Canada planned to launch a national Internet access service called Sympatico. Those events foretold the crushing competition Istar would face, which proved catastrophic for the stock. It closed yesterday at 90 cents.

"I just bought in hoping to make a fast buck because people were clamouring for the stock," Mr. Watson says. "It went against my philosophy, which is to find out a lot about a company before I buy, and buy solid companies with long-term track records."

ADVICE: "Put everything you can afford into the market."

THE PORTFOLIO

Date:	Saturday, November 22, 1997
The investor:	Malcolm Watson, 52.
Occupation:	Retired construction safety engineer.
Investment personality:	"Poor man's Warren Buffett."
Portfolio makeup:	Stocks include Bombardier, Hummingbird, Loewen Group, Magna International, Trimark Financial. Funds include AIC Advantage, Altamira Equity, Dynamic Partners, Elliot & Page Equity, Trimark Fund, Trimark Canadian.
Portfolio size:	Low seven figures, including margin account.
Rate of return:	"20 per cent plus annually."

It's hard to argue with success, and Mr. Watson's is even that much harder to argue with because, well, it just makes so much darn sense!

Whether you're choosing your own stocks or doing it through mutual funds, if most of the money you have allotted for equities ends up in blue-chip companies that are industry leaders, have posted steady gains in earnings and continually make the news with positive developments and deals, you should be more than amply rewarded by steady, strong returns.

THE
Risk-Takers

R ISK-TAKERS put their money into high-risk investments with the hope of making big returns.
Some people like bungee jumping, some people like sky-diving
and some people like tight-rope walking. And, of course, some people like putting their money into risky investments.

What these pursuits all have in common is, beyond ongoing adren-
aline rushes, the results can be thrilling. And if you plan carefully enough,
you may be able to be all-but sure you won't hurt yourself.

All-but, but definitely not 100 per cent. With speculative investments,
like more extreme outdoor sports activities, there's always a chance—
sometimes more, sometimes less—you'll end up going splat.

In this chapter, you'll meet a lot of people who take big risks in an attempt to reap the big potential rewards some investments offer.

Short of the racetrack, you couldn't find a better collection of long shots that have the potential of rewarding you with double, triple or 10 times your original investment than in the stock market. But neither could you find a better way to get rid of a good deal of money in a very short time-frame by backing speculative investments that go down instead of up.

Often, of course, what makes speculative investments so tricky is that the same investment can turn some people into millionaires while wiping out the savings of others. When you pick speculative investments you have to not only pick the right investment, but you also have to bet on the direction it's going in, and get your timing right as well.

If Bre-X did anything positive for the investing world, it provided a lifetime of speculative investment lessons in one simple stock. Those who got in early and out near the peak, of course, made money hand over fist as the stock went from a few dollars to well over $200 before it split. On the flip side, there were many people who were purchasing the stock at $25.00 (after it split) and found, not too long afterwards, their investment was worth a big fat zero.

THE UPSIDE

Diamond Fields, Ballard Fuel Systems, AOL—all of these stocks have rewarded investors who bought early with returns ranging up to 1,000 per cent and higher. Returns like that are dangerously attractive—the stock market's version of the sirens of the sea, entrancing and beguiling you until your stocks founder on the sharp reefs just below the surface.

Even if you approach more speculative investments through mutual funds that offer a higher degree of safety due to their built-in diversification, targeting speculative investments means much higher highs and lower lows. In the year ending September 1995, the returns from larger-cap Canadian equity funds ranged from -8.2 per cent to 18.7 per cent, with an average of 5.7 per cent. Compare that to precious metal and natural resource funds, which focus on companies that are very volatile. The returns for the same one-year period range from -20.0 per cent to a high of 32 per cent, with an average return of -2.3. (More recent returns from this sector, of course, are in a word disastrous, because of the continuing slide in prices for resources and precious metals.)

THE DOWNSIDE

That's just the financial side. Speculative investments can also mean losing sleep, weight and any memory of when you last felt relaxed. They can also become all-consuming.

In the past, your broker may have simply stopped taking your phone calls after hearing from you every hour to get an update on the latest prices of your stocks. But today, with the Internet and on-line brokerages, you can stay welded to your screen and watch the price of your investments change, literally second by second. This is a decidedly unhealthy way to spend your time, plus the inescapable fact is that no matter how hard you squint your eyes and wrinkle your forehead, your stock doesn't know that you're rooting for it every step of the way.

DOING IT YOURSELF

As you can see, investing in speculative stocks and other investments on your own has one huge danger—it can quickly move from being an intelligent way to invest a small part of your portfolio to an all-consuming and pleasure-less method of putting your savings on the line every day.

Limit yourself to only ever having a small portion—say 10 per cent—of your portfolio in speculative situations. This will obviously limit your returns if you pick a couple of stocks that turn in home runs, but it will make your financial and personal lives much calmer and predictable.

Being connected to the on-line world will let you carry out some research and make a more reasoned assessment of a stock rather than just buying it on a hot tip. You can also more easily bail out if things start to go sour, rather than hoping you don't get a busy signal when you try to phone your broker to put in a sell order.

USING A HELPING HAND

Many of our risk-takers rely heavily on a broker or adviser, and with good reason. Often, the best way to get in on speculative investments is on the ground floor, perhaps even at the Initial Public Offering—when a stock is first sold to the public.

Because they live, breath and sleep this stuff, brokers by definition are usually the first to hear of upcoming deals and offerings, as well as news and other developments that may put some pop in a speculative investment. Never forget though, that it is your—not your broker's—money that you are both working with.

HOW THEY PULL IT OFF

To a man and woman, all of our risk-takers like taking risk. This, of course, is a mixed blessing.

Many Canadians could learn to mix in a few more aggressive investments into their portfolio. As long as you don't rely on all of your money being there in the next year or two, and you have seven to 10 years to leave your money invested, you will likely be more than rewarded by expanding your investment choices to include stocks by better returns than if you'll limit yourself to safer investments such as GICs or even bonds.

However, if you are predisposed to liking and embracing risk, then you are starting without one layer of armour most people have that protects them again their own worst instincts. If risk doesn't bother you, then you need to develop some way to bring discipline and diversity to your portfolio.

Here are some of the tried-and-true ways to help bring success to your more risky investments.

- *Be Patient.* Some speculative investments pop up overnight, while others take a while to build up steam for their big run. If you've done your research and the story makes sense, don't just bail out if the stock pulls back a little.
- *Do Your Homework.* Often, the more speculative the investment, the less work people put into checking it out. It's almost as if people know ahead of time they are throwing their money away, so why bother wasting your time on top of your money?

  But if they are to pay off, you need to research speculative investments just like you would any other investment. Only thing is, it will be much harder to do, and you'll have to make your decision on much less information.
- *Don't Risk Money You Can't Afford to Lose.* Speculative investments are not the way to pull together next month's mortgage payment. While they can be tempting as a way to quickly make your financial picture a lot brighter, they will inevitably leave you brooding darkly about why you wasted your money.
- *Limit Riskier Investments to a Small Part of Your Portfolio.* Even if you have a large portfolio to work with, you shouldn't in most cases put any more than 10 per cent into speculative investments.

- *Don't Expect Miracles,* as Matthew van Woollen so eloquently puts it. In the stock market, often the more you hope for something, the less likely it is to come to fruition.
- *Remember that Nobody Can Predict the Future.* Newsletters, experts, gurus and Internet devotees are all ready to tell you what stock will be the Next Big Thing. Problem is, they really are only making somewhat educated guesses at best.

GUSHERS
AND A CAST-IRON GUT

•

STOCK-MARKET SUCCESS for Peter McKenzie-Brown comes from a volatile mix of potential gushers and a cast-iron gut.

The 49-year-old Calgary resident has been speculating on small Western oil and gas exploration companies for several years, and making serious money. But he's quick to warn others he never bets money he can't afford to lose, and a key part of his success is that he's able to keep his ear exceedingly close to the ground.

"I understand geology and I know the players," he says.

It also helps that he enjoys the boom-or-bust nature of resource penny stocks, and that the oil industry has been booming lately. "I'd be bored silly just doing mutual funds."

HOW HE DOES IT: His approach is built on an intimate knowledge of the oil business. He worked for many years as a public-relations executive, and a few years ago wrote a history of the Canadian oil industry.

And in this age of electronic communications, he says being physically on top of the latest developments is also key. "I work out at the 'Y' and a lot of the people I run with are presidents of their own oil companies."

In addition, he taps into the *Daily Oil Bulletin*, a Calgary-based publication, and frequently trades tips with other speculators.

He also relies on as many as five local brokers, including one whom he talks to on the phone up to a couple of times a day. "You have to find somebody who's good at playing high-risk stocks and is on top of it." He usually makes one or two trades a week.

In general, he focuses on Alberta Stock Exchange stocks that are truly pennies—trading below a dollar.

"If you get in at 20 cents, it goes to dust or it doubles," he says. "The one thing I avoid is buying anything that's more than $1.50. When they're at that price, basically they've been overpromoted."

HIS BEST MOVES: Among his recent homers is TVI Pacific Inc. (TVI-TSE, high $3.50, low $1.11, close yesterday $1.30). He bought it early in the summer of 1995 for as little as 40 cents, and sold it last June at $2.56.

He also made a nice quick profit from Canadian Conquest Exploration Inc. (CCN-TSE, high $2.85, low 92 cents, close $2.35), which he picked up at $1.50 in August, and dumped in late October at $2.50. "I made a good buck, and my daughter got a horse."

Not only does he have to move quickly if he hears of a good buy, he also has to be quick to head for the exit, such as with his almost-overnight triple on Oxbow Exploration (OXB-ASE, high $2.10, low 25 cents, close $1.20). He bought it in September at 80 cents, and sold a month later for $2.56. "I was playing a very specific play in Saskatchewan, and I heard before it was common knowledge that the well had tested for salt water and got out."

He is a true believer in buying on rumours and selling on news. "When I know results are about to come out, I get ready to sell," he says.

In general, when a stock doubles, he sells half and puts the proceeds into something defensive. "You use speculation to generate cash and then use growth and conservative investments to protect your capital."

A typical buy for Mr. McKenzie-Brown is Cascade Oil and Gas Ltd. (COL-ASE, high 47 cents, low 15 cents, close 42 cents). The shares of the exploration company are mostly owned by three of its executives, along with a large U.S. company. But while the stock has doubled from his 20-cent purchase price, he's holding on to this one.

In fact, he says it's the only speculative oil stock he would buy currently. "They've got $2 million in the bank and they're very good managers."

He also takes a speculative approach to other investments.

For example, he cashed in all his more conservative holdings and foreign mutual funds, and put the money into Canadian equity funds the week before the Quebec referendum in October 1995. "I didn't realize how close it was going to be, but that's the kind of thing I'm comfortable with."

HIS WORST MOVES: One of his biggest money-losers has been Dynamic Ventures Ltd. (DVL–ASE, high $1.45, low 24 cents, close 30 cents). He bought it a year ago at 60 cents, and was so excited by the potential of a well the company was drilling that he bought more at $1 and held on to all his shares, even when the stock had doubled. It then proceeded to head south, and he sold out at 30 cents. "It was one of those things where I didn't obey my own rules."

He's also been sideswiped by the shenanigans revolving around Bre-X Minerals Ltd. He bought Bresea Resources Ltd. (BSR–ME, high $17.65, low $5.25), which owns 24 per cent of Bre-X, at $15, and the stock has dropped to a closing price yesterday of $9.40. "I thought it was a cheap way to play Bre-X," he says.

ADVICE: "If you know the oil industry and you're willing to take high risks, you can do well in boom markets."

THE PORTFOLIO

Date:	Saturday, December 14, 1996
The investor:	Peter McKenzie-Brown, 49.
Occupation:	Business writer/public-relations consultant.
Investment personality:	"I take high risks but calculated ones, and I can play the oil industry because I know it. I've also got the temperament to go with high risk."

Portfolio makeup:	Growth stocks including Petro-Canada instalment receipts, Onex Corp., Renaissance Energy Ltd.; penny stocks including Cascade Oil, OGY Petroleum, Inspan Investments; mutual funds.
Portfolio size:	Mid-six figures.
Rate of return:	One-year gains of 14 per cent on mutual funds, 36 per cent on all stocks and 76 per cent on high-risk stocks.

To win at speculative stocks, you not only have to get hold of the right information at the right time, but you also have to be able to evaluate it. So, for example, being told at a party that CrashComputerWare has just tripled but is going higher because its logarithmic multiplexer bilateral dual transponder analyzer is the hottest thing going would be a bad tip. (It would be bad even if you knew a thing or two about high-tech stocks, because the above jargon is completely meaningless!)

On the other hand, say you were Peter McKenzie-Brown, you worked and knew the oil business, and went jogging with oil company executives—that would be a good position from which to do some speculating.

And speculating is exactly what he calls his more risky investments. If you try to fool yourself that junior plays on the Vancouver and Calgary markets are anything but, you'll cause yourself a lot of headaches, and probably suffer a lot of losses. Mr. McKenzie-Brown has his eyes wide open, knows the ride will be wild and has the time, interest, contacts and energy to get in early and out early.

HE PLUMBS THE MARKET
FOR SWEET DEALS

•

MOST OF THE TIME that Gerod Floyd puts money into the stock market, he says, it doesn't give him the same sort of returns he gets by investing in his own plumbing and heating businesses in British Columbia's Lower Mainland.

So why would someone who has built up a string of companies worth seven figures play the markets? "Maybe it's just an outlet for me," says the 31-year-old resident of Vancouver. "It's fun, it keeps me in touch with other businesses and I meet some interesting people."

Mr. Floyd prefers to get in early on a deal and out quickly. Long term for him is a matter of months, not years.

"I have a difficult time with the plodding style of investing because it's less proactive—you just pump your cash in and then just wait."

HOW HE DOES IT: Mostly, Mr. Floyd waits by the phone for a call from his broker Wendell Nunes, or Mr. Nunes' partner, Craig Rademaker, who both work for C.M. Oliver & Co. Ltd. in Vancouver. The two are often involved with early-stage deals, and they know Mr. Floyd likes to get in early.

Make that really early. In addition to initial public offerings, Mr. Floyd also likes investing in shell companies that are being used as the vehicle for a new venture or concept. "If there's some potential and a group that works out of C.M. Oliver is getting involved, then I'll get in," he says.

Despite the speculative nature of his early-stage involvement, making a profit often isn't simply a matter of flipping his shares the next week or so, because there are often unexpected delays. "I've got $10,000 in a stock that's been halted for six months," he says.

In general, he holds his investments for six to eight months. "If it's not proven itself or the group hasn't got the deal together, I'll move out of it at that point."

HIS BEST MOVES: One of his best moves was Intercap Resources (IRC-VSE, 52-week high $5.25, low $1.51, yesterday's close $2.30). The company was trying to organize a buyout of an oil production facility, and Mr. Floyd felt comfortable with the investment because the group handling it had put some profitable deals together in the past. He bought in at $1 in the fall of 1995, and sold his position at $4 in March 1996. "The deal eventually fell apart, but they're working on something else," says Mr. Floyd, who has bought back in.

He also did well by buying into the IPO [Initial Public Offering] for Multivision Communications Corp. (MTV-VSE, week high $4.35, low $1.85, yesterday's close $3.40). Run by an investment banking group, the company is involved in acquiring cable companies in the developing world. "I got in because my adviser was handling a part of the deal, and because I felt that the company was going into a growing market." He paid $2 for his shares in March 1996, and took some profits last December at $4.

Mr. Floyd recently cashed in some of his shares of Royal Millennia Group Ltd. (RMGL-Nasdaq, high $4.37 (U.S.), low $3, yesterday's close $4.06) at $4, a nice runup from the $1.50 a share he paid last October. The company had acquired an insurance company in the United States and was looking to get into the reverse mortgage market.

HIS WORST MOVES: Dell Computer Corp. (DELL-Nasdaq, high $91.87, low $20.25, close $91.87) handed Mr. Floyd his worst setback in recent times. He put $40,000 (Canadian) into the computer equipment maker at around $36 (U.S.) a share a few years ago. Unfortunately, he caught the company when its stock was coming off a high, and when he needed the cash a couple of months later, he was forced to sell at $29.

ADVICE: Don't expect a quick turnaround. If there are good fundamentals there, be prepared to hang on longer than you intended to.

THE PORTFOLIO

Date:	Saturday, May 3, 1997
The investor:	Gerod Floyd, 31.
Occupation:	Owner of mechanical plumbing and heating companies.
Investment personality:	"I'm a pretty aggressive risk-taker."
Portfolio makeup:	Intercap Resources, Multivision, Royal Millennium, Paloma Ventures.
Portfolio size:	About $40,000
Rate of return:	"Around 40 per cent over past 12 months."

A key to understanding Mr. Floyd is his statement that he simply enjoys volatile investments. "I like the excitement of the IPOs and the big-ticket movers."

Another reason why the early-stage speculative stuff works for him is that he himself is an entrepreneur. As he remarked to me, "I like to invest in other people's businesses as well as my own, and there are good opportunities at the seed level." He also gets many benefits beyond a pure financial return. Not only does he find it fun, but he also says it helps him learn about other industries and business.

More to the point is his advice to others looking to follow in his shoes, which includes spreading your money around. Mr Floyd says his best returns have always come from putting money into his own companies, but he continues to invest in outside investments because it's a form of diversification. He also advises keeping an eye on fundamentals, not selling on dips if those fundamentals haven't changed, and remembering that many investments—especially early-stage ones—often take longer to shine than you first anticipate.

Funny, isn't it? Almost sounds like some good principles to apply to blue-chip investing. In other words, Mr. Floyd may choose more speculative investments, but he certainly isn't flying by the seat of his pants looking for that overnight killing.

There's a valuable lesson in this for those who find themselves watching the ticker tape on their PC every day. Unless you're wedded—or perhaps the word should be welded—to your monitor, don't keep checking in on your stocks every 10 minutes. Stocks, funnily enough, don't know that you're keeping your eye on them, and won't, like attentive children, respond by performing cute tricks like doubling in front of your eyes. Take a deep breath, take a break and take a look at the rest of your life. Your investments—even your speculative ones—won't notice, but you definitely will feel your blood pressure go down, and your "enjoyment of life" index go up.

PLAYING WITH OPTIONS

LIGHTS HIS FIRE

•

JUST LIKE CHILDREN AND MATCHES, most investors know the worst way they can get burned is by playing with options.

But they certainly don't scare Philippe Denolf, a 21-year-old finance student at the University of Ottawa. (A call option gives the buyer the right to purchase a stock at an agreed-on price, up to a certain date. If the stock moves above that level, the buyer can profit in a big way. If it doesn't, the options can become worthless.)

In fact, options are all he invests in, and although he's been singed a few times, the risks he's taken have largely been rewarded by red-hot returns. "I like them because you can make a lot of money in a small amount of time," he says.

HOW HE DOES IT: The ability to move fast, time to watch the markets daily and an affinity for the wired world are all critical to Mr. Denolf's method.

He starts every day by jumping on the Internet, which he says is absolutely critical to his strategy. "It's my best investment tool," he says. "To play options, you have to be well informed every day."

He checks into the "Briefing Books" on *The Wall Street Journal's* Interactive Edition, as well as Reuters, for the latest news and analysts' recommendations on the dozen or so stocks that he follows. Those stocks include IBM, Microsoft, Intel, Cisco Systems, Dell Computer and Micron Technologies. "I follow large U.S. high-tech companies for two reasons—I like stocks with a lot of liquidity, as well as a good deal of volatility."

What he's looking for is an event that will potentially cause the shares of a company to spike upward. If he finds something, which can be as mundane as a quarterly earnings report coming up, he then looks to see if there are any recent buy recommendations on the stock.

"It's kind of funny, but people forget these things," he says. "Sometimes the momentum only builds into the options one or two days before the news comes out."

Staying on top of the latest events is crucial, because Mr. Denolf likes to be able to move in and out quickly, often only holding his options for a day or two. He tries to pick up his options two to four weeks ahead of their expiry date, when there is little "time premium" left in the price, he says. "You get the most appreciation close to the expiry date if the stock's going up."

A classic example of Mr. Denolf at work occurred just this week. On Monday he thought U.S. Robotics was ready to start moving, and bought March $65 (U.S.) calls for $1.87. The company had been plagued by delays on its new super-fast modems, which the market felt would give competitor Rockwell the edge. That morning, though, Mr. Denolf found out on the Internet that the company had overcome recent technological setbacks, and in fact was set to begin shipping the modems.

The stock soon moved up a couple of dollars, but then, out of the blue, came an announcement that 3Com Corp., a maker of networking equipment, had agreed to buy the company. An ecstatic Mr. Denolf thought the news would push his options through the roof but comments about the overheated market by U.S. Federal Reserve Board chairman Alan Greenspan hit stocks hard, including U.S. Robotics, and Mr. Denolf sold his options Thursday at $2.

HIS BEST MOVES: Early in January, Mr. Denolf saw some momentum happening in Motorola Inc., largely in response to the company's latest results. But it took a couple of buy recommendations before he got excited, and picked up some January $65 calls for 50 cents. The buy recommendations were certainly heeded, because the stock moved up nicely, and he sold his options three days later for $1.50.

Also in January, he bought January $145 call options on Intel Corp. at $3, as the company was preparing to report its latest earnings figures. "The stock was moving up because people had gone bananas on Intel, but I thought the earnings estimates were way too high," he says. So he rode the momentum, but sold out at $5.12 before the earnings came out. A good thing too, because soon after the stock fell by $5.

HIS WORST MOVE: Last September, he thought that investors were beginning to once again take a shine to Corel Corp., after the company had been given a rough ride over its purchase of WordPerfect Corp. from Novell Inc. "Corel and (president) Michael Cowpland were in the news every day," says Mr. Denolf, and when he noticed that a few analysts were praising the company, he picked up some September calls at $1.15. The market, though, didn't jump on board, the stock didn't climb, and his options expired worthless.

ADVICE: "Get hooked up to the Internet—it pays for itself. It's accessible to everyone, and, if you want to play options, it lets you stay well informed."

THE PORTFOLIO

Date:	Saturday, March 1, 1997
The investor:	Philippe Denolf, 21.
Occupation:	University finance student.
Investment personality:	"I'm a high risk-taker. I'm after quick capital appreciation."
Portfolio makeup:	Call options.
Portfolio size:	"Five figures."
Rate of return:	"Approximately 55 per cent a year."

Options are one of the most risky investments out there. Their value can bounce all over the map within a single day. What's worse, they often end up worthless.

You have to be prepared to put in a lot of time and effort to watch over your options, as a little bad news or higher than expected earnings can make them plummet or soar like a jet fighter at an airshow. Whatever you do, only put a very, very small percentage of your portfolio in options. I know a successful money manager who used to play the options market. To give you a sense of how risky it is, he only played with 5 per cent of his portfolio...and kept the rest in 100 per cent guaranteed GICs!

EARLY INTRODUCTION
TO RISK PAYS OFF

•

MATTHEW VAN WOLLEN was introduced to the markets on a first-name basis when he turned 18 and was handed the reins of his trust account. "My father took me down to one of his brokers and said, 'Now he's going to be taking care of his own portfolio,' and I said, 'What?!'"

Since then, Mr. van Wollen has taken to the high-risk stock game like a duck to water. He spends at least half an hour every week on the phone with his broker and he says "I'm learning every day."

Mr. van Wollen, 22, is a student at the University of British Columbia, where he is heavily involved in the school's solar car project. His involvement in "alternative" energy power gives a glimpse at how he is not always a complete believer in the traditional approach to getting somewhere.

He took the Canadian Securities Course three years ago, and vividly remembers studying a chapter on the kinds of asset allocation that would be best for different types of investors. "My model would have had me 50 per cent in high risk, and I'm looking at my portfolio and it's 95 per cent high risk," he says. "Either I have a much different definition of high risk than them, or I'm playing a different game."

While he says he's looking for fast and high returns, he doesn't step up to bat and swing at just anything. "I'm not a yahoo—I'm sensitive to things like gold prices and interest rates," he says, though he's quick to admit that he measures his returns in fun as well as financial terms.

"The excitement that's generated by a huge win is something that you just feed off of."

HOW HE DOES IT: Mr. van Wollen favours companies in the high-tech and mining sectors. "I like high-tech stocks because I'm an engineer and I understand the markets," he says. "And I'm quite comfortable reading the research reports on mining stocks."

To make his picks, he looks for leads, talking to his broker and his father—who works in the venture capital business—as well as reading a lot. He also says living in Vancouver is a great advantage. "It's such a tightly knit community you can almost talk to a stranger on the street to find out what's going on," he says.

However, he's learned enough lessons that he's sensitive to the market's unpredictable nature. "Experience plays a big part and so does luck."

He generally limits himself to stocks trading under $1, looking for at least a 25 per cent return. "I don't hold more than four stocks at any one time," he says. Playing volatile stocks, he believes it's important to stay on top of the market, and, he says, "There's no point spreading yourself too thin because the leverage is better."

HIS BEST MOVES: While Cartaway Resources Corp. (CWA-ASE, 52-week high $26, low 60 cents) carted away huge sums from many investors when the infamous ASE stock plummeted overnight, Mr. van Wollen got in early enough, and out early enough. "I heard they had been drilling and took a bet," he says. He paid $3.30 a share, and watched the stock drift lower to $3.10 over five days. "And then it moved and I sold out at $15."

He has also been able to catch a couple of nice waves off the turbulence kicked up by speculation in Oliver Gold Corp. (OGO-VSE, high $6.95, low $1.55). He first bought it in February 1995 at $1.40, selling out his position when it hit $5. He later bought back in at $2.50, and is still holding the stock. He's also done well with Sierra

Nevada Gold Ltd., based in Grass Valley, Calif. (SDD-VSE, high $1.70, low 34 cents), which he picked up for 25 cents, selling out at $1.

HIS WORST MOVE: No question, his worst step so far has been Consolidated Golden Unicorn Mining Corp. of Vancouver. He picked up 20,000 shares at 20 cents in the spring of 1995, and a week later the company was delisted, and hasn't traded since.

"They've got a really good property and it's really annoying they can't be traded," says Mr. Wollen, who has mentally written off his investment. "It may come back, but today, as far as I'm concerned, it's gone."

ADVICE: "The first mistake people make is they expect miracles to happen. If you've lost, take your money and put it elsewhere. You should know when to leave. It's like being at a bad party—why wait it out?"

THE PORTFOLIO

Date:	Saturday, January 25, 1997
The investor:	Matthew van Wollen, 22.
Occupation:	Engineering physics student.
Investment personality:	"I'm interested in quick, high returns."
Portfolio makeup:	Oliver Gold Corp., Nord Resources Corp., San Fernando, Ace Developments Ltd.
Portfolio size:	Low six figures.
Rate of return:	"Around 30 per cent."

Like smarter speculative players everywhere, Matthew van Wollen takes many concrete steps to reduce his risk, raise his likelihood of making a decent return, and minimize his likelihood of getting into situations better left untouched. Here are just some of the things he's done right:

- He educated himself. While he took the Canadian Securities Course—a great primer in many aspects of the market—it's not so much what he studied but that he studied something. Any books, pamphlets, articles or courses that you work through will add to your knowledge base. And don't forget that learning is an ongoing process.

  Even if you don't have a clue today about the difference between stocks and bonds, if you just read one introductory article a week, in a year's time, you'll have given yourself a first-class introductory lesson in investing. And the more you know about investing, the better able you are to do everything from developing a financial plan and monitoring your investments to ensuring you're getting your money's worth from your adviser.

- He keeps his eyes and ears open. Mr. van Wollen knows that stocks don't exist in a vacuum. Even the most speculative investment still has to play itself out in the larger world. A penny gold mining stock may have the discovery of the decade, but as many junior gold investors discover, that doesn't matter much if the price of gold has been in freefall and the world has just learned that Bre-X was a fraud. The more you stay on top of external influences that may affect your stocks, the less likely you are to get side-swiped by economic, political and general market factors.

- He invests in what he knows. Junior resource stocks and high-tech companies frequently find their way into his portfolio, but he can read and understand mining research reports and, as a student in engineering physics, can quickly grasp the potential for many high-tech companies. The more you know about an industry, the better able you are to judge if the promise of a stock—whether it's an ore body or a killer piece of software—is grounded in reality, or is simply being inflated behind the scenes by unscrupulous types with lungs full of hot air and not much else.

- He stays focused. At any one time, he's unlikely to have more than a handful of stocks in his portfolio, meaning he doesn't try to follow too many developments on too many fronts. Sometimes the news—and rumours—on speculative stocks flows fast and furiously, and you'll drown trying to keep up if you are involved in too many investments.

COMPUTER STOCKS
CRUNCH OUT PROFITS

•

ADIL BURNEY HAS ALWAYS LIKED COMPUTERS, but over the past couple of years, he's grown to really love them.

"I don't know how to program, but I can understand more than the average person what computer geeks are saying," says the 25-year-old Beaconsfield, Que., accountant.

His growing affection for things data-driven is in no small part the result of the fantastic returns he's made by placing most of his bets on the ability of the U.S. technology leaders to grow.

"The industry has setbacks, but I take the long view," he says. And in the long term, Mr. Burney feels the demand for computer-related products will continue to grow, especially given the growing demand he expects to see from developing countries.

HOW HE DOES IT: Although he's only been playing stocks for two years, Mr. Burney has rung up some very impressive returns. He has made some good picks, but his performance has been given a great boost by his patience.

If he finds a leader he likes but is put off by a sky-high stock price, he'll just sit back and wait for one of the regular falling-outs the industry tends to have with investors, and then buy in. Many of his big gains, in fact, were a result of his buying a number of companies in late 1995/early 1996 when the industry was out of favour.

It's important to be selective in the computer world, he says, and one of his key tenets is "the big get bigger." As a result, most of his attention is focused south of the border on large U.S. technology leaders.

He reads up a lot on management to ensure it is continually innovating and runs a tight financial ship as well. And while even in downturns leading technology companies can be expensive, he still feels comfortable buying in if the earnings growth is higher than the price/earnings ratio.

HIS BEST MOVES: Mr. Burney hit a homer with his first at-bat with his purchase of Houston-based Compaq Computer Corp. (CPQ-NYSE, 52-week high $79.56 (U.S.), low $23.68, yesterday's close $75.62.)

He picked up shares of the computer maker in 1995 and 1996 for an average price of $17 (adjusted for splits). One reason the company looked enticing was the stock had fallen from $55 to under $40 (pre-split), which dropped the price/earnings ratio into the single digits for a time. "I'd followed the company for a while, knew it was a leader, and when investors starting getting bearish on the company, I became very bullish."

Strong earnings, cost-cutting and large cash reserves added to the appeal. He also felt the industry was poised for some consolidation, which would further benefit Compaq. "The PC market was growing at 15 per cent to 20 per cent, so I figured Compaq would grow at an even better pace."

Mr. Burney's long-term take on all things technological got him into Applied Materials Inc. (AMAT-Nasdaq, 52-week high $108.37, low $25.62, yesterday's close $108.37), which makes manufacturing equipment for the semiconductor industry. The market at the time was putting the boots to the semiconductor industry, and Applied Materials' stock had been pulled down from the mid-sixties to $20.

That was a clear buy for Mr. Burney, who felt the stock hadn't been overpriced at its high, and in the long run the demand for semiconductors would only grow stronger.

"They are in everything from computers to cars, and they are being used more internationally in countries like China and India," he says.

"Applied Materials is the leader in its field, and my research showed the management was strong, and that the company always weathered the downturns of the industry well." He bought his shares in the $20 range.

The general weakness in the computer industry in early 1996 also gave him some wonderful profits on Intel. "They basically have a monopoly in one of the most attractive fields in the world," he says. Mr. Burney bought call LEAPS (long-term equity anticipation securities) on Intel Corp., the Santa Clara, Calif.-based chip maker (INTC-Nasdaq, 52-week high $102, low $49.06, yesterday's close $93.31) with a strike price of $90 for $3, when the stock was at $50. The stock doubled by the fall, and Mr. Burney sold his positions for $20.

HIS WORST MOVE: Just because a computer company is down doesn't mean it's always going to get back up. In late 1995, Mr. Burney bought software maker Corel Corp. (COS-TSE, 52-week high $12.95, low $5.20) at $20 on the strengths of CorelDraw, which dominated the graphics software market. A week later, the company bought WordPerfect, and the stock began a long steady decline.

"I didn't do my homework on them," Mr. Burney says. "Afterwards, I learned they don't have a very good management team. They're always hyping the stock, and when you do that and don't meet expectations, you get punished." Mr. Burney took his lumps and bailed out early this year at $9, which still looks like a good move, given that the stock closed yesterday at $5.55.

ADVICE: "Buy affordable shares in good companies and in the long term you should do well."

THE PORTFOLIO

Date:	Saturday, October 4, 1997
The investor:	Adil Burney, 25.
Occupation:	Accountant.

Investment personality:	"Aggressive."
Portfolio makeup:	Applied Materials Inc., Ascend Communications Inc., Oracle Corp., Compaq Computer Corp., Intel Corp., Netscape Communications Corp.
Portfolio size:	Low six figures.
Rate of return:	"42 per cent in 1996, 100 per cent year-to-date."

Playing computer and Internet stocks has become almost a national pastime in the United States. But if you want to protect yourself, you have to make a big distinction between stocks that investors are buying up because they might be worth a lot more next year and those companies that actually make and sell something at a profit.

In the former category go stocks like Amazon, the on-line bookseller, that within a year had gone from a low of just under $12 U.S. to a high of $147 U.S.! In that time, it wasn't unusual for it to rise or fall by five, six or seven dollars in a single day! All this without yet having figured out how to make a profit.

In the latter category, you have companies like IBM, which during the same period had a low of $88 U.S. and a high of $131 U.S. Still a big range, and plenty of room for profits, plus they had all sorts of other exciting features like a solid balance sheet, years of historical performance to look at and, of course, profits.

BEWARE THOSE
HONKY-TONK BROKERS

•

LIKE MANY GOOD STORIES, Mike Zichowski's begins with a bar and a young, attractive woman.

Back in 1986, the 45-year-old Thornhill, Ont., man found himself in the former talking to the latter, whose clothes gave off a clear scent of money. "She was standing there and then boom, she passed me her card and said, 'I'm a broker. I want you to be a client and you can drive a BMW just like me.'"

Without further ado, Mr. Zichowski climbed on for the ride, which unfortunately, as it turned out, made the fast investing track seem like the place to be. "We made some quick killings on things like Imperial Oil and Loblaw, and that made me even more greedy."

The first big bump in the road came courtesy of Cineplex. His broker convinced him that Garth Drabinsky was going to buy the company out, and persuaded Mr. Zichowski to buy in at $15.

Mr. Drabinsky's leveraged buy-out attempt failed, however, and he left the company. Shortly after, so did a lot of the air in the stock, as it soon fell to $11. His broker, though, called it just a drop in the bucket. "She said, 'Don't get discouraged. Get back in there and start boxing again.'"

He followed her advice, but lost track of his broker who soon disappeared from the business. Mr. Zichowski only found out where she had gone when she called him up a few years later trying to enlist him in a cosmetics pyramid marketing scheme.

Over the next 10 years, Mr. Zichowski continued to "box" faithfully. The net result? He estimates that he has lost 90 per cent of all of the money he has put in the stock market. "I've got basically nothing to show for 10 years of investing."

A former high school teacher who now is making a living as a freelance writer, Mr. Zichowski is willing to expose his financial failings because he hopes it will help others make wiser decisions.

HOW HE DID IT: Mr. Zichowski says one of his biggest mistakes was putting too much confidence in his brokers. In particular, one of his biggest trip-ups was locking in on the target price his brokers always cited when they were touting a new stock. "There's no such thing as a 'target.' It's just a number anybody can devise," he says.

He also says he was far too agreeable every time the person handling his account moved on, and his brokerage company simply passed him over to another broker. "I should have checked them out a lot more."

In addition to his adviser, he also says it would have been wiser to have been more proactive about researching his investments on his own instead of blindly following his broker's suggestions. "Now, when my broker suggests something, I'll call up a colleague who invests a lot for his advice, and get his broker's advice as well."

HIS WORST MOVES: While there must be many thousands of people who took massive hits on Bre-X Minerals Ltd., Mr. Zichowski is one of the few brave souls willing to admit it. He bought into the infamous scam-of-the-century this past February. The stock had already soared to $23.50, and his brokerage firm was calling for it to head right up to $40.

Even when the first rumours that it was a fraud started floating around, Mr. Zichowski was reassured by his broker that the gold was indeed there. Mr. Zichowski put $20,000 into Bre-X, and all he got out of it was a stock certificate that hangs on his bathroom wall (for another $26 charge, mind you).

In late 1996, gold fever and a strong push by his broker got him into Vancouver-based Channel Resources Ltd. (CHU-TSE, 52-week high $2.45, low 50 cents) at $2.65. "They were exploring for gold in Nigeria and Ghana, and it was supposed to be another Bre-X."

Thankfully, that didn't turn out to be true. The company is still exploring for gold, but nonetheless, like many other junior gold stocks, the price has collapsed, closing yesterday at 65 cents.

Ourominas Minerals Inc. of Toronto (OMI-TSE, high $4.50, low 60 cents) handed him more of the same this year. His broker had a target of $9, based on the company's plans to develop scavenged gold mines in Brazil, so Mr. Zichowski bought in January near the stock's 52-week high. The only thing that has been picked clean so far is Mr. Zichowski's pocket, as the stock is now trading at 70 cents.

HIS BEST MOVES: Mr. Zichowski is still hoping that a few aggressive moves will help him claw his way back, and some recent bets have been paying off. In 1996, he more than doubled his money with junior diamond company, Diadem Resources Ltd. (DIR-ME, 52-week high $8.50, low 90 cents, yesterday's close $1). He bought at $2, and sold out within the month at $4.85. "My broker had said, 'Here's our target price,' and I sort of believed him."

ADVICE: "You have to try and not get drawn in by the excitement. Especially when the markets are flying, it's easy to feel like you are a loser if you're not on board."

THE PORTFOLIO

Date:	Saturday, September 27, 1997
The investor:	Mike Zichowski, 45.
Occupation:	Freelance writer, former high school teacher.
Investment personality:	"I was extremely aggressive; now I'm depressed."

Portfolio makeup:	Cineplex, Northrock, Jannock, NCE royalty trust units, Simmonds Capital, Channel Resources.
Portfolio size:	"Five figures."
Rate of return:	A loss of 90 per cent of all his capital over 10 years.

Mr. Zichowski is one of the bravest and most thoughtful people to offer his financial life up to public scrutiny in *Me and My Money*.

He's brave because it's tough to admit mistakes, especially financial ones. In no other endeavour (save perhaps for fishing) do people tend so much to focus on their positive achievements, often expanding and enlarging on them, and minimize their mistakes and failures. Many people overestimate how well they've done in the market, and quite understandably often put their losers out of their mind.

(In fact, you never really know what goes on behind other people's doors—or inside their bank accounts. Never try to compete with someone else's "returns." You don't know what kind of risks they took, whether those investments are even suitable for you, or whether those returns were actually what they made! On a broader financial front, don't try to keep up with the Joneses. You have to live within your means, not somebody else's. And how do you know that the Joneses aren't keeping up their lifestyle by carrying burdensome loads of high-cost debt?)

Mr. Zichowski is thoughtful, not only because he's spent some time considering his errors, but also because he was willing to talk about those errors, in the hope that others would be able to learn from them.

Here are a few key lessons he has to offer up:

• *Don't Believe Target Prices.* As he rightly points out, the "targets" for stocks and other investments that analysts bandy about are just that—targets. If you've ever tried your hand at archery, you know even the most talented bow-handlers don't hit the bull's-eye every time. Targets for the future value of an investment are arrived at by weighing many unpredictable factors, assigning hard numbers to future events like what a company will earn in the next year, as well as what investors will be willing to pay for those investments. At best, target prices are an educated guess about the possible outcome of several yet-to-be determined developments.

- *Don't Get Passed Around from Broker to Broker.* All too often, I hear of someone whose broker has left a brokerage firm—or the business altogether—and had their account simply passed on, often without them being notified, to another broker.

  If your broker stops handling your account, you're a free agent. It's a great time to review your situation, your investments, and go over what you liked and didn't like about the way you and your broker worked together. Use this information to interview the broker your account has been handed to, and if they don't meet your criteria, look elsewhere. In fact, use the departure of a broker to interview several brokers—cast your net wide to ensure the new broker you hire fits your needs and personality.

- *Don't Feel Like You're a Loser If You Aren't on Board.* Stock highs and top-performing mutual funds are great headline fodder, but nobody ever has their money in all the winners all the time. In fact, if they did, they shouldn't have, because they are taking too many risks. Don't let the markets drive your decision making. Even if they are steaming ahead, that doesn't necessarily mean it's the best place for your money. You have to look at your income, your circumstances, and when you'll need your money before you can begin evaluating just where to invest.

SURVEY ENGINEER
LINES UP LONG SHOTS

•

WHEN HE'S NOT TRYING to lower his handicap on the golf course, Jim Condon spends most of his free time lining up his next "long shot" on the stock market.

"I really enjoy it," the 59-year-old Regina man says. "My wife's into genealogy, and I'm into stocks."

While he's been an investor all of his working life, Mr. Condon only made the switch to picking his own stocks a few years back. He decided he could earn a better return than the mutual funds he owned.

He also felt he wasn't getting the sort of breaking news and recommendations he thought he was paying his full-service brokers for. "Whenever it seemed like there was something attractive, I was at the bottom of the list."

HOW HE DOES IT: Information is the name of Mr. Condon's game. The pub he frequents after work, for example, just happens to be the favourite haunt of a dozen or so other stock jockeys. And many of his colleagues at his survey engineering firm are avid market followers. "Instead of having a coffee break, we'll talk about stocks," he says.

He is also an avid reader of newsletters. He's a big fan of *Carter's Choice*, as well as *The Money Letter*, Kaiser's *Bottom Fishing Report*, and *Gold Stock Report*.

Mr. Condon is rarely without his laptop computer. He regularly logs onto the Internet to see if there is any breaking news on the companies he's following. He also frequently goes on-line to get real-time

quotes for his shares with Toronto-Dominion Bank's MicroMax software program. "I can use it even when I go golfing in Arizona, because
they have local numbers you dial in to," he says.

So how does he choose from all the potential superstars he hears
about? One characteristic he looks for is heavy volume made up of
a large number of trades. "I don't want to see big block trades," he
says. "The more people, the more speculative fervour there is." Beyond
that, though, he says that often the key factor is simply a "gut feeling."

Mr. Condon figures he spends at least an hour or two a day watching the markets, and usually makes one or two trades a week. These
days, he's keeping more than 20 per cent of his portfolio in cash.

"With all the talk of a possible drop, I want to be able to get in there
and buy if the market falls."

HIS BEST MOVES: The problem for many investors like Mr. Condon is
that Bre-X Minerals Ltd. (BXM-TSE, 52-week high $28.65, low $17.70,
yesterday's close $17.75) can be grouped with their best and worst per-
formers. On the recommendation of the *Carter's Choice* newsletter, he
bought into the exploration company at 50 cents. He sold out at $2
when he had made what seemed at the time like a terrific return.

Mr. Condon also got into Arequipa Resources Ltd. in the early
days. He bought into the exploration company three years ago at
around $1, and rode it until the company was taken over by Barrick
Gold Corp. at $30 last August. "Carter was in and out of it, but I hung
in there, because I was so mad after I dropped Bre-X."

He came across Berkley Petroleum Corp. of Calgary (BKP-TSE,
high $40.50, low $11.75, close $34.30) when he was doing some sur-
veying for the oil and gas company, and was immediately impressed.
"They're major players, former employees of Shell Oil, and they are
very astute people." He picked up his shares 18 months ago, paying
between $4 and $5, and is still holding on for further gains.

His circle of fellow frequent traders helped him score a nice double with Cavell Energy (KVL-TSE, high $7.70, low $3.20, close $5.85).
He was golfing with a few friends in Scottsdale, Ariz., last fall, and

phoned his office. One of his partners told him Cavell had paid a
record price to purchase mineral rights in Saskatchewan.

That was a huge positive sign, he says, and although the initial offering was oversubscribed at $2.50, he picked up some shares at $3.40
in November. By Christmas, the stock had risen to $5. "It paid for our
golfing trip," he says.

HIS WORST MOVE: Mr. Condon got caught when he bet real estate stocks
such as Bramalea Inc. and Trizec Corp. could turn themselves around
a few years ago. For example, he bought Bramalea at $3.25 in April
1993, and sold in December 1994, when the stock had fallen to $1.36.

ADVICE: "Most people don't spend enough time on the financial end
of things. They depend on other people and often they're just self-
serving. It's really not that difficult. The calculus exams I've written
are a lot harder than doing a price/earnings ratio."

THE PORTFOLIO

Date:	Saturday, March 15, 1997
The investor:	Jim Condon, 59.
Occupation:	Survey engineer.
Investment personality:	"I'm sort of like a Western farmer—I go by the seat of my pants. I really don't have any master plan."
Portfolio makeup:	Stocks include CAE Inc., Benson Petroleum, Essex Resource, Franco-Nevada Mining, Gerle Gold, Hurricane Hydrocarbon, Jordan Petroleum, Wascana, Western Copper, Yamana Resources, Metallica Resources, William Resources.
Portfolio size:	High six figures.
Rate of return:	"Around 30 per cent a year."

Talk about information overload. If you want to follow Mr. Condon's path, you'll have to wade through a half-dozen newsletters a month, chat it up with other investors, surf the net and track your stocks. Whew! Plus, when you go away, whether you're visiting a friend in another province or vacationing in Scotland, like Mr. Condon did, you should probably follow his packing advice, and make sure a portable computer and modem make it into your suitcase.

In short, Mr. Condon likes and enjoys the stock market. For him, going on-line from Scotland in the middle of trying to win out over its famously tricky links just to see what somebody is willing to pay for the Really and Truly Next Big Thing Company is not just water off his back, he looks forward to it. As he admits "Golf and separating the wheat from the chaff in the stock market are my hobbies."

That kind of ongoing involvement—fun if you're into it, and dreadfully dull and onerous if you're not—is unavoidable if you want to avoid getting pulverized in the speculative markets. You may be able to make better returns—perhaps 1 or 2 per cent, or perhaps 20 percent—with high-risk investments. But those returns don't really matter if it leaves you in a constant state of nervousness.

If you like the excitement and always having an eye on the markets like Mr. Condon—and are careful to limit your losses—that's one thing. But if you keep on putting off that once-in-a-lifetime holiday to Fiji because you're worried that you won't be able to go on-line from your grass hut, that's another. You can let playing the market be a big—and even rewarding—part of your life. Just don't let it take control of your life when you're not looking.

PRINCIPAL BETS ON

GOOD FIRMS GONE BAD

•

GERALD BRISE DOESN'T beat around the bush. When asked about his approach to investing, he quickly responds with "far too risky" without missing a beat.

"I take way too many chances," he says. In fact, when I asked him to pick out his best and worst moves, he said it was a lot easier to find stand-out losers than it was to shortlist his big winners. The problem, he says succinctly, is "I go for the big wins, and usually lose."

But he certainly knows his way around the more speculative edges of the market. *Me and My Money* readers may remember Mr. Brise's name from a few weeks back, when he was mentioned as the adviser to the two British Columbia high-school students who won a stock-market contest using "play" money.

Mr. Brise could, in fact, show some Olympic team coaches a thing or two about succeeding. In the 10 or so years that the teacher and principal has been helping students from Fraser Lake Secondary School compete in the bi-annual competition, he has seen them win four national championships and eight regional championships. "A lot of our success is because we play the options market," he says. "It's the only way I can think of that you can make a heck of a pile of money in short order."

He's also more than aware that luck and good timing are needed to ensure that a pile of money is made, and not lost. Take the stack of pretend money amassed last fall by two of his students, Tyler Romain and Danielle Sansom, in a simulated stock-market contest. The team bought put options on the TSE 35, betting that the market couldn't maintain its dizzying heights, and almost quadrupled their stake in under three weeks. The day they sold (guaranteeing themselves the national championship, incidentally), Mr. Brise decided there was still a lot of downside left in the market and potential profit left in the put strategy. He bought in big, with real money. But instead of the market falling, it headed back up again. "I lost my last year's profits in a day," he says.

Interestingly, Mr. Brise is more than capable of earning solid returns with a conservative strategy. Fifteen years ago, he began looking after some of his mother's savings. He only bought big blue-chip names, and has seen that portfolio easily outperform his own high-risk investments. "It's done very well," he says.

HOW HE DOES IT: Mr. Brise tries to jump on tips and stocks in the news that he feels are going to be home runs. He's also a big proponent of buying big-name stocks when they are beaten down, but not necessarily out for the count. "You always want to have that big win. That's part of the gambling thing," he says. "You think, 'Gee, this is the one that's going to take off. This is the one that's going to do it.'"

Mr. Brise, a graduate of the Canadian Securities Course, is fully aware of what he's up to. "I know what I should be doing," he says, adding that he is gradually changing his approach. "I've been trying to build up some solid stuff and reduce my gambling stocks."

HIS BEST MOVES: It's more than a little interesting that Mr. Brise's winners are all different stories from the "Buy good companies when they are beaten up" book.

For example, he picked up Northern Telecom Ltd. (NTL-TSE, 52-week high $77.75 (adjusted for a two-for-one split in January), low $43.50, yesterday's close $75.80) in the summer of 1993, after hearing on the radio that it had dropped to $29, presplit. "They'd taken a writedown, and everybody was overreacting," he says. "It was a solid company, and had no business being down that low." He was proved right and profited from it, selling half of his position two years later at $52.25, and unloading the rest of his shares in May 1997 at $102.75.

The same buy-low technique also worked with Mitel Corp. (MLT-TSE, high $17.95, low $6.35, close $18.30), which he picked up at $4.70 in late 1994. "I thought it was a recovery story, as they were still a fairly large company and had a reasonable market share for their switches."

HIS WORST MOVES: There is no perfect stock-investing strategy. For proof, look no further than a couple of Mr. Brise's losses, many of which also involve betting on big turnarounds that instead bottomed out with Titanic-like collapses.

"I've got a lot of losers," he says, rhyming off names such as Dome Petroleum, Bramalea and Laidlaw. "I've been a part of every big story."

The one that bothers him the most, though, is Laidlaw Inc. (LDM-TSE, high $22.90, low $17.70, close $20.75). Although he now trades through Toronto-Dominion Bank's discount brokerage, Green Line, he used to use a broker, and in the spring of 1988, he got a call that Canadian Pacific Ltd. was rumoured to be buying the waste management and school busing operation. He decided to play warrants for the extra leverage, and picked them up at $2.82 that April. "It looked like a really good way to make a really good buck," he says. He was emboldened by the words of Laidlaw chairman Michael DeGroote, who Mr. Brise says stated that he would stand by his shareholders after putting the company on the block.

Shortly after, however, Mr. DeGroote sold his controlling interest to CP, wiping out any takeover premium and dropping the stock to below its presale announcement price. Mr. Brise averaged down, picking up more warrants at just 18 cents a month later, and in August got rid of them all for 2 cents apiece.

THE PORTFOLIO

Date:	Saturday, February 28, 1998
The investor:	Gerald Brise, 49.

Occupation:	High-school principal.
Investment personality:	"Far too risky."
Portfolio makeup:	Bema Gold, Bombardier, CAE, Canadian Pacific LEAPs, CIBC, Certicom, Demand Gold, Compton Petroleum, Gennum, Habanero Resources, K2 Energy, Laidlaw, Loadstar Energy, Loewen Group, Magellan Aerospace, National Bank, Newbridge, Nova LEAPs, Precision Drilling, Princeton Mining, Renata Resources, Revenue Properties, Royal Bank, Symmetry Resources, TransAlta.
Portfolio size:	"Six figures."
Rate of return:	Not known.

Mr. Brise is a big believer in being a contrarian. Contrarians like to go where others aren't—buying stocks that everybody else has turned their backs on. The thinking is that if you choose carefully, you will be able to profit from the way the actions of other investors tend to be overdone, kind of like overcorrecting when you're trying to get control of your car in the winter when it starts to spin.

If a stocks get hot, too many investors often jump on board and drive it higher than it has a right to be. And when a stock falls on bad times, investors tend to bail out *en masse*, often driving the price of the stock far below a reasonable level. Contrarians try to take advantage of this by buying shares in companies that the great majority of investors have given up on. Their goal is to locate those that will stage a big-scale comeback like John Travolta did with *Pulp Fiction*. If they pick correctly, then when other investors discover these out-of-favour stocks again, the contrarian investor who bought in low will profit big-time as prices soar.

ARCHITECT SPURNS RISK
FOR SOLID RETURNS

•

VANCOUVER ARCHITECT PETER LOVICK, 45, owes his involvement in the stock market to the persistence of new brokers looking to build up their trading business.

"Somebody I'd done work for became a stockbroker, and so did another fellow I knew who was a geologist," he says. Both brokers got Mr. Lovick to sign on with them, and while his first few investments didn't work out so well, he says he enjoyed the new-found sense of independence.

"Buying individual stocks seemed to be a much better way of having control over your investments," he says. "And it gives you more of a chance to try and make a decent return."

Today, Mr. Lovick works closely with the former geologist—Norm Duncan of C.M. Oliver & Co. Ltd. in Vancouver—to invest both his own savings and the liquid assets of his architecture business.

While in the beginning he favoured more high-risk situations, he says that recently he's begun to feel that the returns simply aren't high enough on average to warrant the extra uncertainty. "I've always said to my broker that if we can be really safe and make 10 to 12 per cent (a year), I'd be happy."

HOW HE DOES IT: He mostly looks to his broker to come up with investment recommendations. The two men generally spend an hour a week on the phone together, reviewing his portfolio and talking about new opportunities Mr. Duncan has unearthed. "We try and buy stuff before it's widely recommended so we're buying before everybody else does."

Mr. Lovick also uses his broker to research companies he gets tips on, rather than taking a flyer without knowing what his money is buying. "Especially when it's a mining company, (Mr. Duncan) is able to do the homework and check them out for me. He can come back and say whether or not they've got good management and good properties."

He also says he looks to his broker to keep his own willingness to take risk in check. "He talks me out of things, and keeps me on the straight and narrow, which has been good."

Still, Mr. Lovick feels that he himself is ultimately responsible for deciding what moves to make. "I always read the business sections in the local papers just so I can try and understand where he's coming from if he calls. If Norm feels I'm making the wrong choice he'll let me know, but I make my own decisions."

HIS BEST MOVES: Having his broker check out a tip was how he scored big with Vancouver-based junior mining company, Gitennes Exploration Inc. (GIT-ASE, 52-week high $6.80, low 70 cents, yesterday's close $5.75).

Gitennes is exploring in Peru and the Northwest Territories. After researching the company, Mr. Duncan came back with two thumbs up on the company's management and properties, and Mr. Lovick went in at around $1. He is holding on for further gains.

He's also done well with Bank of Montreal (BMO-TSE, high $8.80, low $30.37, close $48.80), which he bought two years ago at $23. "My broker just thought the banking industry was solid, and he felt it was a good long-term hold."

Another winner has been Consumers Gas Co. Ltd. of Toronto, which he bought in 1994 for $14. Late last year, the company was merged into Calgary-based IPL Energy Inc., a gas distribution and oil pipeline company. Consumers Gas shareholders received the equivalent of $24 a share. Mr. Lovick took the offered IPL shares in place of cash and is holding the utility, largely because of its healthy dividend.

He got a quick runup on Windsor-based Anchor Lamina Inc. (AKC-TSE, high $7.25, low $4.75, close $7.25), which makes die sets, mould-based components and die-maker accessories. "That was another one where Norm felt it was a really well-run company with loads of potential that nobody was buying," Mr. Lovick says. He picked it up last summer for $5, and sold in January for $7. "It was supposed to be a short-term investment, and that's exactly what happened, and we sold when the stock popped up."

HIS WORST MOVE: Mr. Lovick bought into Vancouver-based junior exploration company San Fernando Mining Co. Ltd. (SNF-TSE, high $1.62, low 92 cents, close $1.04) in 1994 at $2.40. The company is involved in gold and silver exploration in Mexico. "It looked like they were going to come out with some good results," he says. "But then they just kept bringing out worse and worse reports."

He's still holding on to the stock. He's hoping to get his original investment out, helped by the fact that a "big Mexican promoter" is involved with the company, but says that "we probably should have sold it long ago."

ADVICE: "I'm finding out that with the high-risk stuff you often don't make the big hit. The risky stuff still balances out to 15 to 20 per cent (a year) in the long run. There's no such thing as easy money."

THE PORTFOLIO

Date:	Saturday, Febraury 8, 1997
The investor:	Peter Lovick, 45.
Occupation:	Architect.
Investment personality:	"I like taking risks, but the returns don't seem to be there, so I guess in the long run I'm tending to be more conservative."

Portfolio makeup:	Mutual funds include Trimark RSP Equity Fund, Trimark Select Canadian Growth Fund, Global Strategy Japan Fund, AGF Asian Growth Fund, Industrial Income Fund. Stocks include Bank of Montreal, Gitennes Exploration, Mexico Equity and Income Fund Inc., San Fernando Mining, IPL Energy, Intimate Brands.
Portfolio size:	Low six figures.
Rate of return:	18 to 20 per cent a year.

Like many investors before him, Mr. Lovick came into investing from the wrong direction. He began by acquiring more high-risk stocks, but found there were two problems. He didn't like the uncertainty, and he wasn't so keen on the returns, which weren't as great as he thought they'd be. Put them together and you get a not terribly attractive situation—high risk and not-so-terrific returns. As he puts it, "There is no such thing as easy money."

The pretty charts that show speculative stocks that have gone through the roof look enticing, but there aren't a lot of people who manage to buy at the low and sell at the high.

If you're just setting foot in the stock market, learn from Mr. Lovick's experience. Start slow, and start conservative. If you enjoy picking stocks, like risk and have the time, then add some more speculative issues. But don't expect them to instantly change your financial situation, and remember that blue-chip stocks can often offer comparable returns with a lot less headaches.

SAVVY
System
PLAYERS

OUR SYSTEM-BASED investors depend partially—
or entirely—on methods of evaluating stocks
by looking at trends in their price and volume, as well as their dividend yield.

Ali Baba had it easy. Once he figured out all he needed to say was "Open Sesame," the cave doors opened up and he could help himself to pots of gold.

Finding the key that will open the door to investment riches has proven to be a lot tougher. But many investors feel that much of the code needed to crack the market is embedded in the numbers it so endlessly churns out—numbers such as the daily changes in a stock's price, its volume and how much it pays out in dividends.

Some investors find that looking at objective numerical information provides yet another useful tool with which to assess a stock's potential. Others investors, though, depend solely on their number-crunching, and completely ignore so-called *fundamental* factors, such as what the company does, its marketplace and its financial picture.

THE UPSIDE

At best, having a system is kind of like having a round-the-clock body-guard whose only job is to protect you from yourself. Probably the single biggest threat to your financial well-being is your emotions. Fear and greed are the biggies of course, but there are many much more subtle psychological forces that kick in when money is at stake. You may, for example, simply be trying to imitate your parents' financial moves. Or you may be rebelling by doing exactly the opposite of what went on in the family home.

Because systems are usually based on cold hard numbers and statistics, they allow you to fake out your emotions. While they are still trying to catch up to you to twist your arm about what they want you to do, whether it's how much money to put away or whether to get into that high-tech stock, you will have already sneakily made your decision by simply crunching some numbers and moved on.

THE DOWNSIDE

Most systems, particularly those that work with technical analysis, have an endless appetite for raw numbers to crunch. It's only by feeding in information about a stock's price, volume and other vital statistics that a technical system can let you know if it's time to buy or sell.

In order to give the system a fighting chance, you have to be able to provide that data. Various Web sites and computer software programs make this task relatively easy, and in some cases, they let you partially automate the process. Still, it is something you need to take care of on a regular basis.

(One big exception to this is David Stanley's Beating The TSE strategy—he figures his method only takes a few minutes a year!)

Most systems could give two hoots about whether a company is inventing a technique for freeze-drying water or has just developed a software program that actually works all of the time, even when you're facing deadlines. With technical analysis, you're not going to be able to keep your eyes open if what interests you is learning about companies—what they make, how they sell their products and services, and their financial picture. On the other hand, if numbers are to you what notes were to Mozart, you'll get a lovely buzz watching their pretty patterns develop as they sing and dance across your computer screen.

DOING IT YOURSELF

Being handy with computers is pretty much essential if you want to try the technical approach. The good news is there are many ways to get hold of the latest numbers and put them into your PC. Most discount brokerages, for example, allow you to go on-line and download the latest price and volume information.

USING A HELPING HAND

Number-crunching is not something most brokers like to get involved with. Things usually happen too quickly, plus they undermine what most brokerages houses see as one of their major assets—their fundamental research.

HOW THEY PULL IT OFF

All of the investors in this chapter feel that the market is trying to tell them something, and they all have different methods of deciphering just what that message is.

The message though, is usually buried in three basic numbers—a stock's volume, its price and its divided yield compared to other stocks. Following each profile, I've gone into more detail about how these statistics are used.

By and large, our system advocates tend to be rather conservative. They often have larger-cap stocks in their portfolios, and employ strategies to limit their losses. For example, John Beamish relies heavily on what are called stop-loss orders.

Stop-Losses Explained

A stop-loss order is an order you give to a broker to sell a stock, but only if it falls below a certain price level. This can serve to limit your losses if a stock plummets. It can also help you lock in profits. For example, you could set your stop-loss at 10 per cent under the last day's closing price. As the stock price rises, so does the level at which your stop-loss order would get acted upon and your stock sold. By changing the stop-loss regularly, you keep upping the floor price at which you will sell, locking in your profits.

Coldly Clinical Can Be Profitable

Our system-oriented investors also help limit their losses and maximize their gains by using their technical signals to help keep their emotions in line. The most common investment practice known to humanity seems to be the very popular "Buy high and sell low."

This is the logical outcome when you mix riskier investments such as stocks with human emotions. A technical system gives our investors a way to manage and control the risks they are taking. This allows them to lower the stress of equity investing, which helps remove emotions from the equation, which time and again have proven to be easily confused and, at least in the world of investments, lousy decision-makers.

GEOPHYSICIST TAKES
TO TECHNICAL ANALYSIS

•

KAREN BRAWLEY-HOGG has discovered there's a lot of similarity between her work as a geophysicist and her new pastime of using technical analysis to play the stock market.

"In my job, I take a bunch of seismic data—remote sensing of the Earth—and then interpret it. It's not an exact science," the 35-year-old Calgary woman says. "And my investing also involves making interpretations of data and taking risks."

Until earlier this year, she had been investing in mutual funds for more than 10 years, but had grown unhappy with her results. "The funds I was in were reputable, but many times they weren't performing as well as the TSE," she says. "So I thought maybe it was time to take charge."

Immediately catching on to the connection between her professional training and technical analysis, she began picking stocks and was quickly taken with the ups and downs of the markets. "Initially, it was more than a little exhilarating but once I honed my skills, I toned it down a little bit," she says.

She took a course in technical analysis, and became committed to staying on top of her investments. Every night, for instance, she cranks up her computer and downloads that day's market numbers into her investment software program.

HOW SHE DOES IT: She begins by looking at sectors whose indexes are outperforming, and then starts to focus on individual stocks, looking for established companies that are fundamentally strong.

At that point, she breaks out the charts. She likes to see a stock that is trading in a well-defined, predictable pattern, with a moving average that is heading up. "I'm looking for indications that the markets are supporting it to go even higher, such as heavy volume and closing on the highest highs of the day," she says.

However, when stocks are volatile, it's hard to chart where they're likely to go next. "I stay away from stocks that are bouncing all over the place," she says. "Technical analysis doesn't work with every stock."

She admits that her returns so far have been helped by the fact that the natural resource sector has been strong and she understands the industry. "It's a double whammy," she says, "because I'm very comfortable investing in oil and gas."

HER BEST MOVES: Her first move turned out to be a good one. She picked up Bre-X Minerals Ltd. (BXM-TSE, 52-week high, $28.65, low $17.70, yesterday's close $22.40) in February at $150 and sold it in June at $202. "That was definitely one of my gutsier moves," she says.

She nearly doubled her money with Amber Energy Inc. (AMB-TSE, high $21.70, low $8, close $20). She bought the stock for a split-adjusted price of $11 in March, selling it for $19.50 in October. She got almost the same results from Berkley Petroleum Corp. (BKP-TSE, high $33, low $7.62, close $33). She purchased the stock at $14.50 in March, and bailed out in October at $28.75. She is now considering moving back in. "I'll often look at the charts, look at how well I've done, sell the stock, and then watch it again."

She also made a nice, quick profit with Oxbow Exploration Inc. (OXB-ASE, high $2.10, low 25 cents, close $1.24). She bought her shares at 60 cents in June, and sold them in September at 91 cents. Another favourite is Canadian Natural Resources Ltd. (CNQ-TSE, high $39.40, low $19.25, close $36.75). She picked it up in March for $23.75 and is still holding the stock.

She likes using technical charts because they help her cut her losses and move into stocks that offer better potential upside. "No matter how much I like a company, if the market doesn't like it or its sec-tor, it makes no sense for me to park my money there."

In addition, she often sells a stock simply because it has become too volatile for her charts to make sense of it all. "But if I know the company really well, I'll ride it out." However, she is not an entirely cold-blooded investor. "One of the signs for me is if I start getting edgy, I'll get out."

In addition to her basket of stocks, she also has much of her port-folio invested in a private oil and gas company. The company, run by her husband and another partner, is focusing on production.

HER WORST MOVES: When asked, she quickly offers up Micrex Development Corp. (MIX-ASE, high $3.30, low 21 cents, close $1.50). "Here's one where I broke all my rules and I got burned."

She bought the stock after getting a tip, taking a quick look at its charts and "making a terrible decision." She paid $2 for it in October, and sold out recently at $1.35. "I got a little overconfident, but I'm happy to have learned my lesson so young."

ADVICE: "Be very ruthless about keeping your money working and growing. Treat it like a business. Don't be afraid to get out of a loser."

THE PORTFOLIO

Date:	Saturday, January 4, 1997
The investor:	Karen Brawley-Hogg, 35.
Occupation:	Oil-company geophysicist.
Investment personality:	"I follow the markets every day. I love doing it and I have quite a lot of fun."
Portfolio makeup:	Anderson Exploration Ltd., Canadian Natural Resources Ltd., Vermilion Resources Ltd., Barrington Petroleum Ltd., Newport Petrol Corp., Northrock Resources Ltd., Penn West Petroleum Ltd., Probe

	Exploration Inc., Pursuit Resources Inc., Tesco Corp., Triumph Energy
Portfolio size:	Low six figures.
Rate of return:	From end of March to end of November: 29 per cent.

While a big fan of technical analysis, Ms. Brawley-Hogg only uses it as one tool for assessing stocks, not the first and last word on when to buy and sell. As she correctly points out, technical analysis simply doesn't work on every stock. In particular, it can often give misleading readings of stocks that leap all over the place. "Technical analysis doesn't predict the future, it just gives you as many indicators as you can get to minimize risk," she says.

But not being able to apply technical analysis to every stock doesn't bother her because, like most successful investors, she knows there are more than enough "good buys" out there. "There are so many companies to choose from, I might as well stick with those I can use my evaluation tools on."

It's a good point. You should never feel rushed to buy a stock or fund, or feel you need to put it in your portfolio if you haven't really assessed it, or feel unable to evaluate it properly. There is such a huge range of choices in the investment world that if you don't even bother looking at those you don't feel capable of assessing, whether because you don't understand the industry, can't get enough information or can't effectively apply your assessment techniques, don't worry. If anything, it's a blessing as you'll still have more than enough potential picks to look over.

In Ms. Brawley-Hogg's case, for example, she not only limits herself to those where technical analysis makes some sense, but also largely sticks to oil and gas companies that she is well equipped to evaluate given her work as an oil-company geophysicist.

She also knows full well that her techniques and her targets mean a lot of work on a regular basis. "Things can change in a day," she says.

In her case, she enjoys the daily involvement, but if you don't, you should probably give this sort of approach a wide berth. It will quickly become another unwanted chore you have to take care of. At the least, that's probably something you don't need. At worst, you may end up putting off the homework your system demands, leaving yourself open to some large losses.

STOP-LOSSES STEADY

THIS SAILOR'S COURSE

•

SAILING THE HIGH SEAS has always had a romantic appeal. But to safely pilot their crafts between shoals, reefs and rocks, modern-day sailors like John Beamish rely on the objective mathematical assessment of a lot of numbers obtained—and crunched into a usable shape—with modern technology.

Mr. Beamish and his wife, both 71 and retired, winter in Florida. But when they return to their Gananoque, Ont., home every summer, Mr. Beamish can be found six days a week behind the wheel of the Thousand Island 3, a 500-passenger cruise boat.

His reliance on finding his way with mathematics is no doubt partly why, when this certified "Master of Minor Waters" decided to explore the uncharted territory of managing his own portfolio two years ago, he decided to go the technical, computer-driven route.

HOW HE DOES IT: Mr. Beamish uses a combination of three analytical techniques to pick his stocks. The underlying principle that ties them together is his belief that just how much buying and selling of any particular stock is taking place tells, ahem, volumes about where the price is headed.

"People say that the three things that matter most in the retail industry is location, location and location," he says. "I feel the same way about volume when it comes to the stock market."

Every Thursday night, Mr. Beamish happily devours his fax newsletter from Stock Trends. The service analyzes stock prices using moving averages as well as changes in volume to pick winners.When a stock is recommended by Stock Trends, Mr. Beamish uses Green Line Investor Services to download the past year's price and volume data onto his Excel spreadsheet.

He then adds a couple of his own refinements. The first is to assess potential stocks using an approach laid out in *Beating the Dow* by Michael O'Higgins. The book recommends seeking out high-yielding stocks that are trading at a low price, relative to similar companies. Finally, he assesses a stock's "on-balance volume," a statistical method that looks at the weekly closing price over several weeks to determine if interest in the stock is growing or waning.

A blind dependence on the numbers also helps Mr. Beamish navigate safely past a usually dangerous stock market siren, namely hanging on to a loser for emotional reasons. Following the advice put forward by Stock Trends, he religiously uses stop-loss orders, which automatically trigger a sell order if the share price falls below a set level. Every Friday, he adjusts his stop-losses, setting them at 50 cents under the week's closing price for shares trading under $10, and at 5 per cent below the closing price for shares over $10.

HIS BEST MOVES: Thanks to a recommendation from Stock Trends, Mr. Beamish got in on Vancouver-based Ashton Mining of Canada Inc. (ACA-TSE, 52-week high $7.90, low 74 cents, yesterday's close $2.91), at $1.75 at the end of January, just as the stock started to move up in anticipation of good results from the company's diamond exploration in Alberta. He rode the stock all the way up, and got out thanks to his stop-loss at $7.05 in the middle of May.

The stock cratered this week when its final results proved less than dazzling, but Mr. Beamish neither knows nor cares. For starters, he never bothered to find out what Ashton does or where they mine. "I just don't care, all I'm interested in is the price and the volume."

Secondly, once he gets out of a stock, it's on to bigger and brighter things. "Once I sell something it's history," he says. "I don't want to lie in bed worrying about whether the stock will come back around."

Another of Mr. Beamish's winners—Dorel Industries Inc. (DII.A-TSE, high $26, low $12.60), a Montreal-based consumer products manufacturer—came about because of his earlier position as the vice-president of Townsend Textiles, a Gananoque-based manufacturer of fasteners. "They were a customer of ours, and I always thought (founder) Leo Schwartz was a tough guy to deal with, and that meant he probably ran a good business." When Mr. Beamish started to see the company's name pop up on the recommendations in a couple of newsletters, he crunched the numbers and bought in at $18.50 in January. The stock closed yesterday at $23.85.

HIS WORST MOVE: Thanks to the regular use of stop-loss orders, Mr. Beamish says he rarely loses more than $1,000 on any given investment. His biggest recent drop came courtesy of Sidus Systems Inc., a computer equipment maker based in Richmond Hill, Ont. He bought that stock at $5.25 early last June. His stop-loss kicked in and sold out his position just a month later at $4.45.

ADVICE: "Use stop-losses. They're a great way to limit how much money you can lose."

THE PORTFOLIO

Date:	Saturday, June 14, 1997
The investor:	John Beamish, 71.
Occupation:	Retiree, cruise boat captain.
Investment personality:	"I'm very mathematical. I love number crunching."
Portfolio makeup:	Apex Land, CAE, CIBC, Encal Energy, Cineplex, Laidlaw, Loewen Group, NQL Drilling Tools, Norsat, TD Bank, MacMillan Bloedel, National Bank, Nova, Rand A Technology, TransCanada PipeLines, CanWest Global, Fortis, Mark's Work

Wearhouse, Dorel, Ventra, SNC-Lavalin,
Unican Security.
Portfolio size: "Six figures."
Rate of return: "Just over 50 per cent from April 3, 1996,
to April 3, 1997."

Like many technical traders, Mr. Beamish takes a lot of cues from what he considers one of the most important messages the stock market sends out—just how many people are buying and selling the shares of a particular company.

What technical types keep a close eye on is just how the volume of shares traded in a company changes from day to day. One of the most basic beliefs is that "volume precedes price"—in other words, that before a stock makes a big move up or down, the volume will pick up.

If there is a lot more trading in a stock than usual, one possible reason, the thinking goes, is that the so-called "smart money" is buying it. Often, this isn't so much "smart money" as it is money in the hands of people who have extra knowledge or information that leads them to believe the stock is going up. When a stock starts moving up on big volume, people often talk about it being under accumulation. This simply means that big institutions and insiders are "accumulating" the stock in anticipation of it making a big move upwards. Big jumps in the volume of a stock that is starting to move down in price would be read the opposite way—that the "smart money" is heading for the exit doors.

In addition to a stock's volume and the way in which the price moves up and down, technical analysts rely heavily on a stock price's (or an index's) *moving average*. A moving average effectively smoothes out the daily changes in a stock price (or the value of a stock market index) in order to unearth larger trends that may be at work. The result is a somewhat cleaner and more easily understood picture of how a stock's price has been changing in an effort to figure out where it will head in the future.

To calculate a moving average, analysts first add up the closing price for a stock or stock market index for a certain number of days, and then divide by the numbers of days. For example, many analysts look at the 200-day average for indices. Where the "moving" part comes in is that this process is repeated many times. The first day of the series gets dropped off and replaced by the latest day's price. This results in the average being moved ahead one day at a time, thus the term "moving average." The end result allows you to see broader trends, without being distracted by individual days that don't fit any pattern.

A PRUDENT AND
EMPOWERED INVESTOR

•

IF THERE WERE EVER A CONTEST to find a poster boy for the prudent-and-empowered school of investing, David Stanley would likely come out on top.

The 57-year-old resident of Rockwood, a small town near Guelph, Ont., has always enjoyed taking control of his investments. But when he was offered—and accepted—an early retirement package from his job as professor of food sciences with the University of Guelph early in 1995, he decided to become even more studious in his investing.

"I realized that a major source of income going forward for me was going to be my investments," he says. Putting his own nose to the books, he boned up on the strategies discussed in popular titles such as Peter Lynch's *One Up on Wall Street*.

Continuing reading, following on-line stock information and garnering advice from a full-service broker, he has developed a well-diversified portfolio that is posting strong gains and will soon push through the million-dollar mark.

HOW HE DOES IT: Mr. Stanley was taken by the strategy put forth in Michael O'Higgins's book *Beating the Dow*. He couldn't find any Canadian version of the strategy, so he paid $2,000 to buy historical data on the TSE's performance, ran the numbers through his personal computer and came up with a system he dubs "Beating the TSE." "The method simply finds the highest-yielding blue chip stocks, and then picks the 10 cheapest.

"It's very simple, but it routinely outperforms the market," he says. "Blue-chip companies always make their dividends, and if the price is low, those are the ones that have been beaten down and will come back." Does he spend any time getting to know the companies he's buying? "Absolutely not," Mr. Stanley says. "This is a very mechanical approach. You buy them and put them away for a year."

He says it's great for those who don't want to pay the fees associated with mutual funds or spend a lot of time on their investments. "This conservative part of my portfolio also gives me a really strong base from which to pick other investments."

HIS BEST MOVES: Among his best-performing stocks is BCE Inc. (BCE-TSE), which he bought in July 1995 at $43.50. The stock closed yesterday at $63.25. Another big winner has been Toronto-Dominion Bank (TD-TSE). He picked up his shares in June last year at $21.37, and the stock closed yesterday at $34.85.

Among U.S. winners, he bought into what was once one of the Nasdaq Stock Market's brightest stars, Iomega Corp. (IOM-NYSE), last fall at $3.75 (U.S.)—adjusted for splits. The stock closed yesterday on the New York Stock Exchange to $22.50 (U.S.). He's also made a nice profit from computer chip-maker Intel Corp. (INTC-NYSE). He picked it up in August at around $79, and the stock closed yesterday at $115.87.

To select more aggressive U.S. stocks, he employs a variety of methods, including using his computer to visit stock information sites on America Online Inc. For example, he first heard about Iomega through AOL's "The Motley Fool."

He also uses AOL data to carry out earnings projections. Borrowing a page from investment guru Mr. Lynch's strategy book, he takes the five-year earnings estimate plus the yield of a company and divides it by the price/earnings ratio. The higher the resulting number, the more attractive the stock. "That's how I got into Intel—it just popped up on my computer screen, when I did the numbers, as being undervalued."

Mr. Stanley also has a good deal of his money in mutual funds. His strongest performers have been the AIC Advantage Fund, up 60 per cent, and the AIC Value Fund, up over 43 per cent from when he purchased the two funds in 1993.

He holds a number of Altamira funds, with his heaviest weighting in the Altamira Dividend Fund, which he likes for its strong after-tax returns. "I think it's very important for retired people to realize that dividends are taxed at a lower rate due to the dividend tax credit," he says. Retirees have two things working against them—inflation and taxes.

HIS WORST MOVES: Mr. Stanley's biggest loss so far came from Thermo Tech Technologies Inc. (TTRIF–Nasdaq) of Langley, B.C., a company he knew quite well because many of his students work for it in Guelph. Thermo Tech had an attractive concept—turning biological waste into non-toxic byproducts—so he bought in last March at $3.25 (U.S.) a share.

But Mr. Stanley says the company, which trades on Nasdaq, got strapped for cash and flooded the market with shares. The stock promptly plummeted, closing yesterday at 17 cents.

Another loser has been Micron Technology Inc. (MU–NYSE), which he bought a year ago for $57.50, "exactly at the top." The stock closed yesterday at $31.25. "If I had done my homework I wouldn't have bought it, so I have nobody to blame but myself," he says.

ADVICE: "Investors need to empower themselves. My college expertise is in science—I really don't have any in finance. Believe me, if I can invest profitably, anybody can."

THE PORTFOLIO

Date:	Saturday, November 16, 1996
The investor:	David Stanley, 57.
Occupation:	Semi-retired university professor.

Investment personality:	"All my life I've been pretty fiercely independent. And when it comes to investment, I do the work, make the decisions and actively manage my money."
Portfolio makeup:	Registered retirement savings plan is in stripped bonds. In non-registered account, just under half is in stocks, including BCE Inc., Dofasco Inc., National Bank, Northern Telecom Ltd., Telus Corp., Intel Corp., Iomega Corp. Rest is largely in mutual funds, including AIC Advantage Fund, AIC Value Fund and Altamira Dividend Fund.
Portfolio size:	High six figures.
Rate of return:	One-year return of 34 per cent on stocks, two-year return of around 40 per cent on mutual funds.

Mr. Stanley's approach was so interesting that I recently did a column in which I revisited the Guelph, Ont., investor. How did his strategy hold up? Take a look below.

DOGS OF THE TSE

STILL BEAT THE 35 INDEX

•

THIS WEEK, WE THOUGHT we'd pay another call on the Motley Fool of the North. You may remember David Stanley, the semi-retired professor who lives in Rockwood, a small village near Guelph, Ont. When I wrote about him in November 1996, Mr. Stanley was very enthusiastic about the returns he was getting applying the "Dogs of the Dow" approach to the TSE. "It's so easy to do. It takes you five minutes with a computer, and 10 minutes using a pen and paper," he says. So how are things these days? "Really well," Mr. Stanley, 58, says. "The returns haven't been as spectacular as in the first year I used the system, but over that last year, I've still managed to beat the TSE 35 index by over 50 per cent."

The "Dogs of the Dow" strategy has garnered a lot of attention in the United States after being detailed in a book called *Beating the Dow* by New York-based money manager Michael O'Higgins, and adopted by David and Tom Gardner, the brothers behind the America Online-based Motley Fool approach to investing. Mr. O'Higgins, the Fools and Mr. Stanley say beating blue-chip indexes is a breeze. All you have to do is invest in the 10 (or five or even four) top-yielding stocks on the Dow 35 (or the TSE 35). The strategy is founded on a belief—and supported by much evidence—that these companies have above-average yields because their stocks have fallen, but that at some point the companies will come back into favour, and their stock prices will move up at a better clip than their other peers on the index.

HOW HE DOES IT: Mr. Stanley simply applies this theory to the TSE 35, rebalancing his portfolio once a year in late May. Some might argue that, until the past few months, there really weren't any knocked-down stocks on the TSE 35, borne out by the fact that the overall dividend yield has been dropping. The current yield on his "Beating the TSE" basket of stocks is 2.86 per cent—it was 4.6 per cent two years ago, meaning a decline of about 40 per cent. That doesn't concern him too much though, because after adding in the tax benefits of the dividend tax credit, the average dividend yield of 2.86 per cent climbs to 3.86 per cent. As a result, he says, the portfolio only needs to show capital gains of around 1.3 per cent to match one-year treasury-bill rates. Mr. Stanley also says it's all relative, and buying the higher-yielding companies still makes sense. "Where else are you going to put your money?" he asks. "The yield on bonds is also decreasing, and hopefully you won't try to market-time that junior mining stock on the VSE."

When he rebalanced this past May 27, Moore Corp. (MCL-TSE) got dropped from his Top 10 because the company drastically cut its dividend, "and good companies don't do that." Conversely, BCE (BCE-TSE) has been given the boot because the company's performance has been strong and the stock has climbed so much—72 per cent during the year of Mr. Stanley's portfolio ended May 26— that its yield has been driven down too far. However, Mr. Stanley says he likes the company so much he won't sell the stock, but has simply "moved" it into his regular portfolio.

Two other companies have been added—Thomson Corp. (TOC-TSE) and Canadian Imperial Bank of Commerce (CM-TSE)—and once the merger between TransCanada PipeLines Ltd. and Nova Corp. goes through, the most likely candidate to take the tenth spot is Bank of Montreal (BMO-TSE). (For the full list of the stocks in his TSE portfolio, see the Portfolio box.)

For all his work, Mr. Stanley surprisingly still relies on a full-service broker to help him with his other stock-picking. Why? "Every year I get back much more from him than I give him in commissions." Quite simply, Mr. Stanley finds that his broker tells him about special situations, as well as providing him with research that he can't get any-where else.

HIS BEST MOVES: Playing "Dogs of the Dow" north of the border. For the year ended May 26, the stocks in his "Beating the TSE" portfolio have rung up a 27.88 per cent gain. Add in the 4.75 per cent dividend yield, and you get a total increase of 32.64 per cent. Over the same time period, the TSE 35 total return index was up 21.23 per cent.

HIS WORST MOVE: Mr. Stanley likes to buy volatile technology stocks, but has been burned by Seagate Technology Inc. (SEG-NYSE, 52-week high $45.75 (U.S.), low $17.75), the Scotts Valley, Calif., hard drive manufacturer. He bought it last June at $40.18. The stock has since fallen about 40 per cent, and closed yesterday at $20.50. "Just about the time I picked it up along came the great Asian malaise," he says. "I haven't sold it yet though. With a lot of these stocks, you have to give them time."

ADVICE: "If you're in it for immediate gains, get one of those lottery tickets you scratch off."

THE PORTFOLIO

Date:	Saturday, June 20, 1998
The investor:	David Stanley, 58.
Occupation:	Semi-retired university professor.
Investment personality:	"Beat the TSE strategist."
Portfolio makeup:	Beating the TSE: Nova, TransAlta, National Bank, Dofasco, TransCanada PipeLines, Noranda Mines, Imasco, Bank of Nova Scotia, Thomson Corp., CIBC. Other investments: AOL, Andres Wines, Applied Materials, Bay Networks, BC Gas, BCE, Cisco Systems, Corby, Dofasco, EMC, Ensco

International, Gateway 2000, GM, Intel,
IBM, Iomega, IPL Energy, Johnson & Johnson,
Magna International, Northern Telecom,
Seagate Technology, Telus, TD Bank.

Portfolio size: "Seven figures."

Rate of return: "1997 total returns: 48.26 per cent on
stocks, 30.06 on mutual funds. Top 10 TSE
portfolio, May 27, 1997, to May 26,
1998, 32.64 per cent."

A FEW SOLID PICKS
SAVE HIS PORTFOLIO

•

THE PAST TWO YEARS have probably been the best of times and the
worst of times for new investors to start playing the market. Just look
at what Doug Blackmore has been through.

The 50-year-old high-school teacher lives, works and plays in
Halifax, the playing mostly done aboard his 10-metre sailboat, exploring the local waters. "I've seen the whole North American coast,
and this area is as beautiful as it gets."

For years, Mr. Blackmore had simply been putting his savings into
balanced mutual funds, but at the beginning of 1996, he decided to
become a more active investor. He got himself a broker, and on her
recommendation sold his funds, opened up a self-directed registered
retirement savings plan and began building a diversified portfolio of
individual stocks.

A few solid picks later, and Mr. Blackmore was enjoying a first-
class ride on the stock market's 1996 gravy train. "Everything I bought
seemed to go up," he says. The big pay-off from just picking his own
stocks soon had Mr. Blackmore ready to take on more risk—and reap
even bigger rewards—by playing the juniors. "I decided I would take
some of my winnings and start speculating."

Unfortunately, that was in early 1997, and just a few months later,
the Bre-X bubble burst. Largely because of Bre-X Minerals Ltd., and
later the plummeting price of gold, the small-cap mining and resource
stocks spent the year being battered into the ground. "This year my

solid investments have done well, but the speculative side tanked and it's really dragged down my whole portfolio."

HOW HE DOES IT: Mr. Blackmore spends a great deal of time—typically 90 minutes a day—managing his portfolio. Much of that time is spent on the Internet, which he uses to unearth speculative picks. A favourite Web site is the Investor Guru (home.iSTAR.ca/invguru/), which focuses on small-cap movers. "I look at their picks and do my own analysis," he says. "I look for stocks with price movement and volume."

He's also started to use technical analysis. "It basically gives you buy-and-sell signals, but you still have to base your decision on fundamentals," he warns. "There's nothing magical about it." One drawback, he adds, is that there "is a lot to learn, and it takes a great deal of time."

In addition, he's become a subscriber to StockTrends, a technical-based stock-picking advisory service. He has followed its buy-and-sell signals and done well on several stocks, including Denver-based gold mining company Solitario Resources Corp. (SLR-TSE, 52-week high $6.25, low $2.50, last close $3.25), which he bought at $3.60 and sold at $5.20. "I've followed a number of their picks, and (editor Skot Kortje's) methodology is solid."

Mr. Blackmore likes the fact the advisory service has switched from a fax service to E-mail. "I can E-mail the editor back with my questions, which is a very big advantage, especially if you're in the learning mode."

With the choppy markets, Mr. Blackmore says any new money he invests will go into solid companies. And he's decided to turn his back on the resource sector. "Any time I make a profit on my resource stocks, I'll take it out."

HIS BEST MOVES: It seems the banks are a mainstay of *Me and My Money's* best moves. Mr. Blackmore rode the financial sector rocket aboard Canadian Imperial Bank of Commerce (CM-TSE, 52-week high $47.45, low $28.50, yesterday's close $44.55) at the suggestion of his broker, buying the stock at $36 in the middle of 1996. "If you're going to start building a basic portfolio, you want to have some bank stocks in it."

On the recommendation of a friend, he bought Santa Clara, Calif.-based computer-chip maker Intel (INTC-Nasdaq, high $100.50 (U.S.), low $65.18, yesterday's close $72.62) in the spring of 1996 at $50, selling it that fall for $90. "I saw it was at the bottom and coming back up," he says.

Over the same time span, he more than doubled his investment in Greenstone Resources Ltd. (GRE-TSE, 52-week high $17 (Canadian), low $4.85, last close $6.95), a Toronto-based gold mining company. He got into the stock on the advice of his broker, knowing it wasn't a great investment but a speculation. He paid $6 a share, and sold for $14. "It looked like it had made its run and was maxxed out," he says.

HIS WORST MOVE: Like thousands of other Canadians, Mr. Blackmore's worst investment move was believing in the due diligence of others. He bought Bre-X at $18 in the fall of 1996. He says he knew it was still a speculative stock, "but all the mutual fund managers who had purchased it must have done their homework, and must have seen things that told them the company was solid."

Of course, it was as solid as just-made Jell-O, and Mr. Blackmore's shares, along with millions of others, soon were worthless. "If you're up and a stock turns around, get out," he advises, while admitting that that is one strategy that is hard to put into action. "You start believing the story despite the warning signs."

ADVICE: "For the small investor, it's wise to put the largest portion of your money into long-term investments."

THE PORTFOLIO

Date: Saturday, January 3, 1998
The investor: Doug Blackmore, 50.

Occupation:	High-school math teacher.
Investment personality:	"Disciplined."
Portfolio makeup:	Imasco, CIBC, Canadian Medical Discoveries Fund, Service Merchandise, Armanda Gold, Essex Resources, Pacific-Rim Mining.
Portfolio size:	Five figures.
Rate of return:	1996: 50 per cent. 1997: "Between 5 per cent and 10 per cent."

Despite using his various analysis tools to double his money on chancy resource and high–tech stocks, Mr. Blackmore still stresses the importance of diversifying, not just having different investments, but different types of investments. For example, he recommends having a few bank stocks in any portfolio.

His advice about the need for diversification would still make sense if the financial sector hadn't been at the top of the performance charts the last couple of years. Focusing on just one type of investment or sector is gambling. You might not lose a lot of money, but what you are doing is making a bet that you can predict the sectors that will outperform. The end result will be one of two possible outcomes—you'll either do far better than the average, or far worse.

Case in point? In one corner, we've got AIC Advantage Fund. In the other corner, Altamira Equity.

AIC made a large bet—no, make that a huge bet—many years ago on the financial services sector. The Altamira Equity Fund, on the other hand, under the now–departed Frank Mersch, went in the complete other direction and bet heavily on the resource sector in the mid–nineties.

How did they fare? AIC Advantage had a three-year average annual compound return of over 41 per cent to the end of June 1998. Altamira Equity, by contrast, had an average return of just 9.1 per cent. That's not too bad as history goes, but still far below the average Canadian equity fund, which returned over 16 per cent.

AIC bet, and won big. Altamira bet, and lost big, relatively speaking. What is more striking is that up to the last few years, Frank Mersch's stock-picking had made a lot of Canadians a lot of money, and had helped Altamira become a household name. In fact, every year from 1989 up to and including 1995, Altamira Equity's returns put it in the top quartile—or 25 percent—of large-cap Canadian equity funds based on their yearly numbers.

If you could, it would be nice to just have your money on winning bets, whether you choose your own stocks or go the fund route. But they wouldn't be bets if you knew they were going to win. Build some diversity into your portfolio, and ensure you have investments that represent different parts of the economy, as well as different parts of that world. You may not get the spectacular returns AIC has rung up, but neither will you miss being completely out of a sector that rings up above-average returns like Altamira Equity was.

RETIRED ENGINEER

TINKERS AT HIS SYSTEM

•

RETIREE, RESCHMIREE. Eighty-one years young, Earl Johnson certainly is one for setting goals. For example, the centrepiece of the retired professional engineer's backyard in Ottawa is a 15-metre ocean cruiser he's building.

He's also been busy building himself a remarkably sophisticated computer-based stock-selection system. He began work on it in 1992, after being disappointed with the results he got by using professional financial advisers. "I've come to a conclusion that some brokers don't know more about the stocks they recommend than the man in the moon does."

While he says he has made some mistakes investing over the years, he says his errors didn't cause him to give up, but merely alerted him to the fact that, as he puts it, he needed a better method.

HOW HE DOES IT: So, what did he come up with? "Other people have asked me to describe my method, but I don't, because I might make some money from it," he says.

However, he couldn't resist my winning ways—or should that be wheedling?—and agreed to give *Me and My Money* readers a peek under his tent.

He starts with a little Charles Darwin-based analogy. "Look at Darwin's example of wheat stalks," he says. "Some are higher than the others. The tallest ones get more sunshine. They tend to survive and grow taller." Similarly, he says, "Stocks that perform well tend to exceed the overall market's performance."

To find those healthy stalks—oops, stocks—he measures the weekly closing prices of 192 stocks, including those on the Dow Jones industrial average, the Toronto Stock Exchange 35, as well as some Fortune 500 companies and a handful of fast-growth stocks. These are all then ranked against his own, customized "world index," which is based on the Dow, the TSE 35, the Standard & Poor's 500-stock index, the Morgan Stanley World index and the Nasdaq composite index.

With his system in place, he slowly began buying, starting with those stocks at the top of the list—those that had turned in the strongest performance over the past year relative to his world index.

To keep his eye on his stocks, he uses a computer program that draws him a chart showing the stock's price, the score it receives from his system, the weekly change in that score and the weekly change in price. He also tracks how the stocks he watches have fared against his world index over each of the past five weeks. Even if a stock has been beaten five weeks in a row by his index, that's not necessarily a sell signal, he says. More important is just where the stock sits, relative to the other stocks he watches, in relation to his index.

The only stock he's sold using his system so far is McDonald's Corp. He's looking at getting out of Sears Roebuck and Co., which used to have a high ranking but has slipped, and has only beaten his index by 2 per cent over the past year. "I have to tighten up the process so I don't hold ones like that so long," he says.

Indeed, Mr. Johnson is constantly tinkering with his system. He figures it would only take an hour or two a week to plug in all the data, but he spends another five or six developing new programs and formulas. "There's more management of the system involved than I thought," he says. "But I'm going to cut that back now that spring is here."

One modification he's looking into is ranking his stocks monthly instead of weekly. "A stock that gets to the head of my list tends to stay there," he says, noting that Dell Computer Corp. has been on top for 39 weeks now. He has recently started running a parallel program covering 100 new stocks to see whether monthly updates will still turn up the strongest performers.

HIS BEST MOVES: All of his big gainers have been selected using his system. Early in January 1997, Bristol-Myers Squibb Co. (BMY-NYSE, 52-week high $108.62 (U.S.), low $57.25) made it to that top of his list, and he bought it at a split-adjusted price of $33.34. The stock closed yesterday at $106.75.

Compaq Computer Corp. (CPQ-NYSE, high $39.75, low $14.13), another constant chart-topper, was bought at a split-adjusted price of $16.03 in April 1997. It closed yesterday at $25.81. A somewhat less stellar performance was turned in by Pfizer Inc. (PFE-NYSE, high $101.62, low $41.50), which he bought at a split-adjusted price of $45.88. It closed yesterday at its high of $101.62.

HIS WORST MOVE: Mr. Thomas says his worst move was Placer Dome Inc. (PDG- TSE, high $27.30 (Canadian), low $14.95). He bought shares in the Vancouver-based gold mining company at $31 in 1992, on the recommendation of a private money management company, and the stock closed yesterday at $20.10. Why hasn't he sold it? "Laziness," he says with a chuckle. "I've been so busy with my system I haven't got around to it. I'm not one of the fastest workers in the world here."

ADVICE: "Pick only stocks that have proven themselves as growth stocks, and don't pick stocks on the basis of what you feel emotionally."

THE PORTFOLIO

Date:	Saturday, April 4, 1998
The investor:	Earl Johnson, 81.
Occupation:	Retired professional engineer.
Investment personality:	Number-crunching computer-based investor.

Portfolio makeup: Bank of Nova Scotia preferred, Bristol-
Myers, Cisco, Compaq, IBM, Lockheed,
Royal Bank preferred (in U.S. dollars), TD
Bank, Travelers Group, CIBC Canadian Real
Estate Fund, First Canadian International
Growth Fund, Coca-Cola, General Motors,
Merck, Procter & Gamble, Raytheon, Sears
Roebuck, United Technology.

Portfolio size: "Six figures."

Rate of return: "17.4 per cent in 1997, for entire portfolio;
61 per cent annualized gain on stocks
bought using system."

Mr. Johnson is a great example of a growth investor. Not for him seeking out underperforming stocks that the market has yet to figure out
should be much higher in price. Mr. Johnson wants to have his money
in stocks that are going up today, not in stocks that may go up the day
after, or perhaps not until next month or even next year.

The reason that a growth stock moves up faster than average is that
the company's profit levels are increasing faster than the norm. The
result is that its earnings per share (the amount of earnings divided
by the total number of shares outstanding) is also growing at a fast
pace. Investors are willing to pay extra for such a stock because if
the rate of growth continues, then the stock will be worth that much
more in the future.

Of course, that also makes growth stocks more risky than other
stocks. If the growth rates that are anticipated—and which are helping determine what investors are willing to pay today for stocks—
aren't sustained, then these stocks will be abandoned by growth
investors, and their prices will drop sharply.

LONG-TERM

Mutual Fund

INVESTING

L ONG–TERM MUTUAL FUND investors put their money
into mutual funds and leave their investments alone,
depending on the managers of their funds to make their money grow
over the years.

This is probably the investment approach most commonly promoted
by financial advisers, and with good reason. Investing in mutual funds
for the long haul is a low-cost way to diversify your investments and
typically earn good returns with minimal effort.

Unlike other types of investing used by *Me and My Money* investors, this is one approach that you can use on your entire portfolio. If you invest in long-term blue-chip stocks, for example, you'll
still need to figure out how you're going to invest and manage the
part of your savings that you want to have in fixed-income and cash-
type investments.

You can use the long-term mutual fund route, however, to take care of all your investment needs. For example, there are many funds that will meet your cash-type investment needs such as a money market fund, as well as many choices for the fixed income part of your port-folio, such as bond funds and mortgage funds. In short, this is a rela-tively stress-free, minimum-headache way to run your entire portfolio.

HOW MUTUAL FUNDS WORK

Mutual funds are actually quite simple investments. You, along with hundreds or thousands of other investors, hand over some money to a professional money manager. The manager then invests that pool of money, taking his or her fee as a percentage of the money being managed. Your share of the resulting profits is determined by how much money you invested relative to everybody else.

Fund Units and Pricing

When you put money into a mutual fund, you are actually buying units. What those units cost and how you buy them will depend on whether the fund is a closed-end fund or an open-end fund.

A closed-end fund has a fixed number of shares. Those shares are usually traded on a stock exchange such as the Toronto Stock Exchange. The price you have to pay to buy shares in a closed-end fund, and the price you'll receive if you want to sell your shares, is determined by market forces—what others are willing to sell and buy the shares for.

This is quite different from open-end funds. The number of shares—usually called units—in an open-end fund can increase or decrease as people put their money into a fund or take it out. Each unit held by an investor entitles them to a certain percentage of the assets inside a fund. To find out what those units are worth, the fund company simply adds up all of the assets inside the fund and divides by the number of units. Usually this is done daily, but some funds only value their units on a weekly or monthly basis.

But don't the numbers get thrown out of whack if you show up and want to buy a hundred units? No, and here's why. If the units are trading at $15, you'd have to hand over $1,500 to purchase 100 units. The next time the fund was valued, its total assets would have to be divided by the total number of outstanding units, now increased by 100 since you made your investment. At the same time, though, the fund's assets would have increased by $1,500, so your investment hasn't changed the value of the fund's units. Similarly, if you sell your units, there is less money in the fund once you've been paid out, but there are fewer units among which the remaining assets have to be divided.

Aren't Mutual Funds Risky?

I often talk to people who worry about the risk of mutual funds, but mutual funds as a whole can't be rated risky or not risky. What determines the level of risk is the type of investments the fund puts money into. There are, in fact, mutual funds that are essentially 100 per cent risk-free, in terms of the danger of losing any of your original investment. Money-market mutual funds, for example, invest only in short-term interest-bearing government and corporate debt. You can always be assured that you will at a minimum get all of the original amount you put into a money-market fund back.

Fund Types Explained

To appreciate the relative risk of a fund—and the type and potential size of your returns—it helps to have an understanding of the different types of funds. Here's how they break down:

BOND FUNDS: These funds invest in government and corporate bonds. The main reason for investing in a bond fund is the security of income payments. Bond funds, however, may also ring up capital gains. Bond funds are further defined by where they invest.

The average Canadian bond fund had an average annual 10 year compound return of 9.7 per cent up to the summer of 1998. The average compound return over 10 years for international bond funds is 8 per cent for the same period. One other characteristic of bond funds is the range of returns is less than that in, say, the equity fund category. For example, the lowest 10-year compound return of a Canadian bond fund is 6.78 per cent, and the highest, 12.7 per cent.

MORTGAGE FUNDS: These funds invest primarily in first home mortgages just like the one you probably have if you're a homeowner. Some mortgage funds also invest in commercial mortgages. These funds are quite conservative, and the returns come largely in the form of interest payments. Canadian mortgage funds have an average annual compound return of 8.5 per cent over 10 years up to the middle of 1998.

DIVIDEND FUNDS: These funds invest in preferred and common shares that pay dividends. (Hey, kind of getting the hang of this lingo, aren't you? Bond funds invest in bonds, mortgage funds invest in mortgages. It's almost like the Bay Street types forgot to develop jargon for this part of the world to keep average folk confused!)

Dividend funds do earn capital gains, but most of their returns are in the form of dividend payments. Dividends are a great way to earn income, because the dividend tax credit means they are taxed at a much lower rate than interest income or capital gains. As a result, it's best to hold dividend funds outside your RRSP or RRIF, as you don't benefit from the favourable tax rates on dividends if they are earned on investments inside those plans. The average annual 10-year compound return for Canadian dividend funds is 9 per cent up to the end of August 1998.

EQUITY OR STOCK FUNDS: Yup, these funds invest largely in stocks. The profits from these funds come largely in the form of capital gains— the difference between what managers pay for the various stocks in their portfolios and what they are able to later sell those stocks for.

There are many different types of equity funds. The first characteristic to consider is geography. There are Canadian equity funds,

U.S. equity funds, funds that can invest anywhere in the world in-cluding Canada (typically called global funds) and funds that can invest anywhere in the world except for Canada (usually referred to as international funds). There are also country-specific funds, such as Japanese funds, as well as funds that focus on a particular region, such as Europe or Latin America.

The next category is just what kinds of companies the funds invest in. There are dozens of funds that invest in big, well-known companies. These are called large-cap funds. (Large cap simply refers to a company that has a large *market capitalization*—the number of shares outstanding in the company multiplied by the market price per share.)

There are also small-cap funds that invest in smaller companies. In addition, there are funds that focus on a particular sector such the gold mining, resource, high-tech or pharmaceutical industries.

Equity funds offer the potential for higher gains, but also mean tak-ing on more risk, one reason why their returns vary more than other fund types. For example, the average larger-cap Canadian equity fund 10-year average annual compound return, up to the end of July 1998, was 9.5 per cent. However, over that period, the highest return was 19 per cent, while the lowest was 3.5 per cent. Small-cap Canadian equity funds have the same average 10-year return (9.8 per cent), while the 10-year average compound return of international equity funds is slightly higher at 10.9 per cent. U.S. equity funds have a 10-year average annual compound return of 11.3 per cent up to the end of July 1988.

THE UPSIDE

Buying and holding a handful of well-performing mutual funds offers you a whole basketful of benefits. First, you get terrific diversification as your money will be spread among hundreds of different investments.

Second, you can pick funds that match the amount of risk you're will-ing to take on. Third, you don't have to watch carefully over your money as the fund manager is (hopefully) spending every waking moment doing just that. Once you've made your fund picks, you can essentially leave them alone. You only need to check in every few months to see if their returns are still on track, and if the reasons you bought the fund—the managers, the cost and investment style—remain unchanged.

Another advantage of long-term mutual fund investing is that the costs of this strategy are relatively low. Since you aren't regularly buy-ing and selling, you'll keep your trading fees down. What's more, with a little negotiating with your fund dealer, you can often buy many top funds at little or no cost.

THE DOWNSIDE

To be honest, I had to think pretty hard to come up with a drawback to buying and holding mutual funds for the long term. Perhaps one strike against this approach is you may be giving up some potential profits. If you have the time, talent and energy to devote to picking your own stocks, not to mention a little luck, you may be able to earn better returns by doing the job yourself rather than handing over the job to a pro.

The Danger of Dogs

Another potential drawback to this long-term strategy is buying a fund that slowly but surely runs out of gas. Often, particularly with more conservative funds, you won't actually lose any money, but you may not make anywhere near as much as you could have earned by putting your savings into a different fund. This downside will be much more marked if the fund you bought that's turned into a dog has a back-end load. Also known as a deferred sales charge, this is a commission for buying the fund that only becomes payable when you sell your units. A back-end load means you have to choose between hanging in there and hoping the fund turns around, or selling and paying the commission.

Count Your Costs

You have to pay to invest in funds. The commission charged to buy a fund can run up to 6 per cent or higher, but you should negotiate that down. Also, funds charge you an annual fee for looking after your money. In addition to the money paid to the managers—the management fee—there are many other expenses including administration and marketing costs that the fund company charges to people who invest in a fund—the *unitholders*. The total cost—called the management expense ratio, or MER—is a percentage of the total amount of money invested in the fund.

The MER for money market funds averages around 1 per cent. For Canadian equity funds, the average MER is around 2.2 per cent, and for Canadian bonds funds, 1.6 per cent. Everything else being equal, if the managers of two funds earn the same amount of profits, the fund with the lower management expense ratio will have a higher return, as management expenses are deducted from a fund's returns before profits are distributed to the fund's investors.

DOING IT YOURSELF

Picking your own funds is something most people have the capability of doing, and doing quite well. However, with over 1,800 funds now available in Canada, it's easy to be overwhelmed. But there are many good—and often free—resources you can tap to help you separate the wheat from the chaff.

Helpful Tools

A good starting point is *The Globe and Mail*'s monthly *Report on Mutual Funds*. Also useful are the many annual guides that hit the bookstores every fall. Good bets are *Fund Monitor* by Duff Young, *Top Funds* by Riley Moynes and Michael Nairne, and of course Gordon Pape's encyclopedic *Buyer's Guide to Mutual Funds*.

The Internet offers many excellent resources for fund investors. Many sites feature tools that will go through all the funds available and offer you a short-list of funds based on criteria you select, such as the rate of return you're looking for, the expense ratio, and so on. Good fund tools are available at www.globefund.com and www.imoney.com.

If you want to carry out heavy-duty research, you'll need to get hold of a computer program that lets you assess and compare the universe of funds using many different factors. The leading programs available to individuals are BellCharts, Paltrak, and Southam Source Disk. Typically they cost $300 to $400 a year, for which you get a start-up disk containing the program and current data, as well as monthly or quarterly updates. These updates are usually mailed out on a computer disk that you simply upload into your computer, but several companies now allow you to download updates from the Internet.

USING A HELPING HAND

Most financial advisers will be able to find their way around at least one of the mutual fund computer programs mentioned above with their eyes closed. In fact, some probably dream about pie charts and portfolio listings.

The growth and popularity of mutual funds mean that most financial advisers and brokers have a thorough knowledge of fund basics, how they work, and how to assemble a portfolio of funds to meet your needs. You can also use an adviser to help you keep on top of relevant news that may affect your portfolio, such as the departure of a key manager from a fund.

Another very important role for an adviser is to serve as a hand-holder. If a fund suddenly starts underperforming, your initial reaction may be to sell it. Often, this is a mistake, as all funds—even those with strong long-term returns—have weak periods. An adviser can provide an excellent second opinion and often help you keep your portfolio profitable by counselling against selling a fund based on your emotions.

Remember, though, that if you are buying funds that have a commission, or "load," the commission rate quoted in fund company brochures is the maximum allowable commission you can be charged. You can and should negotiate a lower commission.

Some advisers argue that buying load funds with a deferred sales charge—a commission that you only pay when you sell a fund—is a good idea. It is, if the fund continues to perform well and you don't sell it. The benefit is that by not paying a commission when you make your purchase, you put all of your money to work.

However, these "back-end loads" kind of handcuff you to a fund. Even if it's losing money, the only way to dump it is to pay the sales fee. This tends to colour your decision-making process. Also, some companies offer you the choice of buying a particular fund with either a front-end or a back-end load. However, the back-end load fund will often have a higher yearly management expense ratio. For these reasons, back-end load funds may not be the bargains many people think they are.

HOW THEY PULL IT OFF

Successful long-term mutual fund investors put into practice many of the general basics of wise investing. The returns they earn aren't so much a result of their fund picks as it is the discipline with which they stick to some fundamental rules. Those include:

- *Invest in Equities for the Long Term.* Historically, stocks have offered the best returns. If your portfolio is to grow over time, you will need to get more aggressive—or at least a little adventurous—with your investing. Don't forget you should be able to leave your money invested for seven to 10 years, though, so that you can ride out the market's dips.
- *Use Dollar-Cost Averaging.* Once you're selected your funds, consider putting a set dollar amount into a fund or funds every month. You will automatically buy more units when the price has fallen, and less when the price is higher. This will lower your average cost, and ensure you don't put all of your money in when the units are at a particularly lofty price.
- *Ignore Short-Term Results.* If a fund has a bad day, week or month, you should barely notice, much less worry. Not having to follow every bob and weave is one of the great attractions of fund investing. Only if a fund's performance has significantly fallen over a period of many months, if not a year or two, should you reconsider whether that's the right place for your money. Major changes with the way in which the fund is run, such as a manager leaving the company—also mean re-evaluating the suitability of a fund.

THIRTY-SOMETHING
FINDS HER WAY

•

KAREN CUMMING SUSPECTS she isn't alone. The 35-year-old, who works as a television reporter with ON-TV in Hamilton, Ont., bets there are thousands of other thirty-something women out there who are living her story.

"I grew up with two much older siblings, believing that I not only deserved to have the things they were able to acquire in the money-grubbing eighties, but that those material possessions would be mine," she says. "Little did I understand 20 years ago that in 1997 the world would have different plans for me."

A self-described "free spirit," Ms. Cumming says she has largely chosen to "do" rather than to "have." In addition to moving four times for her career, she's also bounced around a lot for fun.

She has spent a year train-hopping around Europe, taken adventure holidays in Mexico and the Rockies, and even worked in the Caribbean with Club Med.

But she didn't expect material wealth to simply appear by virtue of being a boomer. She is surprised, for instance, to find out that not everybody takes a cold, hard look at their financial situation with a financial planner when they are only 27, just entering the working world and still struggling to pay off student loans. "I understood fairly early that I couldn't always fly by the seat of my pants."

That meeting led her to start investing in mutual funds, using an automatic deduction plan to regularly direct savings into her registered retirement savings plan. For the past five years she has also used this method to set aside money to buy a home.

But lately, she has come to a very difficult decision, one that she is sure many women, in particular, will find parallels their own circumstances. "I've realized that a single woman can't manage the monthly mortgage payments and have a life at the same time."

Turning her back on the dream of home ownership was very traumatic for her, she says, because as a baby boomer, owning a home is something that is almost seen as a given. "It takes you a while to really come to terms with it and realize the world has changed."

But she has quickly come to see not owning a home as an advantage, largely because she feels her money will grow better in the stock market.

HOW SHE DOES IT: To find her way in the investing world, Ms. Cumming really only needs to show up for work. Many of her colleagues share her interest in managing their money, and stocks and mutual funds are often a hot topic of conversation around the water cooler.

Her primary resource is fellow reporter George Szostak, who covers the business beat for the station. "If you're interested in investing, you can just walk over and bounce something off him," she says.

On the heels of putting a stop to saving for a down payment, she's started to move into buying individual shares. While she plans to begin with strong, steady companies, she says she has a high tolerance for risk, and would be playing more volatile stocks if she had more money to work with. "It's addictive, it gets into your blood," she says. "You feel like you want to be a player."

HER BEST MOVES: "Slow and steady wins the race," quips Ms. Cumming, so it's true to form when she calls having money automatically siphoned off her pay cheque for her RRSP and investment accounts one of her best moves.

"The key is discipline," she says. "It can mean the difference between a wonderful life and a struggle, and if I have the choice, I'd rather not struggle."

She's also glad she has made the move into stocks. She bought Leeds NT Corp. (XLN-TSE, 52-week high $33.60, low $14.) less than three months ago, and has seen it move from $26.90 to yesterday's close of $31.75. The Toronto-based "financial intermediary" invests in the shares of several banks, as well as IPL Energy Inc. and TransCanada PipeLines Ltd. "If you look at demographics, boomers are looking for a place to put their money, so the financial sector should do well."

More interestingly, her enthusiasm for stocks hasn't been dampened by the performance of Bell Canada International Inc. (BI-TSE, 52-week high $31.70, low $20). The international venture and contract arm of BCE Inc., the company focuses on telecommunications in emerging markets. She picked up the stock at $28.50 a few weeks after it began trading on Sept. 30, but it took a hit when the market dropped and still hasn't recovered, closing yesterday at $20.80. "I wanted to buy a high-tech stock," she says. "They are more volatile, but they are also more likely to come in for you when it's their time."

HER WORST MOVE: Earlier this year, Ms. Cumming was working in an Edmonton newsroom stocked with investors who had gotten in early on Bre-X Minerals Ltd. When the story hit the headlines about the possibility the gold world's emperor wasn't wearing any clothes, she bet $1,000 that the gold was, in fact, there. Although the company is now delisted, Ms. Cumming says her latest statement shows her investment has an estimated market value of exactly $5.30. "It teaches you if you want to roll the dice you have to be prepared to lose."

ADVICE: "Value your financial future enough to be willing to educate yourself."

THE PORTFOLIO

Date:	Saturday, November 29, 1997
The investor:	Karen Cumming, 35.
Occupation:	TV reporter.
Investment personality:	"Disciplined."
Portfolio makeup:	Stocks: Leeds NT Corp., Bell Canada International. Funds: Mackenzie - Industrial Future, Ivy Canadian, Universal U.S., Mackenzie Emerging Growth; Templeton - International Stock, Emerging Markets.
Portfolio size:	Five figures.
Rate of return:	"25 per cent in each of the last two years."

Less than 10 years ago, Karen Cumming was worried about paying down her student loan, and scraping together the money to buy a small car. "At 27, I thought I was lagging behind everybody else."

Today, she's got her finances well in hand and is conservatively investing her savings in her RRSP, which is steadily growing. What did she do right?

She sat down with a financial planner and had to put her financial life down on paper. "It's a pretty sobering exercise to have to commit to paper everything you own."

Sobering, yes, but often a good idea. You can't decide on where you want to get to unless you figure out where you're starting from. And as you can see from Ms. Cumming's case, it doesn't really matter what you're starting with, even if that is no assets and loads of debt.

Take a look at where you are today, where you want to be five, 10 and 20 years out, and then put a plan in place to get you there. It may not seem like you're making progress day to day, or even year to year, but over time, you'll find that you are steadily moving towards your goals. As Ms. Cumming puts it, slow and steady wins the race, and the key to making your plan pay off is discipline.

SHIFTING FOCUS BRINGS

FINANCIAL FREEDOM

•

TWENTY YEARS EARNING an above-average income as a real estate agent in Florida and Montreal and a deeply ingrained habit of conserving her capital gave Christine McDowell the financial freedom to recently change careers.

After doing a lot of "personal growth work" herself, she has set up shop as a counsellor specializing in what she calls neurolinguistic programming and time-line therapy.

"I take people who are confused and angry and help them uncover the limiting decisions and negative emotions that are causing their problems." This doesn't require a long-term investment on her clients' part, she says, and the longest she has taken to put somebody on a brighter path is six hours. "My goal is to have everybody have a smile on their face."

The 43-year-old works out of her largely paid-off home in Pointe Claire, Que., another bonus from her focus on financial self-reliance. "I grew up believing that no one would take care of me. I felt whatever I wanted in life had to come from me so no one could take it away from me," she says. "Even when I was married, I kept my stuff separately."

In addition to changing careers, she's also changed her approach to investing.

She's always been great at salting money away, she says, but in the past, the one and only quality she looked for was security. "I put a lot of money away, but I wasn't investing. It went into GICs and silly things because I really didn't understand investing," she says.

It was the "Holy bananas!" reaction to her investments by a financial planner she had met at a seminar that woke her up. "I don't know if a lot of women are like me, but I had a fear that if I couldn't see my money it would disappear," she says. "I wanted to know I could get to it."

But no more. Together with her financial planner, and spurred on by her accountant, she now has a self-directed registered retirement savings plan full of mutual funds. In fact, wise investing outside of her plan even paid the way for her career change. "The return on my money has been unbelievable compared to what I used to be getting."

HOW SHE DOES IT: She depends on her adviser, whom she met while attending a seminar on investing for women. "When she talked, she was very honest and up-front," Ms. McDowell says. "That was so different than me. I was very closed with what I did with my money because I felt women weren't allowed to make money.

"She was shocked when she saw what I was doing with my money," Ms. McDowell recalls. "She couldn't believe I had it all just sitting there."

Her adviser soon moved Ms. McDowell into a handful of largely big, conservative funds. "Whenever she suggests a fund, I ask about the history," she says. "Stability is the key for me, because I get worried about losing my money.

"Maybe it would be different if I were married and my husband was working, but I don't know where I'm going to be when I'm 50, and I've never had a job where I've had a pension."

HER BEST MOVES: The financial freedom to leave her old career and take two years setting up her new business came courtesy of Templeton Growth Fund and Trimark Select Fund, which have five-year average annual compound returns of 18 per cent and 20 per cent, respectively. Starting in 1990, she began putting $250 a month into each fund, and the end result was a nest egg of $45,000 that she has been using to pay her living expenses.

"They are perfect for me because they are blue chip and very stable," she says. "Where else could you invest money for five years and get that kind of return?"

Inside her RRSP, her favourite fund is Templeton International Stock Fund, which has a three-year average annual compound return of 13.3 per cent.

HER WORST MOVE: Ms. McDowell put a small amount into C.I. Pacific Fund in June 1995. "My broker said that it had gone flat, and when it had gone flat in the past it had a tendency to then take off, but she didn't know when it would take off." The fund is still preparing for liftoff, as its two-year average annual compound return is 6.8 per cent.

ADVICE: "Money is there for a reason, and it's not to go out and spend it. It's there to give you some freedom."

THE PORTFOLIO

Date:	Saturday, October 11, 1997
The investor:	Christine McDowell, 43.
Occupation:	Personal growth counsellor.
Investment personality:	"Conservative."
Portfolio makeup:	Funds: C.I. - Canadian Growth, Canadian Balanced, Global, Pacific; Dynamic - Canadian Growth, Partners; Industrial Mortgage Securities; Ivy Canadian; Templeton - Emerging Markets, Growth, International Stock; Trimark - Select Balanced, Select Canadian Growth, Select Growth.
Portfolio size:	unavailable
Rate of return:	"14 per cent to 15 per cent a year."

Ms. McDowell has relied only on herself from an early age. That has had some very good results—she has saved a lot of her income, and paid off her home. The downside is that coupled with her lack of knowledge, her self-reliance led her to put most of her savings into GICs and other guaranteed investments. While her principal was protected, she later learnt that that also shut herself off from the longer-term returns that come from ownership-type investments like equities. As she remarked, "If I'd started doing this when I was 20, holy bananas! I wouldn't like to think about how much money I would have."

But thankfully, she knows that what is past is past, and has educated herself and moved into equities in order to help her savings grow much faster. She's learned to counter her earlier fears about the risk associated with equities, and knows that over time, the short-term volatility of her equity funds will be more than made up for by longer-term gains that will be far more than what she would have made in guaranteed investments. If history is any indicator and you take the long view, the short-term weaving and bobbing doesn't really matter. What is important is that in the years ahead, if you pick good equity funds, they will on average be worth much more than they are today.

What she hasn't done, though, is try to argue herself into putting money into investments that would stop her from sleeping, another smart move. There is no point in taking on more risk if personality-wise it starts to eat away at you. For one, it's just not worth the added stress. And two, the risk and associated worries may cause you to make rash decisions that wipe out those extra gains, and perhaps drop your return below what you could have earned on less risky investments.

To illustrate, just listen to her down-to-earth reasoning about why she chooses equity mutual funds over individual stocks. "It would take a certain type of understanding, and I don't think I was put on this earth to do that."

TIME IS THE
GREAT WEALTH BUILDER

•

BEV ROWDEN KNOWS the real dollar value of a good education. Not that she is against knowledge for knowledge's sake. But the 34-year-old, who lives in the village of Springfield, near Kitchener, Ont., says her practical approach to investing owes a lot to some unusually practical lessons she learned in her last year of high school.

"I had an economics teacher who taught us how to do a tax return," she says, still surprised at the dearth of "real-life" lessons in money management for students.

That prompted her to take a tax course with return-processing giant H&R Block, where she worked part-time for several years. "I got to see how people could make the same amount of money and pay very different amounts of tax."

She also was exposed to mutual fund investing, and learned about the relationship between time and money, a concept that quickly captured the automotive engineer's eye.

"You know those charts that show you how if you start early enough you can easily accumulate $1 million? I caught on to that early on," she says. "And my goal was to hit that million."

And she's right on track, thanks to a basket of solidly performing mutual funds. Success for her isn't measured in home runs, but in steady, long-term growth.

"I like to see somewhere between 12 to 15 per cent a year," she says about her ideal return. "I wouldn't like to drop below that."

HOW SHE DOES IT: Ms. Rowden is an enthusiastic advocate of mutual funds. "They give you diversity because you don't have all your eggs in one basket," she says.

She also likes funds because they offer a cost-efficient way to have her money carefully—and continually—watched over. "I don't have the time, energy or desire to do the research and go through company statements and reports," she says. "And I'm not one of those who runs every day to *The Globe's* financial section to see whether I'm down a nickel."

To pick funds, she first looks at the fund family's philosophy. She doesn't want funds without a long-term view.

"I heard an investment manager once say, 'We buy cheap,' without even saying whether that meant undervalued or whatever, and it made my skin crawl," she says. "I think it's much more important to buy companies that are solid and have a future."

That's why Trimark, with its emphasis on value, is one of her favourite fund families. President Arthur Labatt talks about finding good companies and investing for the long term, she says. "That's the kind of thinking I like."

She also looks for low volatility. She examines many different performance periods to find funds that offer steady returns, rather than a string of peaks and valleys. "That's important to me because if I ever need to get my money out, I don't want to be in one of those valleys."

HER BEST MOVES: Two of her best investments came when her company pension plan was converted to a group registered retirement savings plan in 1990. She put some money into London Life Diversified Fund, buying her units at $71.62. The units were priced this week at $138.63. She also bought units of London Life Equity Fund, paying $122.66. The units have since risen to $259.93.

More recently, she's also done well with 20/20 International Value Fund. She purchased units for $19.67 in December 1994, and they were valued Thursday at $26.04.

She keeps surplus cash and expense money in the Industrial Cash Management Fund, a money-market fund she likes because it offers convenient cheque-writing privileges. "It's useful for big stuff like property taxes on the house that come once a year," she says.

Not only does she get better interest from a money market fund than from a regular chequing account. "It's far enough away you don't think, 'Hey, I've got a lot of money,' but it's close enough so you can use it when it's needed."

HER WORST MOVES: The Toronto Stock Exchange used to encourage people to invest in the stock market by offering the chance to buy small numbers of shares without paying any commissions. Back when the TSE did travelling money shows, she attended one in London, Ont., and picked up shares of three or four companies.

"The next year there were no more road shows, and I was stuck with five shares of this company, and 10 shares of that," she says. "I had to hold on to them long enough just to cover the brokerage cost to get rid of them."

ADVICE: "Decide what your financial goals are, decide how important they are, and then stick to them, stand by them and don't listen to anybody else. Time makes far more money than anything else does."

THE PORTFOLIO

Date:	Saturday, December 21, 1996
The investor:	Bev Rowden, 34.
Occupation:	Automobile plant engineering analyst.
Investment personality:	"I don't mind taking a little risk, but I'm not in for the real highs and lows."
Portfolio makeup:	Families and funds: 20/20 (Canadian Growth, Foreign RSP Bond, International Value); Mackenzie (Ivy Canadian, Industrial Bond, Universal World Emerging Growth);

Trimark (The Americas, RSP Equity);
Templeton (Emerging Markets); London
Life (Diversified, Canadian Equity).

Portfolio size: Low six figures.

Rate of return: One-year return of 15 per cent.

Bev Rowden and long-term fund investing were made for each other. She went looking for a cost-efficient way to invest in a well-diversified group of stocks, and one that didn't require her to spend a lot of time monitoring her money.

Those are exactly the needs mutual funds satisfy best. While more and more attention has been focused lately on short-term fund returns and the most recent top-of-the chart performers, you can't ever really know in advance just which funds are going to come out on top. A much better approach is to look for funds that will generally outperform the pack. Measure your success, like Ms. Rowden, not in funds that post out-of-this-world six-month returns, but in those that consistently do well over the longer haul.

But even funds with solid and consistent longer-term numbers can have very different short-term volatility characteristics. If, like Ms. Rowden, you have an aversion to volatility, a good way to find funds that offer steady returns is using the charts on Internet sites such as www.globefund.com or www.imoney.com.

PEACE OF MIND
IN PINCHER CREEK

•

"WE DO WHAT WE LIKE TO DO, go where we want to go and live where we want to live."

That's what 74-year-old Bert van der Horst says has been the defining credo for his wife and himself since he retired four years ago. "When I stopped working, we travelled all over North America and had a ball," he says.

Their wanderlust exhausted, they now call home a trailer park nestled in a small woods in Pincher Creek, Alta., where he keeps occupied in the winter building model ships.

The basis for all this freedom will have most financial planners biting their tongues to avoid saying "Told you so."

Mr. van der Horst and his bride of several weeks arrived in Montreal from their native Netherlands in 1953 with $300.

Over the years, Mr. van der Horst did well professionally, working for a number of construction companies before starting his own construction management company, where he often made more than $100,000 a year. He would have been well-off no matter what, given his view that one should pay off one's mortgage, have no debt and spend less than what one earns for peace of mind.

However, he says his financial success was largely founded on grasping the implications of registered retirement savings plans when they were created in the sixties.

"I read all about them, and thought they were amazing," he says. "I realized I didn't have to do anything but put in as much as I could and I'd be fine."

HOW HE DOES IT: Mr. van der Horst says in different circumstances he could see himself being an active stock jockey. "I love playing with money." But 18-hour days in the construction business when he was working precluded stock-picking, so he went the mutual fund route, and has stuck with it.

In the earlier years, he relied on his company's lawyer and accountant to help direct his fund purchases. Then in 1988 he met a salesperson from Investors Group Inc., and has been with the Winnipeg-based fund company ever since. "The salesman looked at my portfolio and said I'd done very well—around 14 per cent a year."

Up to that meeting, he had been with AGF Management Ltd. and then with Mackenzie Financial Corp., but was ready to make another switch. While with Mackenzie, a new tax ruling meant he had to move a good deal of money from a deferred profit-sharing plan into an RRSP. Despite his protests, the fund company hit him with $4,300 of loads on the transfer. If that wasn't enough, he became increasingly upset with the money Mackenzie was showering on its sales forces.

"Mackenzie was making so much money they had a party for everybody and also went to Honolulu," Mr. van der Horst says. "They were bragging so much, and I was teed off that they were going to Hawaii on my money."

He was more than aware that Investors Group ran a captive sales force, but liked the fact that someone was taking an active look at his portfolio. "They're sort of like Avon," he says. "They pay their people good money and that's fine," he says.

These days, his wife's money is all in income investments, while he has his money in two equity funds, two bond funds, one dividend fund and an income fund. "But I tell my son who is 42 to invest all in equities because that will be the place to be over the next 20 years," he adds.

HIS BEST MOVES: Overall, Mr. van der Horst says it hasn't been so much his individual picks as two basic principles he put into play over many years that have left him and his wife so well off. "All I did was play the RRSP provisions to the hilt while working my butt off in construction where I made good money." And, he adds, simple money management also played a part. "I was brought up in the Dutch way," he says. "I was taught to never spend money until it was in my hot little hands."

HIS WORST MOVE: Mr. van der Horst believes in tapping financial professionals to manage one's money. The trick, he says, is to ensure it's the right person with the right knowledge. He says his worst mistake was allowing his bank manager to put one of his yearly RRSP contributions into a guaranteed investment certificate. "My conclusion from that was a bank manager is not suited to give advice on investing."

ADVICE: "With old-age security disappearing and the Canada Pension Plan in limbo, try to put in your limit to your RRSP."

THE PORTFOLIO

Date:	Saturday, November 8, 1997
The investor:	Bert van der Horst, 74.
Occupation:	Retired owner of construction company.
Investment personality:	"Conservative."
Portfolio makeup:	Funds: Investors Growth - Government Bond, Corporate Bond, Canadian Equity, Mutual, Dividend.
Portfolio size:	unavailable
Rate of return:	"14 per cent a year over 20 years."

I wasn't kidding when I said financial experts would have a tough time not telling their more wayward clients "I told you so" after reading Mr. Van der Horst's story.

Here are just a few of the things he's gotten very right:

- He maximized out his RRSP.
- He never spent money he didn't have. (Borrowing, though, can sometimes be OK. Try to stick to using debt only to buy things that will go up in value—a home for example—and try to minimize borrowing on things that will go down in value—a car, for instance.
- If you're going to play stocks, you have to have the time. If you don't, stay away from the stock game and stick to funds.
- Know when you need help. As he puts it, "If you want to build a hospital, come to Bert. If you want to invest, get somebody who does nothing but look after money." As he says of his adviser, "He makes good money, but he doesn't steal it, he earns it."
- If you have many years to leave your money invested, a good chunk of your savings should be in equities as they will pay off the most over the long haul.

SHE'S CREATING
HER OWN SAFETY NET

•

NANCY LEPPAN HAS FOUND out first-hand how simple, wise and re-warding it can be to put some basic financial planning lessons into practice.

Eight years ago, she decided it was time to start managing her money. The 52-year-old resident of London, Ont., was leaving her job with the provincial civil service to work as the sole assistant in a pediatrician's office. Single, she found herself focusing on her financial future and realizing the leap meant jumping without a safety net.

"Working for the province, I always felt that nebulous 'They' would take care of me," she says. "But when I decided to work in an office without a pension, I became really aware of the fact that only I'm going to look after me."

She received a lump-sum payout of her public service money-purchase pension plan. Going to a financial planner for advice, she was told to sock it away in Trimark RSP Equity Fund.

Since then, she's used an automatic monthly purchase plan to build a strong portfolio of mutual funds, whose value has recently pushed into six figures. She's also invested in real estate to give her-self a rent-free place to live, as well as a stream of income when she retires.

"A few years after I'd been doing steady investing, someone lent me a copy of *The Wealthy Barber* and it was fun realizing I was already doing what it recommended," she says.

HOW SHE DOES IT: Ms. Leppan relies heavily on her financial adviser to recommend funds. "She gives me the history, tells me about the managers and we look at it together," Ms. Leppan says. "I wouldn't know how to buy without her."

Once she's made her picks—generally, large Canadian equity funds—Ms. Leppan sets up a preauthorized purchase plan so that a set amount of money is used to buy units in the funds every month. "Once it comes out of my bank account, I never think of it as real money. I think of it as locked away some place."

Each month, she puts $350 directly into funds she holds inside her registered retirement savings plan. Another $100 goes into a fund outside her RRSP as a sort of emergency pool. If she hasn't had to spend that money by year end, she puts it—along with her bonus from her employer—into her RRSP.

With her automatic purchase plans in place, she largely ignores her investments until she has around $10,000 in any fund. Then, she and her adviser start to look for a new fund to add more diversity.

"I don't want or need to follow the markets or read *The Globe's* stock charts."

In real estate, she owns the home she lives in, which is divided into four units. She lives in one and rents out the other three. She also co-owns a neighbouring rental building with a silent partner.

Her home will be paid off in nine years, and at that point she hopes to be at least semi-retired, she says. "And I can probably manage on the income from next door."

HER BEST MOVES: Ms. Leppan says her best moves came when she invested a small inheritance. She put $5,000 into Trimark Select Canadian Growth Fund in the spring of 1992. She picked up her units at just above $6, and their value Thursday was $9.04. "I put $5,000 in and it's now worth more than twice that," she says. "In hindsight, I only wish I'd put a lot more money in."

The same spring, she also bought units in BPI Global Equity Fund in the $13 to $14 range. The price Thursday was $20.18.

She's also a big fan of her two MD Management funds, MD Equity Fund and MD Growth Fund, which have a one-year return of 23.2 per cent and 15.4 per cent, respectively, to October 31. While the funds are restricted to doctors and their families, she was able to purchase them through a plan set up by her pediatrician employer. "I wanted to invest where the people with really big money invest," she says.

HER WORST MOVE: Ms. Leppan says she's never put a foot wrong on the investment front so far. But she regrets taking her first steps just in the past few years. "The only mistake I've really made is not getting started early enough."

ADVICE: "Buy mutual funds using a preauthorized purchase plan. Then your money is gone, spoken for and otherwise taken care of. You don't even have to write a cheque. You have to look after yourself. Don't count on a pension and don't count on an inheritance. Start saving sooner rather than later."

THE PORTFOLIO

Date:	Saturday, December 7, 1996
The investor:	Nancy Leppan, 52.
Occupation:	Pediatrician's assistant.
Investment personality:	"I more or less leave it up to my investment adviser. I don't want to do it on a day-to-day basis, and I never want to wake up and find that I've been paying so little attention that I'm in the hole."
Portfolio makeup:	RRSP: 20/20 American Tactical Allocation Fund, 20/20 Canadian Growth, Trimark RSP Equity Fund, Universal Canadian Growth Fund Ltd., Canada Trust Everest Stock Fund, MD Growth Fund.

Non-registered: Trimark Select Canadian
Growth Fund, BPI Global Equity Fund.
Portfolio size: Low six figures.
Rate of return: Ranges between low to mid-teens.

It's amazing the peace of mind that people get from following a few simple basic financial strategies such as investing regularly over the long term. As Nancy Leppan makes clear, you don't need to stash away mountains of cash. A few hundred dollars a month will grow over time.

She's also another terrific example of why for most people the best advice is to have a set amount taken out of your account and invested automatically. You side-step the temptation of spending the money, plus you take advantage of the benefits of dollar-cost averaging. Each month, you'll buy more units of a fund when the price is lower, and fewer units when the price is higher.

Another smart move Ms. Leppan makes is not trying to jump into every second fund that comes along. Not only does this strategy risk putting your money into hot funds that often soon cool off, you can easily end up overdiversifying, not to mention paying too much in fees and commissions. Ms. Leppan's approach is not to even consider a new fund until she has at least $10,000 in her chosen funds. This helps steady her hand and ensures she gets the benefits of being in strong, steady performers over the long term rather than bailing when they hit a rough patch. Selling a fund when it stumbles, is, of course, not that difficult to do. The real challenge and one that few can pull off is to decide when to get back in!

Small-Cap

INVESTING

S MALL-CAP INVESTING involves taking on the added risk of buying smaller, less proven companies for the chance of above-average returns.

When you stay in a hotel, you typically have two choices. One is to go with a well-known chain like Holiday Inn or Sheraton. If you do, you have a pretty good idea of what you'll get. The staff will be well trained, if somewhat mechanical, and whether you're in Belleville or Beijing, you'll get the same sort of service, treatment and amenities. You might even get the same type of bedspread. That's kind of how blue-chip stocks work. They're well known, well understood and trusted by millions.

Small-cap stocks—the stocks of small, less well-known companies—are more like boutique hotels. Each one is unique, and unless you do your homework, you won't know if you're checking in to Shangri-La or a flea-bag motel run by Basil Fawlty, John Cleese's infamously inept hotel manager.

What makes everything more interesting, intriguing and challenging, is that "boutique hotel" you're checking your money into is constantly evolving and changing. You have to keep an eye on it. If you don't, the next time you show up for a weekend getaway, you may find that it's closed for renovations, or simply shut down altogether!

Of course, you're hoping the exact opposite happens. You are betting that management will make the place so pretty and attractive it's attracting visitors from near and far, and demand is so great you can't get a room for weeks.

SMALL CAPS DEFINED

To start off with, just what is a "small-cap" stock? Well, it's simply the stock of a company whose market capitalization is relatively small.

Don't you hate so-called "helpful" financial articles that give you that kind of dead-end explanation? Well, not here, no sirree!

"Capitalization" Explained (*In English!*)

A company's *capitalization* is simply the current price of its stock multiplied by the number of shares held by investors (or *outstanding*). Take Nepalese Vests-R-Us. If its shares were trading at $10 and it had 15 million shares outstanding, the funky-but-chic clothier would have a market capitalization of $150 million.

People often refer to a company's market capitalization as its value. The reason is the market cap is what it would cost you, if you were so inclined, to go out and buy that company.

There are two basic ways to invest in small caps. You can do it on your own. You'll have to sift through an awful lot of information to come up with companies worth investing in, and you'll have to keep track of them on a regular basis.

If you don't have that kind of time and energy, you can invest through a mutual fund that focuses on investing in small-cap companies (helpfully called *small-cap funds*). Going the mutual fund route is also a good idea if you don't have a large amount of money to put into this volatile sector. Diversification is crucial for small-cap investors, as focusing on just a few companies risks having one bad apple do serious damage to your entire portfolio. Also, if you go it alone you'll have to buy and sell your stocks more frequently, and the trading costs can quickly add up.

Small-cap funds usually have their own idea of what specifically constitutes a small-cap company. Some funds will limit themselves to investing in companies worth $500 million dollars or less, while others may consider a company with a market capitalization of up to $750 million a small-cap company.

WHY SMALL CAPS PACK A PUNCH

Small caps tend to be less covered by analysts, less reported on by the media and less followed by investors. In short, there are far fewer people evaluating small-cap stocks than larger-cap stocks. That means the market may not be as efficient at collectively deciding just what they are worth, making it more likely you'll be able to turn up an under-priced gem or two.

Another reason small caps can give your portfolio some extra punch is because of the rules surrounding mutual funds. Funds aren't generally allowed to own any more than 10 per cent of a company. If you are running a big fund, you'll have to put your money into a huge whack of small-cap companies in order to get fully invested. As a result, the larger the fund, the more they tend to stick to big companies. What you hope will happen, of course, is that your little fish will turn into a whopping great big swordfish that everyone wants to reel in. The bigger it becomes, the more it's worth the while of fund managers to get involved. More buyers, more demand, higher price. Simple.

Unfortunately, many small-cap investors are looking for short-term profits. So if bad news comes along, the company runs into a short-term setback, or the hype around a company quietens down, investors may leave in a rush, driving a small-cap's price down...waaaaaay down.

Of course, the exact opposite also comes into play. A bit of good news, renewed interest or a view that a company's earnings and revenue will jump in the future can quickly move the price up as well.

Buy small caps cheap enough, and it becomes easy to see why they can help put a little extra wind in your portfolio's sails. If they drop—even by a substantial amount—if they only form a small part of your portfolio, the damage should be minimal. On the flip side, if a small-cap stock or fund makes a move, it can often be a hey-the-joint-is-really-rocking-tonight type move. And a strong runup can help pick up your entire portfolio's return.

DON'T WALK IN BACKWARDS

Funnily enough, the first stocks people often buy are small caps. And that's usually a result of being told that "this baby's going to fly" or some such other catchy little phrase.

Doing this is sort of like deep-sea diving without first having taken some basic lessons like learning how to swim. And even if you could front-crawl from here to eternity, you'd probably want to take it step-by-step and try snorkelling and scuba diving first.

The same is true with small caps. In order to be successful, you'll have to educate yourself because you'll need extra tools in your investment assessment kit to perform the needed checkup on small-cap stocks. And if you're like most folks, you're probably better off going slowly. Begin by dipping your toe into the mutual fund waters and then getting your feet wet with blue chips before finally diving into small-caps.

THE UPSIDE

Small-cap stocks and funds typically offer more potential upside, and more potential downside than most other investments. That includes large-cap stocks and large-cap equity mutual funds. However, it's hard to pick that out when you look at recent performance numbers. Blue-chip stocks were on a tear up until 1998, and the small-cap rally that many were expecting failed to turn up.

THE DOWNSIDE

Investing in small caps means taking on much more risk than sticking with blue-chip stocks. There are three basic reasons why smaller, less well-known companies are much less of a sure thing than more established companies.

LACK OF EXPERIENCE: Small-cap companies are often run by entrepreneurs who have suddenly found themselves trying to pilot what was a speedy outboard but has since been transformed into a large in-board cabin cruiser. Running the company becomes much more complex and demands many more and often different types of skills. The managers are faced with many tests, which include realizing what skills they are lacking and ensuring they hire the right talent to keep the company on track, manage growth and seize new opportunities.

LIMITED ACCESS TO CAPITAL: The higher risk and relative "newness" of these companies mean they often have a harder time raising funds. In business, often the key ingredient to making it through a rough patch is access to money, whether to pay suppliers, build inventory or help push through a new marketing program that will lead to a big boom in sales.

VOLATILE SALES: Many small-cap companies rely on a handful—and in some cases, a single—product or service. If what the company is selling is only being bought by a few customers, then the danger is even greater. If the product or service goes out of fashion, or a large customer suddenly stops buying, then sales can plummet overnight.

All of this means that if you don't know what you're up to, don't buy small caps. Also, stay away from them if extra risk makes you more than a little uncomfortable.

Even if you understand them forwards and backward, they still take a lot of time to evaluate and to monitor once you're bought them. Like one of those Asian fighting kites, you have to keep your eye on them a lot more than you do your standard issue wind sock.

HOW THEY PULL IT OFF

For winning at the small-cap game, here are two basic rules to follow:

- *The Smaller the Cap, the Larger the Whisper Effect.* Don't buy a small-cap stock just because you've heard it "looks good." You have to do more homework, not less, when appraising a small-cap stock.
- *Look for a Solid Balance Sheet.* Nice jargon that, but what does it really mean? Essentially, it means that the company is in good shape financially. Here's how to tell.

Molehills—not Mountains—of Debt: The way to suss out a company's debt situation is by looking at its debt-to-equity ratio. This is simply its debt divided by the total shareholders' equity. A safe range is a debt-to-cash-flow ratio of 2.0 or less.

High Operating Margin: The higher a company's operating margin, the more money it's pulling in. A company's operating margin is its earnings (before interest, taxes and depreciation are deducted) divided by revenues.

Growth is Good: You want to buy small caps that aren't going to stay small. Look for companies where earnings and sales are both growing from year to year, preferably at a rate of 15 to 20 per cent, but 25 to 30 per cent would be nicer.

Don't Forget Diversification

If you are going to buy individual small-cap stocks, you should have a fairly large portfolio to work with. The reason is that in a more conservative portfolio, small caps should only represent a small percentage of your total investments. In turn, the portion of your savings you want to have in small caps should be spread among a minimum of five companies. That way, if four don't perform—as is likely to be the case—the fifth one will hopefully more than make up the loss with hefty winnings.

...And Patience

If you invest conservatively and buy quality, you should also be prepared to hold your small caps for several years. If you have done your homework, you have to give the companies time to let their strategies bring in increased profits.

Tips for Maximizing Your Small-Cap Profits

GO FOR QUALITY: Sure, the more off the beaten track a small-cap stock, the larger the potential profits. But the hot stock of the month is more likely to burn you than it is to sizzle.

WATCH YOUR TIMING: Typically, small caps start to move after larger-cap stocks have been moving up for a while. The reason is twofold. First, the upside potential of the larger-cap stocks starts to diminish. At the same time, investors start to become less cautious and more willing to buy more aggressive investments such as small-cap stocks and funds, helping move their prices higher.

WATCH THEM CLOSELY (BUT NOT *TOO* CLOSELY!): Small-cap stocks are kind of like corks. They bob up and down with the slightest ripple. Contrast that with blue chips, the ocean-going liners of the investment world. They cut through the waves with nary a thought, and can maintain a steady course through sun, wind and rain.

You have to keep an eye on your small caps as they bounce up and down on the waves of investor sentiment. The trick is to know when to hang on and when to sell. That last ripple may have been the time to sell, as your stock enters becalmed waters and sits there forever. On the other hand, a huge tidal wave of support may spring up that drives a stock to record highs.

LONE WOLF TAKES

PSYCHOLOGICAL ROUTE

•

AS A SOCIAL WORKER, Richard Schwindt, 40, spends lots of time trying to figure out the emotions and motivations of the people he's counselling.

And what's surprised him since he began investing is just how much psychological factors affect the stock market. "I had always assumed that there were very concrete things that moved the market—that if you quantified it you'd understand everything."

Finding that wasn't the case was good news, says Mr. Schwindt, noting that most social workers aren't known for their wizardry with numbers. "But if the company has a good story and profits are going up, even a simple guy like me can figure out that's good for stocks."

Another surprise for Mr. Schwindt, a confessed lapsed leftist, is just how much he's enjoying investing. "I appreciate people who are innovative and creative and looking to grow in the world, and I think that comes out in capitalism," he says. "And I've learned about all sorts of things from gold mining to drug development."

HOW HE DOES IT: Calling himself a hands-on learner, Mr. Schwindt decided when he began investing five years ago to go it completely alone—doing his own research and using a discount brokerage. "I feel if I learn on my own, I'll learn better," he says.

The biggest lesson he's learned to date, he says, is to have some patience and think about the long term. "When I've sold prematurely or in a panic, and sold at a loss, I've usually lived to regret it."

For the first four years, Mr. Schwindt stuck to mutual funds as he familiarized himself with the investing world, branching out a year ago into individual stocks.

Not being handy with numbers, Mr. Schwindt pegs his picking strategy on finding innovative companies with a good story to tell. A typical recent buy was Micrologix Biotech Inc. (MBI-TSE, 52-week high $5.25, low $2.75, yesterday's close $5.10). The biotechnology company is developing powerful drugs designed to work on the growing number of infections that have become resistant to current antibiotics. "My approach is that if you buy solid innovative companies run by good people, your patience will pay off."

That patience is important given that he lives in Sioux Lookout, an isolated community in Northern Ontario, Mr. Schwindt says. "I'm never going to be the first one to have information so I have to look for companies that will reap the benefits of their innovation in a few months or years." His patience is obvious when he notes that his return from his first year of investing in individual stocks has been a big fat zero. "I don't feel bad because this is my year to learn and position."

HIS BEST MOVES: Royal Bank (RY-TSE, high $68.40, low $34.50, close $64.20) has been a stand-out among his stocks. "The thing that caught my eye was they had significant diversification with a strong portfolio of international holdings," he says. "Even if interest rates rise and the economy does its cyclical thing, Royal Bank will do well in time."

Mitel Corp. of Kanata, Ont. (MLT-TSE, high $10.85, low $6.35), caught Mr. Schwindt's eye when he read a number of comments from analysts that its semiconductor division was wildly underpriced, and that the company was into a lot of new technologies, partly because of its acquisition of assets from Gandalf Technologies Inc. "They make so many critical components for different things—including things like my pacemaker."

He bought in at between $7.30 and $7.70 this spring and summer, and the stock is now trading in the high $9 range, closing yesterday at $9.60.

Mr. Schwindt bought Sleeman Breweries Ltd. of Guelph, Ont., (ALE-TSE, high $7.20, low $4.90, close $6.30) this past spring at $5.40. "They are good marketers, they throw all their money back into expansion, they have limited product line and they know who their customers are."

HIS WORST MOVE: His biggest loser to date has been Vancouver-based gold producer Placer Dome Inc. (PDG-TSE, high $36.50, low $19, close $21.65), which he picked up last November at $27. "Gold was at a low so I was trying a contrarian approach, plus they were jockeying with Barrick for a piece of Bre-X." He sold his shares at $21.50 last April.

In addition to the refusal of the price of bullion to show any buoyancy, Mr. Schwindt notes that the company is involved in a lot of litigation. "I wonder if the management is arrogant, or lack the knack for the cross-cultural relations international gold companies need to be able to manage," he says.

ADVICE: "Find out the context your company exists within, and think about what they're making."

THE PORTFOLIO

Date:	Saturday, September 13, 1997
The investor:	Richard Schwindt, 40.
Occupation:	Social worker.
Investment personality:	"I enjoy investing because I learn about the world."
Portfolio makeup:	Stocks: Sleeman, Vedron, Micrologix, Avenor Cabre Exploration. Funds: Green Line Global Select, Altamira Capital Growth, CIBC Mortgage Fund.
Portfolio size:	"High five figures."

Rate of return: "15 per cent to 20 per cent a year on funds,
nil on stocks for the first year."

It certainly helps that Mr. Schwindt enjoys learning about companies and exactly what they do. Understanding what a company is selling and to whom is a key to protecting yourself again nasty surprises in the small-cap world.

Take Mr. Schwindt's purchase of Micrologix Biotech. He heard about the company in the newspaper, and then set about researching it very carefully. What he found was a company that was trying to make headway in developing the next generation of antibiotics. The market is obvious and huge, given how quickly many diseases are becoming immune to current medicines. He knows he invested early—at the "idea" stage—but as he put it, he felt the ideas were brilliant. "The company will either do unbelievable things or turn into nothing."

That couldn't sum up many small-cap stocks any better. A large number of companies in this area have a very small number of products or services, and often they aren't even proven, much less earning the company a profit. It's those sort of factors that mean small caps should never be a huge part of your portfolio. Mr. Schwindt, for example, has a good deal of his savings in mutual funds. "If I have that conservative anchor there, I can take on more risk with direct investments."

Another factor to consider is that many small caps are only in the development stage so patience is a necessity, not a virtue. A drug company can find the approval process takes much longer than expected, an industrial concern may have problems getting quality products off the production line, a technology company may discover the market isn't quite ready yet to beat down the walls to buy its software. "People in my profession look for the capacity to defer gratification in people," notes the social worker. "If you can hold off and say 'I don't have to have the profit tomorrow,' investing in these stocks can work."

One final thought from Mr. Schwindt on the difference between speculating and small-cap investing. "I look for interesting companies that are innovative and are perhaps down a little on their luck, but not speculative shots in the dark," he says. "To avoid those, you have to think about what the company makes or creates, who they are going to sell it to and the larger context the company exists in, including its competitors and the trends that may influence its fortunes."

ENTREPRENEUR GAINS
BY TAKING CONTROL

•

NANCY SINGLETON likes to be in charge.

The 48-year-old entrepreneur has done everything from owning a restaurant to operating 12 Money Mart outlets in Toronto to running a petro-chemical service company in her new hometown of Calgary.

And now that she's said goodbye to running her own businesses, she's busy taking control of the capital she has accumulated from the sale of her many enterprises.

When the first proceeds flowed in as she divested herself of her various companies in the early nineties, she put the money into a conservative balanced fund run by a private money management company. "It wasn't at all my style, but they never fished that out of me when we talked," she says.

Along the way she also got involved with a real estate limited partnership in Arizona, which she has quickly grown to hate. "It's totally non-liquid, nobody's in control but the people that are handling it, and the returns have fallen steadily from 7 per cent to around 1.5 per cent a year."

She's been much happier since she moved the bulk of her capital into mutual funds, but is keen to start building a portfolio of individual stocks. Besides finding stock picking fun, she feels it's a financially wise move.

"I think if the market does correct, you have more control if you choose your own stocks because you can make decisions faster," she

236 ME AND MY MONEY

says. "I am also hung up on all the high expense ratios the funds charge." She's enjoying the business of investing so much, in fact, that she plans to make it her next career. "I hope to work as a retirement planner, because it covers the whole gamut and makes investing meaningful."

HOW SHE DOES IT: To equip herself for stock-picking, Ms. Singleton has completed the Canadian Securities Course and the Canadian Investment Management Program, both offered by the Canadian Securities Institute. "The courses give you a wonderful overview of how the markets work," she says.

She also follows the financial press closely, and spends a good deal of time reading up on potential picks at the University of Calgary's library. In the near future, she intends to cut herself off from the safety net of using a full-service broker and do her trading through a dis-counter. "I think it will be a good learning process."

She finds herself drawn to penny stocks, because she likes the volatil-ity and the chance to bet on entrepreneurs making it big. Ms. Singleton reads the *Penny Stock Reporter* newsletter faithfully.

She also favours small-capitalization stocks because she feels blue-chip companies are currently overpriced. "The market is out of bal-ance and there's going to be a restructuring," she says. "I think the big companies are getting too much capital, and the CFOs are getting paid too much."

HER BEST MOVES: Yogen Fruz World-Wide Inc. (YF-TSE, 52-week high $7.20, 52-week low $2.80, yesterday's close $6.70) caught her eye when she read about the Toronto-based yogurt franchisor in the *Penny Stock Reporter.* "They said it was a worldwide franchise and that it was expanding into over 80 countries," she says. She bought in last March at $4.44. "I thought it would go up, but certainly not that quickly."

Her broker also alerted her to Denbury Resources Inc. (DNR-TSE, high $25.00, low $16.20, close $22.80), an oil and gas producer with properties in Canada and the United States. She bought her shares at $16.90 in March. "They had absolutely no debt at all and that was very intriguing to me," she says.

Of her funds, BPI Canadian Small Companies is a stand-out, earning her a 70 per cent return on her initial investment over three years. "It was recommended to me by my adviser at the time," she says. "I didn't even understand mutual funds then, but I researched it after."

HER WORST MOVE: In addition to her limited partnership, Ms. Singleton has been completely under-whelmed by the return from her investment in BPI Canadian Resource Fund. "It's just been a terrible performer."

She has been in the fund, which has a one-year return to the end of July of minus 18.8 per cent, since last August. However, she blames no one but herself for her loss. She had thought the fund was invested largely in oil and gas companies, and was surprised to learn that half of the fund's assets were in mineral companies. "I simply didn't do my homework," she says.

ADVICE: "When you buy a stock, set a target 'sell' price and follow through on it."

THE PORTFOLIO

Date:	Saturday, August 30, 1997
The investor:	Nancy Singleton, 48.
Occupation:	Entrepreneur.
Investment Personality:	"I'm very growth-oriented and I have the re-sources to be that way."
Portfolio makeup:	Funds: AGF RSP International Equity; BPI - Canadian Equity Value, Canadian Resource, Global Equity, Canadian Small Companies; C.I. - Global, Emerging Markets, Hansberger Global Small Cap, Hansberger Developing Markets; Fidelity - Far East, International

Portfolio, European Growth, Latin American
Growth; Trimark Discovery. Stocks: Denbury,
Yogen Fruz, Laurasia.
Portfolio size: "Low seven figures."
Rate of return: "Between 20 and 25 per cent."

One of the biggest arguments both for and against investing in individual stocks is it's much easier to sell them than it is to dump a fund.

At the very least, when you put an order in to sell a fund, it's generally not done until the end of that day. Some funds also have extra costs that make you think twice about quickly selling. Often, there is a charge for selling a fund within a few months of purchasing it. Others may have a deferred sales charge—a commission for unloading your units.

Individual stocks, however, can be sold much more easily and quickly. Put in a market order, and your stock will be sold in a matter of minutes. For Nancy Singleton, this is a big advantage to buying individual stocks. You can move very quickly to sell a stock in reaction to bad news, whether it's a lost contract, poor drilling results or lower-than-expected earnings.

However, this liquidity also poses a potential danger. Just because a stock dips or even drops a good deal doesn't in itself mean a year, a month or even a week out it won't be much higher. One of the most common mistakes admitted by *Me and My Money* profilees is selling too soon. This is usually an emotional, not an intellectual decision, and, as many people point out, your emotions almost always exercise bad judgement when it comes to the market.

TEACHER HAS LEARNED
HIS LESSONS WELL

•

A COUPLE OF YEARS AGO, Sang Kim realized his parents weren't in particularly great financial shape as they headed into their retirement years.

Not only did that make the 30-year-old London, Ont., high-school physical education and science teacher take a hard look at his own situation, but he realized that his upbringing hadn't entailed much in the way of a financial education.

He quickly made preparing for his own retirement a high priority, and set his sights on becoming an informed investor. He started reading the *Report on Business* every day and signed on with the Canadian Shareowners Association. He also joined the Ivey League, an investment club composed largely of fellow teachers.

Soon, Mr. Kim had not only developed a sound approach to the markets, but also equipped himself with a number of useful tools he uses to guide his investing.

HOW HE DOES IT: Mr. Kim has what at first may seem an unusually heavy overweighting in small-capitalization stocks and funds, but it is part of a well-thought-out asset-allocation strategy. "My wife and I are both teachers, and since we both plan on teaching for a long time, I look at our defined pension plans as just like a GIC," Mr. Kim says. "That means we can look for aggressive growth with the rest of our savings."

Any stock he is considering will likely get put through the Canadian Shareowners Association's stock selection guide.

He also applies several financial tests detailed in a book called *How to Make Money in the Stock Market*, written by William O'Neil, the founder of Los Angeles-based *Investor's Business Daily*. One of Mr. O'Neil's rules that Mr. Kim likes to stick to is focusing on companies with less than 30 million shares outstanding. "Historically, they've usually turned in the best performance."

Another of his personal tests on a prospective buy is to see if it is held by his four favourite small-cap fund managers: Steve Misener (BPI funds), Wayne Deans (Marathon Equity, O'Donnell Canadian Emerging Growth), Allan Jacobs (Sceptre Equity Fund) and Bill Andersen of Driehaus Capital Management Inc. of Chicago (20/20 RSP Equity and RSP Aggressive Smaller Companies).

For further investigation, he usually turns to the Internet. Some of his favourite sites include Canada Stockwatch, Canoe and Canada NewsWire. "I probably put in anywhere from 30 minutes to an hour a day managing my portfolio," he says. "I treat it like a part-time job."

HIS BEST MOVES: Mr. Kim remains firmly attached to Newton, Pa.-based magnet maker YBM Magnex International Inc. (YBM-TSE, 52-week high $15.25, low $5.90, yesterday's close $11.70), which has gained a lot of attention largely because of its low-cost manufacturing plant in Hungary. He bought the stock in November at $7.50. He first heard about the stock from his broker, who in turn had come across the company in BPI's annual report. "It met all my criteria, and I expect it to continue to perform well for several years."

Speaking of BPI, Mr. Kim has gotten a nice ride from the fund management company itself, Toronto-based BPI Financial Corp. (BPF-TSE, 52-week high $4.25, low $1.25.). He picked it up at $2.65 in December, and it closed yesterday at $4.39.

He's also done well with Drug Royalty Corp. (DRI-TSE, 52-week high $3.25, low $1.05, yesterday's close $2.10). The Toronto-based company receives a portion of the royalties of a number of different pharmaceutical companies in return for helping finance their drug development and marketing efforts. "It's terribly undervalued, and it's a good way to be in the pharmaceutical industry without taking too much risk."

Having been born in South Korea, Mr. Kim remains interested in Asia, and invests in the region through C.I. Pacific Fund. His average cost is around $7.50, and the fund units are now valued at $20.93. "I started picking it up when it was in the dumpster, and it's been doing well lately, particularly because Hong Kong has been so hot."

HIS WORST MOVE: Eighteen months ago, Mr. Kim was tipped off that Markham, Ont.-based Legacy Storage Systems Inc., a data storage concern, was set to take off, and picked up some shares at $2.65. The company failed miserably to live up to its promise, though, and after a 10-for-one consolidation last fall, the stock is trading in the same range under a new name, Tecmar Technologies Inc. (TTI-TSE, 52-week high $3.45, low $1.30, yesterday's close $1.70). "I didn't have my system set up back then," he admits. "And although I did a lot of reading, I didn't understand the numbers."

ADVICE: "If you want to invest in the stock market, you can avoid a lot of risk just by doing some research."

THE PORTFOLIO

Date:	Saturday, July 26, 1997
The investor:	Sang Kim, 30.
Occupation:	Secondary school teacher.
Investment personality:	"Aggressive."
Portfolio makeup:	Stocks: YBM Magnex, BPI Financial, Insulpro, Tecmar, C.M. Oliver. Mutual Funds: C.I. Pacific, BPI Canadian Small Companies, BPI American Small Companies, 20/20 Aggressive Smaller Companies.

Portfolio size: "Mid-five figures."
Rate of return: "30 per cent over the past year."

Mr. Kim has done many things right. Most of them stem from his understanding of the value of a good education, something I'm sure he sees first-hand every time he runs into one of his old students.

Here's a cheat sheet from his investing lecture:

- *Take a Moment and Consider What Kind of Financial Education You Received from your Parents.* If you are lucky, they passed on to you a good understanding of the basics like regularly saving a part of every pay cheque. If not, you may have developed many dangerous financial attitudes and habits. If this is the case, the sooner you realize it, the sooner you can start re-educating yourself to build a better financial future.
- *If You Want to Expand Your Understanding of Money, Start Looking at the Big Picture First.* Too often, people focus on one small aspect of their financial situation when they start to take control of their money. For example, you may suddenly realize you have been missing out by having your money only in guaranteed investments and want to quickly put the situation right. But rushing out and quickly buying a bunch of stocks would be a mistake. You can't decide on specific financial moves until you assess your complete situation, and develop an overall plan.
- *Take Your Money Seriously.* Saving money, given our high level of taxation, is tough, no question about it. So it makes sense to try to make the most of what you've managed to put away by helping it grow. To do that, you'll have to put in a little time educating yourself about your best course of action. You also need to put in some time watching over your investments.
- *Consider Equities for the Long Haul.* If you have savings that you can invest for at least seven to 10 years, consider putting a good chunk of it into equities. They offer the best potential for long-term growth.

HE'S LEFT THE PONIES
TO BET ON THE STOCKS

•

MURRAY MILLIGAN STARTED to invest in the stock market because it presented more opportunities for higher returns and a lot less risk than what he was used to.

What's less risky than the stock market? Try the racetrack, which was for many years Mr. Milligan's investment of choice.

As a high school student, he thought nothing of betting $500 at the track. When he joined the working world, he even bought his own horse, aided by his well-paying union job with an auto-shipping company in London, Ont. "All of our guys make $65,000 or more, and with real estate cheap here, that's good money," he says.

He eventually realized, though, that the racetracks were also making good money. "The house takes 20 per cent out of every dollar, so even if you break even, you're only getting 80 cents on the dollar."

Not that every cent got spent on horses. He also picked up three rental properties along the way, but the house, or, rather "houses," also took their cut of his take. "I'd hate to add up all the money I spend on fridges, doors and paint," he says, adding that the labour he puts in probably pays him less than 50 cents an hour. "I would have done better to put that money into mutual funds."

And that's exactly what he's begun focusing on, along with starting to pick his own stocks. "Instead of racing programs, my favourite reading material is now the *Report on Business*," he says.

HOW HE DOES IT: To pick his funds, he simply transferred his racetrack research methods to the markets. "When I bet horses, I looked very closely at who the trainer was, and at its past positions," he says. "If it hadn't raced well over the last six starts, I would look to see why."

All he needed to do was substitute "fund manager" for trainer, and "yearly compound return" for "finishes," and he had a ready-made investment mindset.

He also carried across his willingness to bet long shots. "But you don't just bet a horse—or a fund—because it's long odds. You have to have a reason," he says.

Mr. Milligan likes to scour the newspaper looking for innovative ideas for his stock picks. For example, he recently bought into IBI Corp. (IBI-CDN, 52-week high 31 cents, low 5.5 cents, yesterday's close 10 cents), a Toronto-based company that trades over-the-counter and is involved in developing gold and timber resources. "I noticed that John Turner had signed on as a director, and I thought there must be a good reason why such a big driver got on this horse."

He also shares ideas with his work colleagues, many of whom have recently taken to the markets with enthusiasm. They've even formed an investment club of 20 people, putting in $10 each week. The club meets monthly to buy one stock.

"Some guys used to only care where the next beer hall was, but now they're all talking about investing," he says. "*The Globe and Mail* is very well looked at, and nobody knew it even existed before."

HIS BEST MOVES: Forsys Software Corp. (FORS-CDN, 52-week high $2.35, low $1.25) was brought to his attention by his investment club. The company sells software to restaurants that helps them crunch numbers on everything from when chicken wings sell best to the take from different servers. Mr. Milligan did his own research, including talking to the management of local restaurants that used the system, and bought in February at $1.50.

A big fund winner has been AGF Asian Fund, which has doubled his investment in four years. He bought because at the time, he was hunting for a new financial adviser, and eight of the 12 he interviewed suggested Asian funds were poised to perform well. "My wife is

Japanese, and it helps her understand and feel more comfortable about my investing because she knows the companies," he says.

He's also a big fan of Trimark's Select Canadian Growth, or any Trimark fund, for that matter, saying he likes the numbers the whole family turns in. "Even the AGF guys all relate themselves to how Trimark does it," he says.

HIS WORST MOVE: In addition to his rental properties, Mr. Milligan took a beating on his very first stock, Calgary-based Dome Petroleum Ltd., which was eventually taken over by Amoco Canada Petroleum Co. Ltd. He invested in the failing oil company in the eighties on the advice of a broker who insisted the company would bounce back, but "it just kept going down and down." Mr. Milligan, who lost 90 per cent of his investment, says his big mistake was not doing any research himself. "I thought only brokers could pick stocks."

ADVICE: "The stock market is nothing to be afraid of. You can find stocks that suit whatever level of risk suits you."

THE PORTFOLIO

Date:	Saturday, July 12, 1997
The investor:	Murray Milligan, 39.
Occupation:	Auto shipping company employee.
Investment personality:	"Enthusiastic."
Portfolio makeup:	Stocks: Forsys Software Corp., National Challenge, IBI Corp. Mutual Funds: Trimark - Select Balanced, Advantage Bond, Americas; AGF - Asian Growth, Japan, European Growth, Growth Equity; Dynamic - Real Estate Equity, Europe; AIC Advantage II.
Portfolio size:	"Mid-six figures."
Rate of return:	"Over 20 per cent over the past two years."

When you assess investments—whether it's a small business, real estate, or stocks and bonds—one factor people often overlook is the pain-in-the-neck factor. Just what you have to put into an investment in terms of time and energy and what that investment will return to you financially and otherwise are key considerations if your investment life and the rest of your life are to match.

Mr. Milligan, for example, got out of the real estate market because it is so labour intensive, and he figures he was getting far less than minimum wage for his work.

From young to old, people I speak with usually have a very good idea of just how involved they want to be in managing their money. At one end are the truly passive types who want to hand everything over to a fund or private money manager and never have to think about it again. At the other end are those who can't think of a better way to spend a couple of hours a day than researching and tracking stocks.

Knowing where you lie on the passive-active spectrum will go a long way to helping you choose the right investment approach. You'll enjoy—rather than be annoyed by—your portfolio. What's more, you'll be more likely to make profitable decisions.

COUPLE TAKE THE
TEAM APPROACH

•

SYLVESTER AND DARLA PETRYK aren't stockbrokers or mutual fund salespeople, but they likely spend just as much time studying the markets as people employed in the financial industry.

The couple, both in their fifties, live in Senneville, Que., on the western end of the Island of Montreal. He still occasionally works as a consulting civil engineer and she does some part-time bookkeeping, but making their money grow is now their chosen profession. "Managing our portfolio is a full-time job," Mr. Petryk says.

HOW THEY DO IT: The Petryks have an extremely methodical, well-planned team approach to managing their investments.

It begins with Mr. Petryk, whose job it is to stay abreast of the business news. "I read a ton of financial papers and that's probably my biggest source of finding stocks that attract my interest," he says.

What he is continually scanning for are changes in a company that he feels will have a significant impact on the company's growth and its stock price. "There's usually something that happens in a company and we try to project what the future impact of that will be," he says.

That can be anything from a jump in earnings or management changes to increased insider buying. "To me that's a signal, as the insider has more information in the company than anybody else," Mr. Petryk says. "He makes a commitment and he'll look after it if he takes a significant position."

Once something catches his eye, Ms. Petryk steps in, contacting the company and obtaining a complete package, including annual and recent quarterly reports, press releases and investment reports.

At this stage, many companies get set aside because the Petryks find something they don't like. This is often a management conflict of interest such as a software company where the president owns the software and the company only has the right to market it. "I just drop it at that point," Mr. Petryk says.

If a company gets this far, he then spends five to 10 hours doing an in-depth analysis of its finances, which often includes a phone call to the vice-president of finance. "I make a projection on what the performance of the company will be and what will be the corresponding effect on the stock price."

If the company then meets their minimum projected return target of at least 20 per cent, then it becomes a serious buy candidate. At that point the two then decide whether to make a buy, put the company on their watch list of about 100, or add it to their files of several hundred companies they track.

THEIR BEST MOVES: Montreal software company Metrowerks Inc. (MWK-TSE, 52-week high $18.55, low $11.75, yesterday's close $12.30) has been one of the Petryks' best performers. They bought in late 1994 at around $1.80 when the company traded on the Vancouver Stock Exchange, and sold most of their position at $5.37 in May 1995. Then, after the Quebec referendum, they bought back in at $5 on November 2, 1995, and then sold out their position a couple of weeks later at prices ranging from $8.62 to $9.12.

They've also done well with Scintrex Ltd. (SCT-TSE, high $28.75, low $8.12, close $21.15). Mr. Petryk had followed the maker of high-tech detection instruments for a long time, and got in when a new president was appointed in 1993. "From that point the turnaround started," he says. The Petryks bought in at just under $3, and sold the stock throughout this last summer at prices ranging from $5.87 to $7.75.

Another high-flyer has been air charter carrier Transat A. T. Inc. (TRZ-ME, high $32, low $5.37, close $9.65), which the couple have been trading in since 1987. They took a big position in the stock in mid-1993—buying at $6.62 and picking up more shares all the way down to $2.65.

They've been slowly decreasing their position, starting in October of last year when they sold some shares at $5.75, and sold out a large portion in February of this year at between $10.25 and $12.

Buying into a falling stock is not unusual for the couple, who say they stand by their research. "It's just fundamental analysis—the lower the price, the more attractive the stock," Mr. Petryk says.

They also have a pretty firm idea of when they will get out. Once a stock reaches their target, then a partial sale is considered. If the stock then goes up another 25 per cent, anywhere from half to all of their remaining holdings are sold.

THEIR WORST MOVE: The most precipitous drop for the Petryks came courtesy of the tailspin Canadian Airlines Corp. (CA-TSE, high $3.65, low $1.05, close $2.25) has been in. They had owned PWA, which was taken over by Canadian, buying it from the high teens down to as low as $1.70.

They then proceeded to buy more shares in Canadian at 62 cents in 1994. "The cost of operation per passenger mile was consistently more efficient than Air Canada, and I felt they would reach profitability," Mr. Petryk says. The company did a 20-for-one share consolidation in 1995. "We lost somewhere over $30,000," Mr. Petryk says.

ADVICE: "The most important thing for a beginner is to find a good broker because 99.9 per cent of people don't want to follow the financial news. If a person is interested in spending time reading the financial papers and researching, I'd say the basic rule is use fundamental analysis and a logical approach to investing."

THE PORTFOLIO

Date:	Saturday, December 28, 1996
The investors:	Sylvester and Darla Petryk.
Occupation:	Retired; managing personal portfolio.
Investment personality:	"I feel we have a very logical approach. If we're impressed by a company, I'll take a position. If the price drops, I'll buy more. To us, that is logical."
Portfolio makeup:	Large holdings include AVID, ISG Technologies, TSI, Inacom, Goodfellow, Hy & Zels, Synex, Sidus, XL Foods, Inventronix.
Portfolio size:	"Substantial."
Rate of return:	Compound average return of 23.8 per cent since 1978. One-year return of 36 per cent.

Talk about tough sells. A company has to be on its very best behaviour to make it into the Petryks' portfolio. Beyond positive news that they feel will drive stronger growth, they want to see a strong financial position, one that will allow that growth to succeed and to drive up the company's stock price. But even that's not enough. They then do a lot of number-crunching and analysis to ensure a stock offers better potential than others that have passed their tests.

The Petryk's disciplined approach is the key to their success. But to duplicate their earnings, you'll have to be prepared to put in a lot of work, from tracking news reports to analyzing balance sheets. It's not for everyone, but their approach has meant they've uncovered many interesting buys—a lot of them from the small- to mid-cap sectors, and made very impressive long-term returns from their efforts.

KIWI STOCKS PLEASE
EDMONTON WOMAN

•

FREELANCE EDITOR Philippa Fairbairn, a professional dotter of i's and crosser of t's, used to like her investments all lined up, nice and neat.

"Security was my prime consideration," says the 58-year-old Edmonton woman. "I wanted guaranteed safety, and, of course, interest rates were a lot higher until the last few years."

She doubts whether she would have ever changed course if it hadn't been for an inheritance. When her mother died in 1990, Ms. Fairbairn and her two siblings were left the bulk of her parent's estate, the large majority of which was in New Zealand blue-chip stocks.

Her sister got the family home, and she and her brother took the shares. "I tend to let things happen, so I wasn't prepared to make a decision to say 'sell' when I inherited the stocks."

It helped that Ms. Fairbairn, who moved to Canada from New Zealand in 1970, was familiar with many of the companies in her mother's portfolio. "Having lived in New Zealand and Australia, I felt more comfortable because they were mostly names that I'd grown up with."

Included in the inheritance were shares in Westpac Banking Corp., a large Australian bank, as well as a newspaper company, a forest and building products company, and a brewery.

Ms. Fairbairn has since gone on to purchase several stocks on her own, as well as filling out her portfolio with a handful of mutual funds. "Interest rates were falling, but it really took the inheritance to break the ice and get me into stocks."

HOW SHE DOES IT: A lot of what defines Ms. Fairbairn's approach stems from a financial strategy course she took back in early 1987. "The teacher was predicting a crash, but he also said a crash was the time you could do extremely well."

That left her wary of high price/earnings ratios, and an eye for bargains. But her concern over stocks that move up strongly has often hurt her, she admits. "Because I've got this sense that things are going to fall, I often get out too soon."

If anything, she says her best returns have followed from the "hold" strategy she has taken with her New Zealand shares. "It was essentially forced on me because, until recently, I didn't have a New Zealand broker," she says. "In Canada, my buy-and-sell strategy has been much less successful."

Besides the sheer technical complication of trading her Kiwi shares, their relatively low price-to-earnings ratios and strong dividends have also contributed to her long-term approach. Along the way, the performance of the New Zealand part of her portfolio has been given a nice boost by the appreciation of the Kiwi dollar.

In 1990, the New Zealand dollar was worth 70 Canadian cents, and has recently been as high as 95 cents. Ms. Fairbairn says the renewed competitive spirit in New Zealand has its drawbacks, though. "It used to be a very caring society, but it's changed from what I grew up in," she says. "It's very hard-nosed and business-oriented now."

HER BEST MOVES: In total, her inherited New Zealand shares have moved up a total of 115 per cent since 1990. One of her top performers from down under has been publisher Wilson & Horton Ltd. The company's interests include the Auckland-based *New Zealand Herald*, the country's largest newspaper, which interestingly was the company where Ms. Fairbairn's father worked.

Her shares were worth around $5 when she inherited them, and she sold her position in late 1996 for $10.50 when Irish Newspaper conglomerate Independent Newspapers PLC made a takeover offer. Including a stock split, her total return was 160 per cent.

In 1993, Ms. Fairbairn got a tip that Baytex Energy Ltd. (BTE.A-TSE, 52-week high $22.50, low $11.25, yesterday's close $19.35), a Calgary-based oil and gas producer, deserved a look because it had good management and solid prospects. She bought in at $3, hung in even when the stock dropped to $2 and sold in 1995 at $5.50. "I was told the stock was going to double, so when it did, I got out."

Like many tips, this one proved to be wildly off target, but unfortunately on the low side, as the stock is now trading at more than $20. "Sometimes it seems that once I sell a stock, it takes off, while the ones I hold on to fall."

That certainly seems to be the case with another of her winners, Toronto-Dominion Bank (TD-TSE, 52-week high $51.90, low $30.30). "I needed a bank for diversification and my broker recommended it because it was one of the cheapest banks."

She paid $20 for her shares in January 1995, selling them in September 1996 at $26.90. TD's shares closed yesterday at $50.70.

HER WORST MOVE: Sometimes tips work out, but often they don't. Ms. Fairbairn bought Guyanor Resources (GRL.B-TSE, 52-week high $15, low $2.15) at $11.50 in the spring of 1996. A few months earlier, the stock had already soared to almost $20 on hopes for its diamond prospect in French Guiana, and Ms. Fairbairn's source said it was set to rise once again. Since she bought in though, the stock has continued to drop, closing yesterday at $2.55.

ADVICE: "Stick to what you know. I haven't made a fortune out of the companies I know, but they haven't let me down."

THE PORTFOLIO

Date:	Saturday, October 25, 1997
The investor:	Philippa Fairbairn, 58.
Occupation:	Freelance editor.
Investment personality:	"Tentative."

Portfolio makeup:	Funds: Royal - Energy, Canadian Equity; Trimark RSP Equity, Dynamic Partners; Fidelity - Far East, European Growth, Global Strategy World Bond. Stocks: Barrick, Fletcher Challenge, Guyanor Resources, Niko Resources, TransAlta, Westpac Banking, Takla Resources, TransCanada Pipelines, Forest Regeneration Fund Trust units.
Portfolio size:	Six figures.
Rate of return:	Canadian stocks in 1996: 20 per cent in RRSP, 7 per cent outside. New Zealand stocks 140 per cent from 1990 to present.

As I said in the introduction to this book, there are many investors whose stories could have been used as successful demonstrations of many different investing strategies, and Ms. Fairbairn's is one of them.

That in itself is often a very good sign. A balanced approach that has you investing in different types of investments and using a variety of strategies will help lower your portfolio's volatility while hopefully providing some opportunities for growth. In addition to her small-cap stocks, Ms. Fairbairn has a nice mix of domestic and international mutual funds.

(By the way, she recently sent me a note saying that the suffering stock markets and falling currencies in New Zealand and Australia have hurt her Kiwi holdings, as has the Asian crisis. However, rather than selling and simply locking in her losses, she sees this as a buying opportunity.)

Fund Timing

THE SEARCH FOR
MEGA MUTUAL FUND
RETURNS

INSTEAD OF HOLDING THEM for the long haul, fund timers try to only hold funds when they are going up in value, and sell those that are treading water or declining.

If King Arthur were a denizen of the twentieth century and had to hold down a nine-to-five job (due to cutbacks in the freelance crusader business), his "Holy Grail" would undoubtedly have been to seek out and return home carrying high a system for timing mutual funds.

While it certainly lacks the symbolic overtones of a blessed chalice, a method for being able to predict the peaks and valleys of funds would certainly assure our latter-day hero of a reception worthy of, well, a king.

Just like individual stocks, mutual funds generally don't rise steadily in value. Their returns run up, stall and fall back with regularity. It's only when you look at one-, two- or even five-year average annual returns that the gains seem to be on a smooth path. And with some funds, the returns just don't stop-and-start, they soar like a glider that's hit a huge thermal, and then plummet as if the thermal has called it quits and the plane's wings have been chopped off, to boot.

If you could know when a fund was set to rocket, you could make a lot of money by getting in at the right time. You could also profit by being able to sell when a fund had peaked. In fact, you would benefit twice over by being able to predict when to dump a fund. Not only could you avoid losing money by bailing before the fund entered a losing period, but you would also free up cash that could be moved into a fund just getting set for a profitable run.

But as history buffs will tell you, King Arthur never found his Holy Grail. Yet that hasn't stopped many of today's more courageous investor-types from pursuing this ideal.

And be warned—many financial advisers and fund pros will tell you it just can't be done. If it could, goes the standard argument, the winning system would quickly get snapped up by a large brokerage house, packaged and sold. At its most extreme, if there was a "perfect" system out there, it would cause endless problems in the financial world, as everyone would rush to get in on the funds going up and stampede for the exit on funds due for a downfall. But that doesn't stop the brave few, by any means.

THE UPSIDE

Consider this: If in the late spring of 1997, you had put your money into C.I.'s Global Telecom Sectors Shares fund, by May 1998 your money would have increased by over 60 per cent. Whew! And there are other examples. The top one-year performance for a Canadian fund was 49 per cent, turned in by the Chou RRSP fund. In the U.S. equity fund sector, a number of funds also posted returns in the 40 to 50 per cent range.

And many funds don't even need a full 12 months to sparkle. Resolute Growth, a Canadian equity fund, returned 31.5 per cent in just three months, from March to the end of May 1998.

But short-term losses are just as easy—if not easier—to ring up. If you don't particularly like money, a good place to have invested for 12 months would have been Cambridge Special Equity, which lost 28.3 per cent for the year up to the end of May 1998. But that looks positively beatific compared to the Year of Suffering hugely endured by Asian and Pacific Rim funds. They lost an average of over 32 per cent over the year. And a lot of damage can be done in just a few short weeks. Many Far East funds dropped by 10 to 20 per cent in just the three months ending May 1998. In fact, in August 1998 alone the average large-cap equity fund lost 17.3 per cent.

THE DOWNSIDE

I noted above how one of the reasons market timing with mutual funds is so enticing is that done correctly, your returns are doubly improved. You bail out of a fund—perhaps one that that will continue to have a good return over the longer haul—and save yourself the loss as the fund enters troubled waters. That extra money you've freed up, if everything works right, gets put into a fund coming out of a tailspin and heading for the starts.

Getting it wrong twice is also another distinct possibility—selling a fund before its time and moving your money into a fund just as it drops.

You also have to consider our old friends time and cost. You have to stay on top of your portfolio and input data regularly. And the more you trade, the higher your fees. Except for a small number of discount brokerages, you have to pay a commission—either as a commission based on the size of your transaction, or as a flat fee, when you buy funds. (Market timers avoid back-end loads, as they can be quite high for those wishing to sell a fund one or two year after purchasing it—which is a long time to be in a fund for a timer!)

Some fund families and a small number of brokerages will allow you to switch into other funds at no charge. There are often limitations on the number of switches you can make, and, as well, you may find that the charge-free transaction only applies if you hold a fund for a minimum period—say three months.

DOING IT YOURSELF

In a way, this is really the only option available to those looking to time their fund transactions as financial adviser and planner-types would much rather be seen assembling a portfolio with an Ouija board than admitting to being fund timers.

At a minimum, you'll need a system, most likely a computer-based mathematical program that will crunch the numbers and spot the trends for you. You'll also need to find time to enter updated performance numbers on an ongoing basis, run your comparisons and make adjustments to your portfolio.

Consider distributing your money between three or four fund families that offer a large number of different types of funds. This way you can minimize your commission charges by taking advantage of the free switching allowed between funds run by the same fund company. If you are going the discount route, call a few brokerages and compare their trading costs. Higher fees will definitely cut into your overall performance otherwise.

USING A HELPING HAND

As noted above, most advisers feel timing funds is out there enough to qualify for the topic of an episode of *The X-Files*. An adviser, though, may be able to assist you in obtaining up-to-date performance and volatility numbers. They may also assist you in using more fundamental factors to help you choose between several similar-looking funds that make it to the top of your buy or sell charts.

HOW THEY PULL IT OFF

Our three mutual fund timers have a lot in common. They all have a head for numbers, they all use computers and they all have developed their own programs that take in fund data and produce indicators of which funds are hot and which funds are not.

Two of our timers use variations on the same theme—assessing a fund's relative strength. What this means in English is they all look for funds whose units are starting to appreciate quickly. "Well, duh!" you may be thinking. "Aren't we all!"

Yes, but by the time most people can tell that a fund is starting to post better numbers, it may have six, 12 or even 24 months of top-notch returns under its belt. Buying a fund that has been leading the pack for that long often assures you of only one thing—you're climbing aboard a sinking ship. Funds that are at the head of their class are often there because they take big risks, and those risks have started to pay off. But they won't always and a couple of years is a pretty good run at the top of the charts.

What fund timers do is try to find funds that are going to outperform a month or two into their record-breaking stretch. Every week, or month, they look at the numbers and compare the increase of the price of a fund's units to its weekly or monthly increases in the past. The larger the more recent increases compared to its historical increases, the hotter a fund looks.

Because they are trying to only get in on a fund's hottest periods, they will often only hold a fund for a matter of months. And because they want sprinters, not long-distance performers, they focus in on equity funds, typically those in specific sectors that are synonymous with volatility. For instance, in their portfolios you'll see a lot of funds that are known for having periods of terrific returns contrasted with some stomach-churning drops. Those include resource, gold, small-cap, science and technology, and emerging market funds.

One other thing: if you are going to try market timing, the worst thing you can do is do it on a casual basis. Listening to your gut, say our fund timers, is likely to lead to a stomachache. Your gut, you will likely find, has dirt for brains.

PROGRAMMED

FOR QUICK PROFITS

•

DAN WALO'S APPROACH to investing in mutual funds stands conventional wisdom on its head.

Most experts advise buying broad-based funds and holding them for the long term. Mr. Walo, however, uses a computer program to invest in highly volatile sector and regional funds, and almost never holds them for much longer than six or seven months.

"Five years ago, I got a computer and when I used it to apply some of the technical techniques I'd used trading commodities to mutual funds, I found that they worked," says the 49-year-old financial adviser in the Ontario government, who lives in Ajax, just outside of Toronto.

"By trading on momentum, I have a double screening process," he says. "The manager makes his best choices, and then I hang back and wait until the market validates those choices and ride the market up."

HOW HE DOES IT: Mr. Walo buys into funds when their unit price starts to move up strongly. He does this by tracking the momentum using regression analysis and standard deviation formulas. Each Friday, he puts the closing price of about 50 funds into a Lotus spreadsheet program, then his computer model kicks out a chart.

The program creates an imaginary line for each fund. "If it is at more than 90 degrees, it's time to consider getting in, and if it's less than 90 degrees, it's time to sell."

Because he's trading on momentum, he only tracks the most aggressive funds. In addition to sector funds specializing in gold, precious metals, natural resources, technology and health sciences, he tracks some emerging market and Far East funds. He also follows a handful of aggressive small-cap funds, including Saxon Small Cap Fund, Altamira Global Small Company Fund and BPI Global Small Companies Fund.

He developed the system about five years ago, when he came into a small windfall of $5,000. He decided to try mutual funds after going through a long period of trading commodity futures and only breaking even. The program has its own decision maker. Mr. Walo simply has to choose from the half-dozen or so funds the program puts at the top of its list every week. "I don't care who the manager is, the investing style or what interest rates are doing," he says.

The program also limits his losses, he says, because it alerts him if a fund drops by more than 3 to 5 per cent. At this point, he sells. "I know when I get in what my maximum risk will be."

In general, his holding period for any fund ranges from three to six months. He trades through Toronto-Dominion Bank's discount brokerage, Green Line Investor Services Inc., which charges him $45 to buy or sell no-load funds, and 2 per cent up-front on load funds.

Because he feels he can manage his risk, he also borrows to invest and is currently margined up to 70 per cent. He doesn't have a problem with being margined up to 100 per cent, but is holding back to see if gold funds will start taking off again. He recently bought Dynamic Global Precious Metals and Dynamic Global Resources funds, as well as Cambridge Precious Metals Fund.

Mr. Walo says the program—which has not been assessed by any third-party auditors—only falters when he tries to out-think it. "I was into Royal Precious Metals, which was up 60 per cent, and AIC Advantage, which was up 40 per cent," he says. So, he started selling AIC and buying more Precious Metals. At that point, Precious Metals started to go down.

HIS BEST MOVE: This unconventional strategy really paid off when he started to play gold funds late last year. In November, he jumped into Royal Precious Metals Fund at $20 a unit, cashing out six months later at $33 a unit. He also bought Green Line Precious Metals Fund at $10.13 a unit in December 1995, and sold it last July at $19.15.

But his successes haven't been limited to bullion. He has done well with AIC Advantage Fund, which is heavily invested in mutual fund companies and technology stocks. He bought it at $25 a unit last fall, and sold early this summer at $38. Another winner has been the C.I. Latin American Fund, which he bought at $4.40 in June 1995, and sold a few months later at $5.58.

HIS WORST MOVE: He took a $6,000 profit made by shorting stocks in the crash of 1987, and put it all into commodity futures. He lost it all.

"It's tough playing commodities because you become paranoid about risk," he says. "I just couldn't play the market."

ADVICE: "Either stick with a traditional strategy of dollar-cost averaging and hold for a long time, or use a technical approach. Don't do any kind of intuitive guessing—you'll get killed."

THE PORTFOLIO

Date:	Saturday, October 19, 1996
The investor:	Dan Walo, 49.
Occupation:	Financial adviser with the Ontario government.
Investment personality:	"I really like risk but I like to manage it. I'm very aggressive and very conservative at the same time."
Portfolio makeup:	100 per cent in mutual funds. Currently about one-third in each of Dynamic Global Precious Metals Fund, Cambridge Precious Metals and Dynamic Global Resources Fund.
Portfolio size:	$50,000.
Rate of return:	One-year return of 40 per cent.

What's interesting is Mr. Walo's contention that his method gives him a great way to avoid backing the wrong horse. Fund managers invest in stocks, hoping the price will rise. But Mr. Walo says he doesn't have to bet on the fund manager's choice until those choices are proven to be good ones. In other words, his system allows him to spot funds that hold stocks that the market in general is starting to bid up in price.

But take a look at his portfolio. While he may have—make that probably has—changed it much since his column ran, it underscores the volatility that can come from this method, and how you have to stay on top of your investments.

Consider Dynamic Global Precious Metals fund. Talk about jumping all over the map (not the manager, mind you, just the returns). To the end of May 1998, the fund had a one-year return of negative 34.6 per cent (largely attributable to the slide in the price of gold).

However, even in that time frame, there was a way to make some money. For example, in the last six months of that period, the fund actually returned 10.9 per cent. And that's all the more remarkable because in just the last three months, it dropped by 5.2 per cent.

HE SPOTS SECTOR FUNDS
BEFORE THEY EXPLODE

•

BILL CARRIGAN'S APPROACH to investing can best be summed up with an old saying that has served farmers working the fertile soil around his home of Vineland in Ontario's Niagara peninsula: "Make hay while the sun shines."

Not for Mr. Carrigan the buy-and-hold school of long-term investing. Over the years, he's played with commodities, index options and plenty of gold stocks with varying degrees of success in his search for harvestable profits.

More recently, he has focused on timing the mutual fund markets. Mr. Carrigan, 55, uses a mathematical system for assessing the relative strength of funds that he developed and shares with his investment club.

He began putting the system to work with real dollars at the end of December 1992, and has stuck with it ever since. By the end of September, his initial $50,000 investment had grown to a total of $129,704.

HOW HE DOES IT: In general, he prefers not to trade quite so often. His computer program generates a buy/sell indicator each month, "but we only do changes every six months because we don't like to overtrade." He has been using his system for almost four years, and has done a total of 15 trades in that time.

The average hold time for a fund is 18 months, for an average gain of 43.7 per cent. To date, his switching fees and commissions amount to a total of $6,549. Mr. Carrigan trades through a full-service broker because he likes the higher level of service. "With a discount brokerage, you get somebody different every time you call."

His system evaluates the relative strength of funds, as well as their volatility.

"We want to find a fund that's been very volatile historically and gets very quiet," he says. "If the relative strength numbers turn up, that means the sellers are exhausted and the early buyers are getting in."

Mr. Carrigan says this approach helps him avoid one of the biggest mistakes of performance chasers—namely, jumping into a volatile fund that has rung up sky-high gains right at the point where the fund starts to head south. "A lot of people find they're always in the wrong funds, because they chase the hot funds and hot funds always cool off."

In his view, sector rotation is more reliable than following managers. (Sector rotation means spotting rising sectors such as gold, energy or technology and riding them as they go up). "The funds themselves tell us where the proper rotation is going."

HIS BEST MOVES: Goldfund Ltd., one of the initial purchases using his system, has definitely been good to Mr. Carrigan. He bought it at $3.70 in December 1992, and sold it two years later at $7.65, for a gain of 106 per cent. This past summer, the volatile fund once again sent a buy signal to his system, and in June he got back in at $3.70.

Universal Canadian Resource Fund has also been profitable for his system. Also one of his initial buys, he bought in at $5.43 in December 1992, and sold just a year later at $10.27, for a gain of 89 per cent.

His quickest profit so far has come from Dynamic Precious Metals Fund. He got in at $1.06 in December 1992, and sold six months later at $1.82, for a profit of almost 72 per cent.

HIS WORST MOVE: "The worst trading I've ever done is index options," Mr. Carrigan says. "With options, you have time running against you. Even if you call the market right, the premium is shrinking."

He estimates he lost in the neighbourhood of $35,000 playing index options before he gave up on them.

ADVICE: "I think many people trade too much. We don't bother with daily or weekly changes because they can never tell you what to buy for the longer term. Let the market do the talking. Don't try to tell the market what to do. Listen to what it's telling you."

THE PORTFOLIO

Date:	Saturday, November 2, 1996
The investor:	Bill Carrigan, 55.
Occupation:	Musical equipment importer.
Investment personality:	"I only use mathematical techniques. Some people want to get involved with all the fundamentals and know the whole story, but I don't really pay attention to things like fund managers or a company's projected earnings."
Portfolio makeup:	RRSP: BPI Canadian Resource Fund Inc., Trimark Canadian Fund. Non-RRSP: 20 per cent in gold stocks, rest spread among Admax Global Health Sciences Fund, C.I. Emerging Markets Fund, BPI Canadian Resource Fund Inc., Universal Canadian Resource Fund, Goldfund Ltd.
Portfolio size:	Over $200,000.
Rate of return:	One-year return of 40 per cent.

Interesting! When I recently caught up with Mr. Carrigan, he had not only stopped trading funds, but he had got out of them entirely, and turned his hand to trading stocks. "You can't just stick with one strategy. When the markets change, you have to change your approach."

He made the shift because over the last couple of years, the markets were rising so much, it was just a matter of being in the boat—errr, fund—that would rise the fastest.

Now that the markets have stopped going straight up and become somewhat more volatile, Mr. Carrigan wants to be in stocks where he can get in and out in minutes. By contrast, if the markets tumbled and he wanted to bail out of funds, he'd have to wait until the end of the day to have his transaction processed, by which time the losses that his funds had sustained during the day would be locked in. "I feel like the big banks and companies like Bombardier are getting tired, and the game of making easy money on them is over."

He actually loves to trade stocks, and feels that the current market is ripe for short-term buying and selling. The problem two years ago, he says, is that there was no point in selling stocks once you had bought them because they kept going up!

He is trading some resource stocks, although he feels that "people are still a bit shy of drill results." He is also looking at companies in the pharmaceutical industry.

BOLD FUND

SWITCHER WINS

•

LEAVE YOUR MONEY in a mutual fund, live with the ups and downs, and look for long-term growth? No way, says Doug Watson.

Not only is jumping from losing funds into winning funds a good strategy to boost growth, argues the 66-year-old resident of Nepean, Ont., but it's downright patriotic.

"By moving your money into strong funds, you put capital into the hands of good companies and make the economy more competitive. It's a win-win situation."

Until a few years ago, Mr. Watson says, between his job at Computing Devices of Canada, enjoying his cottage in the Rideau Lakes, playing baseball in summer and skiing in winter, he had little spare time. So he took a largely passive approach to investing, putting most of his money into guaranteed investment certificates.

But when he retired, he decided to become more active, focusing on playing mutual funds. "I felt I didn't have the knowledge and expertise to pick my own stocks," he says.

What he did have, however, was an engineering background and a familiarity with cranking out spreadsheets on a computer. So he took those skills and developed a method for timing funds.

Mr. Watson limits his investing universe to no-load funds. "No-loads give me the freedom to move from one fund to another without incurring any extra costs."

He invests almost exclusively in equity funds, seeing little upside in the near future in the bond market.

While he acknowledges that frequent switching is an aggressive approach to mutual fund investing, he feels three steps bring his risk down significantly. First, he spreads his money among a large number of funds—often more than two dozen.

Second, he spreads his money around the world. Currently, he has 60 per cent of his portfolio in Canada, 20 per cent in the United States and 20 per cent in Europe. He has no Asian funds because he feels "the timing is wrong."

Finally, he cuts his risk by making his investments over a number of months.

HOW HE DOES IT: At the beginning and middle of each month, he takes the unit value of all the funds he tracks out of the *Report on Business*. He then calculates the percentage gain or loss for each fund relative to its unit value one year earlier. (Distributions are factored in at the end of each year.)

The results are then laid out on a performance graph. "Plain numbers don't tell you the dips and dives funds take throughout the year," he says. The charts "also make it easier to compare Canadian, U.S. and European funds."

The graphs were such a hit with friends and acquaintances that at the beginning of this summer, he set up his own Web page where the results can be seen at www3.sympatico.ca/doug.watson2. (If you visit the site, be sure to allow it to fully load.)

The benefit of the charts, he says, is that they make it easy to see the best-performing funds. If he has money in a fund that has been under performing for several months, he will take 50 per cent of it out and start moving it into a leading performer, giving the straggler another six months to catch up before closing his position completely.

HIS BEST MOVES: At the top of his charts is Sceptre Equity Growth. He began buying the fund in June 1995, and it's currently his top holding, representing close to 20 per cent of his portfolio. The fund has a one-year return to the end of June of 30.4 per cent, and a three-year average annual compound return of 30.2 per cent. "It's hard to complain about returns like that," he says.

His second pick is Scudder Canadian Equity, which he began purchasing in March. Launched in October 1995, the fund's one-year return is 47.3 per cent.

His third-place fund is Green Line Value, which he started buying in February. The fund has a one-year return of 39.8 per cent. "The charts are showing it is turning in a strong performance."

HIS WORST MOVE: His worst bet to date has been Altamira Asia Pacific. Its numbers suggested it was heading into a strong phase, but it didn't pan out. The fund has a three-year loss of 9 per cent, and a one-year loss to the end of June of 5.3 per cent. He sold his units in September 1995, after having lost $300 of his original investment.

ADVICE: "If you have a mutual fund that isn't performing as well as it should while others are doing better, I'd say it's time for a change."

THE PORTFOLIO

Date:	Saturday, August 16, 1997
The investor:	Doug Watson, 66.
Occupation:	Semi-retired mechanical engineer.
Investment personality:	"Systematic fund investor."
Portfolio makeup:	Major fund holdings: Altamira Management Ltd. - Alta Fund, Dividend, North American Recovery, European Equity, Science and Technology, U.S. Larger Companies; Bissett & Associates Investment Small Cap; Green Line Investor Services - Canadian Equity, Value, North American Growth, Science and Technology; Saxon - Small Cap, Stock; Sceptre Equity; Scudder Greater Europe.

Portfolio size: unavailable
Rate of return: "22 per cent in 1996."

___

Mr. Watson's Web site (www3.sympatico.ca/doug.watson2) is still up and running, and, in fact, getting better. For example, you can visit his site and ask him to send you—free of charge—his new Money Analyzer, a program he developed that will evaluate which of your funds are performing above and below average.

The beauty of Mr. Watson's charts is their simplicity. They vividly paint a very clear picture of the one-year return of each fund, with its price a year ago being assigned a value of "100," and its percentage climb since then represented on a graph. A strong performer, for instance, might be hitting the "140" line, meaning it has appreciated by 40 per cent. To short-list his best picks, he simply takes a look at the funds offered by the 20 no-load companies he tracks, and sees which funds have the best-one year returns by looking at which fund's graph lines end up at the highest point. He currently offers four best-of lists: Canadian equity funds, European and International equity funds, U.S. funds and high-risk funds.

On any given day, Mr. Watson would say the best buy is the fund that has climbed the highest over the last year. When I asked him if that didn't mean risking climbing into a fund that had just had a great runup and was set to pull back, this is what he said: "If a fund is doing well, it's probably got a selection of investments that are doing well, and they may continue to do well for many months."

What's neat about his system is if a fund is plummeting, it will soon bring down its one-year return to a point where it is no longer a serious contender in Mr. Watson's books, so it will be replaced by a stronger performer. You could, though, buy into a leading fund using his system, and have to endure a few months of bad returns before that took place.

For those without access to the Web, the Canadian equity funds he liked, as of July 1998, were Green Line Dividend, Scotia Dividend,

Altamira Large Cap Growth, Altamira Dividend, Bissett Canadian Equity, Scotia Dividend, Saxon Small Cap, Royal Dividend and Scudder Canadian Equity.

On the European and international front, which is garnering increasing attention, his top picks include First Canadian European Growth, Green Line European Growth, Scudder Greater Europe, Altamira European Growth and Royal European Growth.

THE TOP TEN RULES
OF SUCCESSFUL INVESTORS

·

AFTER READING THIS BOOK, you've probably picked up on something that I regularly come across every week when I put another Me and My Money column together. Whether they're dabbling in the risky options market or are devotees of risk-averse guaranteed investments like GICs, the success individual investors achieve is often a result of following a handful of basic rules.

What's great is that these rules work regardless of your personality, outlook or circumstances. Apply the fundamentals of successful investing and you will be rewarded with fewer headaches, more profits and a sense that you are controlling your money, not the other way around.

Here are the top ten rules followed by successful investors:

1. *Start By Looking At Your Big Picture:* Make sure you are properly protected against risk, have paid down high-cost debt and have done what you can to minimize your taxes. You'll also need to take a look at your saving habits.

2. *Get To Know Yourself:* In addition to considering how comfortable you are with risk, assess how much time, interest and energy you want to devote to managing your own money. Picking a strategy and buying investments that fit your personality will mean less stress and a higher comfort level. And because you'll be more comfortable with your investments, you'll be less likely to make bad investing decisions based on emotions.

3. *Educate Yourself:* No one cares about your money as much as you do, and it's you who will have to live with the results of the many investing decisions you will make over your lifetime. Reading a basic financial planning book and spending five minutes with the business section of your paper is a good way to start. And, of course, you should always learn about the specific characteristics of any investment you are considering before you buy it, not after.

4. *Set Goals:* Knowing what you plan to do with the money you invest will help you choose good investments. (Are you buying a house now, or saving for your retirement?) The key is to consider when you will need your money and choose the right investment(s) for your time frame(s).

5. *Allocate your Assets:* Decide how you want to divide your savings between the three major types of investments-cash, fixed-income investments and equity investments. In general, the younger you are and the less money you need to get your hands on in the short-term, the larger percentage you should invest in stocks and other long-term ownership-type investments.

6. *Diversify:* The money you have in stocks, for example, should be invested in U.S. and international stocks as well as Canadian stocks, and the money that you have allotted for Canadian stocks should be in a number of different companies that operate in different industries. Your goal is to prevent a big downturn in any one company, industry, or even country from taking your portfolio with it.

7. *Focus on the Long Term:* You should have a minimum of five years, but preferably seven to ten years to leave your money in the stock market. This will mean you hopefully will be able to ride out any corrections and won't have to sell your equities when the market is in a downturn.

8. *Have Realistic Expectations:* Historically, the long-term return on stocks has been about ten per cent. Keeping this in mind can save you from many common mistakes like jumping into a

volatile gold fund because it has a sky-high one-year return, only to find the next year its returns—and your principal—have shrunk dramatically. You also will be less tempted to take on unnecessary risks for results that are simply unachievable over the long term.

9. *Try To Understand and Accept Risk:* The best place to invest to make your money grow long-term is the stock market, but it also comes with more risk that the value of your investment will fluctuate. Even guaranteed investments, though, are not risk free. GICs and Canada Savings Bonds, for instance, also pose some risk to your principal, since their rate of return may not keep up with inflation. Familiarize yourself with the different types of risk associated with different types of investments and how to accept that risk in order to achieve the returns you are after.

10. *Remember Nobody Has A Working Crystal Ball:* Nobody knows where the stock market is going to be an hour from now, so don't try to figure it out yourself or make major investing decisions based on short-term movements. Even in the longer term, trying to time the market—buying at the lows and selling at the highs—has been shown to be a losing game. It's time in the market, not how you time the market, that counts.

GLOSSARY

•

Active management: This phrase is typically used to refer to mutual fund managers who actively buy and sell securities in order to outperform the general markets. The opposite of active management is passive management. Passive management is used by people such as index fund managers who simply hold the stocks in a stock market index in order to approximate the index's returns.

Annuity: When you buy an annuity, you hand over a lump sum in return for a series of regular—usually fixed—payments. The payments can be for a set number of years, or until you and/or your spouse die. The size of the payments will be determined by the amount you use to purchase the annuity, as well as interest rates, how long you wish the payments to continue for and whether you want the payments to increase with inflation.

Arbitrage: People who are practitioners of arbitrage—namely arbitrageurs—try to make money by trading in securities, commodities or currencies that are trading at different prices in different markets. The term arbitrage has recently taken on a broader meaning, and is often used to describe the process of speculating in highly volatile securities, such as the stocks of companies rumoured to be takeover targets. People involved in this type of arbitrage typically use many aggressive strategies, including short selling and buying on margin.

Asset allocation / Asset mix: Assets are simply anything with value. In the personal finance world, assets usually refer to three broad categories: stocks, income-bearing investments such as bonds, and cash or cash-like investments such as money-market mutual funds. Asset allocation refers to how you spread your money among these three basic categories.

Automatic reinvestment: Many investments produce gains. For example, preferred shares produce regular dividends, and mutual funds often produce interest income, as well as capital gains and dividends. Instead of having these earnings sent to you, you can have them automatically reinvested. The earnings are simply used to buy you more of your investment.

Back-end load: A commission for buying units of a mutual fund that is only payable when and if you sell your units.

Balanced portfolio: A portfolio in which there is a mix of the three types of assets: cash, fixed income and stocks. The idea is that the three classes will tend to level out your portfolio's ups and down, while providing reasonable returns.

Bear market: An extended period during which the prices of stocks are generally dropping. Typically, the measurement used is a stock market index, such as the TSE 300.

Blue-chip stocks: The stocks of large, stable companies that have a record of good earnings and regular dividend payments. Blue-chip companies are usually companies whose products or services are recognized and bought nationally or internationally. Typical blue-chip companies are IBM, Ford and so on.

Bond: A bond is a contract between the issuer and the buyer. The buyer lends money to the issuer. The issuer, in turn, promises to make regular interest payments to the buyer, as well as paying back the original amount, known as the principal, when the bond matures.

Bottom-up investing: People who use this style of investing focus primarily on the financial picture of individual companies. They usually spend little time evaluating economic conditions or the outlook for a specific industry. They are seeking companies whose stocks look "cheap" and likely to appreciate.

Bull market: A period when the general price of securities such as stocks, bonds or commodities has been rising.

Buy and hold: One of the nicer financial bits of jargon, as it actually means exactly what it suggests. Buy-and-hold investors buy stocks or other investments and hang on to them for many years. Two of the major benefits of this approach is it reduces the day-to-day worry about how your investments have performed over the last 37 minutes, and it also saves on commission charges.

Call option: This gives the holder the right to buy a specific investment at a set price, up to a specific date.

Certified Financial Planner (CFP): Generalists who have a broad understanding of many areas of personal finance. The CFP credential is handed out by the Canadian Institute of Financial Planning.

Closed-end fund: A mutual fund that has a set number of units. After its launch, to buy units of a closed-end fund, you have to find an existing owner who is willing to sell his or her units. Units of closed-end funds usually trade on stock exchanges.

Common shares or stock: A type of stock that gives the holder ownership, or "equity" in the company. While some common stocks pay regular dividends, most investors hold common shares in the hopes that the market price will rise.

Current or "indicated" yield: There are two common investments on which it is useful to know the current yield: money-market mutual funds and bonds. The current yield for a money market-mutual fund is calculated by taking the actual rate of return over the last seven days and converting it to an annual percentage. With bonds, the current yield is simply the bond's annual interest payments divided by its current market price.

Cyclical stocks: Shares of companies whose fortunes rise and fall in reaction to economic conditions.

Deferred sales charge (DSC): A commission charged for buying a mutual fund that you only pay when and if you sell your units. A typical DSC might be 4.5 per cent of the value of your units if you sell them within the first year of your purchase. For every year that you hold on to the fund, the DSC is often reduced, typically by half or a full percentage point. Think of DSCs as exit fees, as opposed to entrance fees.

Disability insurance: Insurance that provides an income if the policy-holder becomes unable to work due to illness or an accident.

Discount brokerage: A company that acts as the intermediary between buyers and sellers of financial products such as mutual funds, stocks and bonds. Discount brokers typically charge lower commissions than full-service brokerages, but provide little research, guidance or advice.

Distributions (from mutual funds): Income, dividends and capital gains that are realized by a mutual fund and handed over to unitholders. You can either choose to receive these distributions as cash or use the money to buy more units of the fund (called automatic reinvestment).

Diversification: The strategy of investing your money in different types of investments to reduce your overall risk.

Dollar-cost averaging: This refers to investing a set dollar amount at regular periods. For instance, you could dollar-cost average by buying $100 worth of units in a particular mutual fund every month. The benefit of dollar-cost averaging is that you automatically buy more units of any investment when the price is lower, and fewer units when the price is higher.

Equity mutual funds: Mutual funds that invest primarily in stocks.

Financial planner (or financial adviser): Someone who can help you get your personal finances in order, and help you develop a plan to achieve your financial goals. "Financial planner" isn't a designation, but simply a generic term. Anyone can call himself or herself a financial planner.

Fixed-income funds: Mutual funds that invest largely in investments that produce regular income payments, such as mortgages or bonds.

Front-end load: A commission for buying units of a mutual fund that is payable when you make your purchase.

Futures: A futures contract is simply a deal to buy (or sell) a particular investment or commodity on a particular date in the future at an agreed-upon price. In the movies, tycoons try to win big by buying things like orange juice and pork bellies on a commodity exchange. Unlike an option contract, both the buyer and seller have to go through with their agreed-upon deal on the exercise date.

Growth investing: A stock-investing strategy of buying companies that have above-average future growth potential. A growth investor may be willing to pay a higher price for a stock if he or she believes that the company's earnings will grow strongly, which will help justify an even higher stock price.

Growth stocks: Stocks of companies whose earnings are expected to rise faster than those of other companies.

Guaranteed Investment Certificate (GIC): A GIC is an investment that will pay interest at a specified rate up to a specific date (the maturity date). GICs can run for a period of three months to five years. They are sold mostly by banks and trust companies.

Income splitting: A strategy of reducing a household's tax bill by shifting income from the hands of someone in a higher tax bracket to someone in a lower tax bracket. For example, a higher-earning spouse can put some of their allowable RRSP contribution amount into a special "spousal RRSP." As long as the money inside the plan is withdrawn no earlier than three years after it's contributed, when the funds are taken out of the RRSP, they are taxed as income to the spouse, not the person who made the contribution. The result is the withdrawals are taxed at a lower rate, boosting the household's overall after-tax income.

Index: A basket of stocks on a particular exchange. The overall performance of these stocks is measured to give an indication of the market's performance. For example, when people talk about the Toronto market, they are usually referring to the TSE 300 Composite Index, which measures the price movement of the stocks of 300 of the largest and most well-established Canadian companies listed on the exchange.

Index fund: A mutual fund that simply tries to mirror the performance of a particular stock market index, such as the TSE 300 or the Standard & Poor's 500 index, by holding the same securities as the index. The management fees on most index funds are lower than the fees on regular equity funds, as index funds do not need to be actively managed.

Inflation: A sustained increase in the price of most goods and services. The higher the rate of inflation, the less a dollar today will be able to buy in the future. You need to factor in inflation when calculating how much money you will need in the future.

Leverage: The use of borrowed funds in order to boost the returns on an investment.

Liquidity: The relative ease with which an investment can be bought or sold. For investors, the critical factor is the time and cost of turning an investment into cash. Real estate, for example, is highly illiquid. It takes a lot of time and effort to sell, and you often won't see the actual money for several months after you strike a deal. In contrast, units of a money-market mutual fund are extremely liquid. You can sell the units whenever you wish, and have the money in your bank account usually by the next business day.

Load: A commission charged to buy or sell units of a mutual fund.

Management expense ratio (MER): The total of all the costs of operating a mutual fund, including management fees, expressed as a percentage of the fund's total assets. Management fees are deducted from a fund's profits before its performance is measured, and before distributions to unitholders are calculated. MERs vary greatly. For example, the average MER for Canadian equity mutual funds is 2.21 per cent, but they range as low as 0.11 per cent and as high as 3.92 per cent. If two funds' gross profits are the same, the fund with the lower MER will provide investors with a better return.

Management fee: The money paid to the people—the managers—who are responsible for investing a fund's assets. The management fee is paid out of the fund's assets. The management fee is included in a fund's MER.

Marginal tax rate: The rate at which your last dollar of income is taxed. (There are several marginal tax rates. The rate on the first $30,000 or so that you make is taxed at a lower rate than the next $30,000, for example.)

Market timing: A strategy of moving money from one type of investment to another as market conditions change in order to maximize returns.

Money-market fund: A mutual fund that invests in short-term interest-earning investments such as T-bills. Money-market funds are a good, safe place to park cash for the short term.

Mutual fund: A pool of investments managed by a professional manager on behalf of the investors who contribute money to the fund.

Net asset value (NAV): The total value of the investments owned by a fund, minus its liabilities.

Net asset value per share (NAVPS): The market value—or net asset value—of a fund's holdings, divided by the number of units outstanding in the fund. If a fund has a net asset value of $100 million and has 20 million units outstanding, its NAVPS is $5. The NAVPS is the current cost of buying units in the fund, as well as the price you would get if you sold your units.

No-load fund: A mutual fund that can be bought and sold without the investor having to pay a commission. (A load is mutual fund jargon for a commission.) No-load funds are typically available directly from mutual fund companies that sell their funds without commissions. No-load funds are also available through brokers and planners. Many no-load funds compensate these people for selling their funds by paying them annual trailer fees—typically 0.25 to 1.0 per cent of the value of the client's funds. (Load funds also generally pay trailer fees.)

Option: An option gives the buyer the right to buy or sell a particular security at a specified price up to a particular date. The right to buy a stock or other security from somebody else is called a "call" option. The right to sell something at a set price is called a "put" option.

Unlike a futures contract, an option holder doesn't actually have to exercise his or her rights. Why would someone choose to do this? Say you paid $5 a share to be able to buy some Humungous Bank stock at $100. You are hoping that before the options expire, the stock is worth at least $100. (If it's over $105, of course, you've made a profit as your total price will only be $105—the price you can buy the stock at, plus your option dividend of $5.) But if the price is below $100, there is no point in exercising the option, since you could buy the stock cheaper (if you wanted to buy it) on the open market. In this case, you would just let your option(s) expire.

Portfolio: A term that refers to all of the investments owned by a mutual fund, financial institution or individual.

Price/earnings ratio (P/E): The market price of a stock divided by its earnings per share. For example, if a company's stock was trading at $10 and its earnings per share was $0.66, its P/E ratio would be 15. A company's P/E ratio is also referred to as its multiple.

Prospectus: A legal document offering a detailed description of an investment. The prospectus for a mutual fund, for instance, will contain information about its investment objectives, the types of investments it will purchase, the cost of buying or selling units in the fund, the management expense fees, as well as administrative details such as how to purchase units in the fund.

Real estate investment trust (REIT): A type of closed-end mutual fund. A REIT will own, operate, manage, develop and invest in real estate properties. Units of REITs trade on stock exchanges.

Real rate of return: The return on an investment after taxes and inflation are deducted.

Registered financial planner (RFP): RFPs are sort of like all-star financial planners. In addition to taking courses and complete exams, they must agree to abide by a code of ethics laid down by the Canadian Association of Financial Planners, as well as carry liability insurance.

Registered retirement income fund (RRIF): A special account registered with the government. Money in an RRIF must be transferred in from an RRSP or a registered pension plan. The owner, or annuitant, must withdraw a certain minimum amount set out by the government. Money that is inside the RRIF can be invested and the income, dividends and capital gains are sheltered from taxation. When money is withdrawn from an RRIF, it is taxed as income.

Registered retirement savings plan (RRSP): An account that is registered with the government. You can contribute money to the plan, up to certain annual limits. You can then deduct your contributions in any year from your income for that year before your income tax is calculated. In addition, money inside the plan can grow tax-free. Tax only becomes payable when you make withdrawals from an RRSP.

Risk: The likelihood that you will lose some or all of the money you put into an investment.

Risk tolerance: A measurement of how well you can tolerate risk—or volatility—in your investments.

Sector rotation: An investment style in which a greater proportion of a portfolio is invested in a sector that is expected to perform above average due to economic conditions. This is also know as top-down investing.

Segregated funds: Mutual funds sold and run by insurance companies. Segregated funds come with a handful of unique features. In addition to being somewhat creditor-proof, segregated funds offer a guarantee. They promise that when your fund matures (or if you die before it matures), the fund company will return a guaranteed percentage of your principal. Most segregated funds guarantee to return 75 per cent of the money invested, but some guarantee 100 per cent of the original investment.

Self-directed RRSP: An RRSP run by the planholder. The benefit of a self-directed plan is it gives you a much wider choice of investments than a mutual fund RRSP.

Strip bond: A bond that pays no actual interest. The coupons have been removed, or "stripped," and sold to another investor. The coupon-less bond is sold at a discount to its face value—what it will be worth when it matures. Your return is the difference between the price that you pay and the face value, which you will receive when the bond matures.

Top-down: Top-down investors choose their investors by first looking at "big-picture" factors, such as the state of the economy, interest rates, economic growth and so on. They use this analysis to decide which countries, economic sectors and industries are likely to perform better than average. Only then will they choose individual investments.

Trailer fee: A fee paid by a mutual fund company to individuals or companies that have sold units of its funds. Trailer fees range from 0.25 to 1.0 per cent of the value of the units sold. They are paid on an annual basis until the investor sells his or her units.

Treasury bill (T-bill): A short-term debt security sold by governments. T-bills don't pay interest. They are sold at a discount to their face value. The return is the difference between the purchase price and the face value. The return is treated as interest income, and taxed accordingly.

TSE 300 Composite Index: The TSE 300 is a basket of stocks of 300 of the largest and most well-established Canadian companies trading on the Toronto Stock Exchange. The index measures changes in the market value of the 300 stocks. The effect of the change in a particular stock's price on the index will depend on the number of outstanding shares of that company.

Value investing: A conservative approach to buying stocks. Value investors try to buy companies that have strong fundamentals, but whose stocks are somewhat out-of-favour and that are "good buys." For example, if the average price/earnings ratio of companies in a particular industry is 15, and the stock of one company that is performing well has a P/E ratio is 10, value investors would say it represented a good buy.

Volatility: A measurement of how often—and how much—the value of a security changes.

ME AND MY MONEY

RESOURCES

•

BOOKS

Beating the Dow
Michael O'Higgins
HarperPerennial Library

Beating the Street
Peter Lynch
Fireside

Fund Monitor
Duff Young
Prentice Hall

Buyer's Guide to Mutual Funds
Gordon Pape
Prentice Hall

How to Make Money in Stocks
William O'Neil
McGraw Hill

The Motley Fool Investment Guide
David and Tom Gardner
Simon & Schuster

One Up on Wall Street
Peter Lynch
Penguin

Personal Finance for Dummies for Canadians
Eric Tyson and Tony Martin
IDG Books

Top Funds
Riley Moynes and Michael Nairne
Addison Wesley

The Wealthy Barber
David Chilton
Stoddart

NEWSLETTERS

Canadian Mutual Fund Adviser

One-year subscription: $127

416-869-1177

(FAX: 416-869-0456)

133 Richmond St.W.

Toronto, Ont. M5M 3M8

Carter's Choice

One-year subscription: $450

403-288-7255

Mistaya Publishing

c/o Silver Springs

P.O. Box 71070

Calgary, Alta. T3B 5K2

Contra The Heard

416-410-4431

680 Queen's Quay West

Suite 425

Toronto, Ont. M5V 2Y9

E-mail: bens@revtrack.on.ca

The Fund Counsel

One-year subscription: $149

416-977-7337

The Financial Player Inc.

35-A Beverly St.

Toronto, Ont. M5T 1X8

E-mail: editors@fundcounsel.com

The Investment Reporter

One-year subscription: $279

416-869-1177

(FAX: 416-869-0456)

133 Richmond St.W.

Toronto, Ont. M5H 3M8

Investor's Digest of Canada

One-year subscription: $137

416-869-1177

(FAX: 416-869-0456)

133 Richmond St.W.

Toronto, Ont. M5H 3M8

Stock Trends

One-year subscription: $199

416-533-9985

(FAX: 888-269-6857)

Stock Trends Publications

163 Sterling Road, Unit 29

Toronto, Ont. M6R 2B2

E-mail: info@stocktrends.ca

www.stocktrends.com

The Successful Investor

One-year subscription: $99

416-222-3759

6021 Yonge St.

Toronto, Ont. M2M 3W2

E-mail: success@rogers.wave.ca

www.successfulinvestor.com

WEB SITES

Briefing Book (U.S. site)
www.briefing.com
(Quotes, volume statistics,
upgrades/downgrades)

Canada Newswire
www.newswire.ca
(Good source of current releases)

Canadian Securities Institute
www.csi.ca
(Information on various
CSI educational courses)

Doug Watson's Mutual Fund Charts
www3.sympatico.ca/doug.watson2
(Fund timing charts for Canadian
funds)

The Fund Library
www.fundlibrary.com
(Lots of articles and commentary
on funds)

The Globe and Mail
www.globefund.com
(Good mutual fund tools, plus
access to columns and stories)

i|money
www.imoney.com
(Quotes, fund filters, portfolio
tracking, personal finance articles)

The Investment Funds Institute
of Canada
www.mutfunds.com/ific/
(Site of the Canadian mutual
fund industry association)

quote.com (U.S. site)
www.quote.com
(Quotes, portfolio tracking)

Silicon Investor (U.S. site)
www.techstocks.com
(Stock forums)

Stockhouse
www.stockhouse.com
(Forums, on-line newsletters, news)

The Street.com (U.S. site)
www.thestreet.com
(Quotes, market commentary, articles)

Wall Street Journal Interactive
Edition (U.S. site)
www.wsj.com
(On-line edition of the
Wall Street Journal)

Yahoo Finance (U.S. site)
www.quote.yahoo.com/?u
(Quotes, Motley Fool, filings,
upgrades/downgrades)

INDEX

•